# My Time to Sing

A Daily Guide to Living
a Happy & Productive Life

Vicki Kralapp

My Time to Sing: A Daily Guide to Living a Happy and Productive Life
Copyrighted © 2020 Vicki Kralapp
ISBN 978-1-64538-010-8
First Edition

My Time to Sing: A Daily Guide to Living a Happy and Productive Life
by Vicki Kralapp

All Rights Reserved. Written permission must be secured from the publisher to use or reproduce any part of this book, except for brief quotations in critical reviews or articles.

For information, please contact:

Ten16 Press
ten16press.com
Waukesha, WI

Photo credits: Vicki Kralapp

The author has made every effort to ensure that the information within this book was accurate at the time of publication. The author does not assume and hereby disclaims any liability to any party for any loss, damage, or disruption caused by errors or omissions, whether such errors or omissions result from accident, negligence, or any other cause.

For all of my friends and family who patiently listened
to me and waited with me to heal.

In memory of Pastor Bruce Pangborn,
my counselor and friend.

*I was broken, but now I'm whole.*
*I was hurt, but now I'm healed.*
*I was lost, but now have found my way.*

These past few years have been a journey of healing and enlightenment for me. For so many years, I longed for a chance at happiness and a way to heal from the demons I carried. This book and the next book are a compilation of the insights I have gained along the way. I share my story in the hope it might touch even one person struggling with life's challenges.

# Part One

## Health, Happiness and Healing

*Anyone can find
joy and happiness
again, wherever
they are in life.*

When I began this journey of self-enlightenment and healing, I had a short list of goals I wanted to achieve when I was done. The top of that list was to be happy and know what joy was again. I had forgotten how. Such a simple, everyday emotion that should be one of everyone's inalienable rights, I could no longer feel, because I had dealt with physical and psychological pain for so long.

However, I must warn you, if you are going to make a request like I did, you must be willing to dig through all of the trash that made you unhappy in the first place. I have cried a million tears and have gone through mountains of Kleenex during these past few years to find my joy again. You also must be willing to work very hard in order to feel better: to push through the fear and the pain in order to experience forgotten joy. It won't be easy, but it is possible for anyone. I know I am the happiest I have ever been in my entire life, and anyone who knows me can attest to that!

The past two Decembers I decorated two Christmas trees in my apartment: the first one was to celebrate the Christmas season and the other to remind myself of all the joy and happiness I've found and the rebirth within myself!

*Don't let the demons
drag you down, soldier.*

Stephen King once said, "Monsters are real and ghosts are real too. They live inside us and sometimes, they win."

I grew up with those kinds of monsters. Many were a product of circumstance: an abusive teacher, a neighborhood family that was murdered, a parent with PTSD from two wars, a mother who had breast cancer, and a neighborhood that was more like the Wild West than the outskirts of a rural city.

I had a great family and loving parents, but life somehow found its way in, as it always does. It took me well into my fifties to figure it all out. But everything I have been through has made me into the person I am today. If it would mean losing even a part of myself to correct the past, I wouldn't change a thing! It has made me the strong, independent woman I am, ready to take on new challenges and adventures.

My first grade teacher had serious problems and passed them on to us. She should never have been allowed to work with children. When she became frustrated and angry with us, she would take it out on us by pulling our ears or hair, shaking us until our teeth felt like they would rattle, and hitting us with rulers or pointers. She once dragged a boy down the hall by his ear. I hated her. I think she hated some of us more than others. I have been told I was one of the unlucky ones she picked on often. Fortunately, I blocked out most of what she did to me, but one of my friends from that time remembered and saved those memories for me so I could heal. We grew up on the Oneida Nation Reservation, but only a few Native Americans went to our school. The boy who sat to my left was a beautiful Oneida Native American who got the brunt of her anger.

One day in February of that same year, the neighbor boy from across the field came home and shot his entire family. I was devastated, as they were some of our closest neighbors and I was just getting to know the twins in the family well enough to call them my friends. Unfortunately, this mass shooting was a result of a dysfunctional family, mental illness, and the time of year when frigid temperatures and lack of sunlight create deep depression in Wisconsin. I still remember the horrific pictures in the newspaper of white sheets covering the family's bodies with blood spilling out from under them and the feeling of terror that enveloped me. It was like living through 9/11 every day for the next few months. The images and emotions from that day have haunted me my entire life.

My father was a product of his generation and of two wars, World War II and the Korean Conflict. He returned home from the latter with two bronze stars—and with terrible PTSD. PTSD is an acronym for Post-Traumatic Stress Disorder. According to the National Center for PTSD, the following are some of the symptoms:

- Reliving the event
- Avoiding situations that remind you of the event
- Negative changes in beliefs and feelings
- Feeling keyed up (also called hyper arousal)

My dad displayed all of these signs and more. Although he never talked much about his experiences in the wars with us, it was ever present in his behavior. He was a very angry person. When we dropped things in the house, as children often do, he would jump and shake; he sometimes came to tears when a car backfired outside. We didn't understand he was ill because we were just kids. It affected my older brother and myself the most, as the healing took place very slowly over many years. The two branches of the United States Service he served in didn't have programs nor did they even recognize this as a disorder until quite recently, so many families like ours with former service men and women suffered in silence.

Mom was a strong woman, but cancer was a menacing monster that left her disfigured and hurting for the rest of her life. She had found a lump in her breast when I was fourteen, and for a year the doctors wouldn't take her seriously when she insisted it was cancer. Only after two second opinions was she finally able to find someone who would perform a biopsy. During the surgery, the doctors found an advanced form of cancer and, while she was still under anesthesia, performed a radical mastectomy on her right side. While she was in recovery, one of the sutures slipped, and she began bleeding internally.

Both my father and pastor were called in to give her last rites and say good-bye, as she had no pulse. She had to go through a second surgery without anesthesia, as there was no time to put her under. She eventually pulled through with the help of quick-thinking doctors and several transfusions. Afterward she was given radiation, which turned her back black. I remember helping her change her bandages and brush her back with a hairbrush to stimulate the feeling in it. Because her lymph nodes were gone from her arm, she lived with one arm that was always swollen and gave her problems until the day she died.

There are numerous other traumas in my life I could relate, but these are the ones that have affected me the most and those I have needed help to overcome. If you have survived a traumatic past like I have, first, kudos to you! If past traumas are still bothering you and interfering with your life, then you should probably talk with someone to help you heal. First, understand that you are extremely strong to have survived this far on life's path by yourself. Tell the friends you trust and open up to them about your fears and how your past has affected your life. You may be surprised by how supportive a true friend can be. My best friend and my sister were truly helpful and checked in on me often to see how I was healing.

If, however, you can't talk to a friend or family member, or they are not enough, then you will need to find a good counselor. Find a professional who will listen to you, one who will validate your feelings and pain, someone who will give you the skills to deal with the problems in life. Find people who shared your trauma if you can. I found friends who shared the trauma of my neighbors' deaths. They filled in the blanks I couldn't. Follow your counselor's directions and assignments. These will go a long way to help you heal. Then write, paint, or sing about your past. Creativity releases a lot of emotions and helps you to remember past events long buried. Finally, forgive and *let go*. That is the hardest thing to do but by far the most healing. You will discover a whole new you, one free and unburdened, ready to face each new day with joy.

*There is no set time for how long it takes to heal. Take as long as you need to mend.*

Healing, whether it's physical or emotional, takes a great deal of time. Individuals are unique in the length of time it takes to recover from trauma or what helps them heal. What works for one person may not work for another. Whether one has been hurt by a death, a breakup, abuse, the battlefield, or at work, it really doesn't matter. These all register in our mind and heart the same way: pain. Some pain will lessen with the years and some won't. We will just have to learn how to endure it. Some pain may be brought back to the surface by just a word, smell, music, or a name, and some pain is buried so deep inside it takes a small miracle to find it.

My dad was a veteran of World War II and the Korean Conflict, as I mentioned earlier. I don't believe he ever got over all of the pain he endured on the battlefields of Korea. However, shortly after my mom passed, he met the second love of his life, and though she never took my mother's place, she filled a hole that was left by my mother's passing. His new love was a war veteran as well and could understand what he went through in a way my mom never could, so blessing him with some healing shortly before he left us. As for me, it took me two years before I stopped grieving my mother's passing. However, it took me over fifty years to get over the murder of my friends across the field when I was eight. Some things are just so tragic it takes special guidance to overcome them.

So please be patient with yourself and take all the time you need to glue the pieces of your heart and life back together. Seek counseling if needed and do all the things you can to help yourself heal. Don't listen to others who compare themselves to you. I remember when I asked for two weeks off from work to help with all of the activities of my mom's funeral and burial and to have some time for myself, another colleague commented he had taken only a day off for his own father's funeral. I instantly wanted to make some nasty comment to him about being such a Grinch, "with a heart two sizes too small", but I bit my tongue. He may not have needed the time off but may have needed to work through his grief in a different way instead. As I said, everyone is different. So listen to your own body and heart and let them lead the way. They will tell you what you need to do.

*Cry if you need to.
There is no shame in
releasing emotion.*

Why is it that we feel we need to hide our emotions? Perhaps we think others may not understand and consider crying or being emotional a sign of weakness. We may be afraid such displays of emotions may invite questions or may make others feel uncomfortable. Whatever the reason, most of us are very careful about who we allow into our private worlds. When we were young, most of us didn't care. We hadn't learned the skill of guarding our hearts yet.

Crying actually is quite good for us. It's nature's way of clearing out toxins from within our bodies. Most of us don't cry as much as we should.

The following is a section taken from Net Doctor (www.netdoctor.co.uk/healthy-living/wellbeing/a10637/the-health-benefits-of-crying/):

> According to the article "The Health Benefits of Crying," crying can help to wash chemicals linked to stress out of our body, one of the reasons we feel much better after a good cry. Higher levels of adrenocorticotrophic (ACTH) have been found in emotional tears (compared to reflex tears). Removing this chemical from the body is beneficial because it triggers cortisol, the stress hormone – too much of which can lead to health problems associated with stress. 'Crying can help release tension and stress, as well as expressing emotions,' says Dr. Abigael San, chartered clinical psychologist. "When you're upset and stressed, you have an imbalance and buildup of chemicals in the body and crying helps to reduce that."

When I was young, I cried all of the time. I imagine people thought I was weak for doing so. But it wasn't that at all. I cried because I was so frustrated by my circumstances I could hardly bear it. I didn't know how to express myself in a way that others could understand. I wasn't allowed to act out, so all I could do was cry. I was also afraid and I perceived there were far too few safe places for me. So I cried then too. As an adult, I don't cry nearly as much, although after breakups and parents passing, I have cried an ocean of tears. Now I still catch myself tearing up at times when I think of my parents or when I have an overwhelming disappointment, but like other people, I almost always do this behind closed doors or with people who make me feel safe.

I won't suggest that you cry more or less, but when you feel the need and are someplace safe, don't feel the weight of social stigma and choke back your tears. I have spent a great deal of time crying in various places such as my shower or bathtub. However, the best place to be is in the arms of someone who understands and cares about you. Your tears are healing and will wash away all of the toxins within you and will cleanse and help mend your heart.

*There are a great
many people who
love you, no matter
what you may think.*

Consider all of the people you have in your life: all of the people who love you or care about you. You might be surprised by the number of people to whom you've made a difference. There are people you have known all of your life: your family; extended family and relations; others from grade school, high school, college, or beyond; some from work or clubs; others may be shared friends with your spouse; and still others may have been met on trips or on social media. All of them care about you in some way or they wouldn't have remained friends with you. Then consider all of the people you have touched in your life and all of the other people you have known. Can you even count that high? I recently received a note from a childhood friend whom I have reconnected with; she wrote she only had good memories of me growing up. I also received a note from a friend in Texas saying I had been a great friend. I was so surprised! And why is that? Did I really think so little of myself or that I was so unlovable?

Last year in the midst of my depression, I pictured my funeral with only my immediate family in attendance. I was terrified that no one really cared whether I lived or died; that I would leave this world just like poor Eleanor Rigby in the Beatles' song. It's amazing what lies we believe when we are distraught and depressed! I couldn't have been more wrong! This past December I received over one hundred birthday wishes on my Facebook page for my birthday. Also, many students have since told me how much of an impact I have had in their lives while I was teaching. (Bless their hearts!) If you have lived with negatives for a long period, it's so much easier to believe the lies in your head rather than the truth.

So the next time sadness or distress overtakes you and makes you believe you aren't loved; that the people you know wouldn't care whether you lived or died, and the world would be better off without you, don't believe it! Hold on for the help that is sure to come along or ask someone else to help, and for heaven's sake, don't believe no one will care. Because they do!

*Unfortunately, no
one ever said life was fair.
But then, we can't see
the big picture.*

We have all heard ourselves exclaim, "It's just not fair!" or "Why did this happen to me?" However, if you really stop to think about it, no one ever promised life would be fair. It is what it is, that's all. Some will be born with a silver spoon in their mouths, never wanting for anything. Others will be born into poverty, not knowing where their next meal will come from. Some people will be born without arms or legs and have deformities they must overcome. Some will have accidents in their lives or be shot on the street. Who is to say why? Life is far from fair.

But if we try to figure out *why* all of these things happen and why life is or isn't fair, we will go insane. Some people blame themselves for events in their lives and go through the "woulda, shoulda, couldas" and some blame others. But no one ever promised us life would be fair or even easy for that matter. I personally believe questions like these are beyond our understanding. We will only understand these when we see the big picture upon leaving this earth and perhaps not even then.

Sometimes life just stinks and there is not a thing we can do about it except to take a deep breath, go to sleep, and reboot! Today has been a long day in a series of very long days. Troubles for me usually come in economy packs. In the past two weeks, I have been bitten by a pit bull and am going through rabies shots. I threw my back out picking up my sister's Havanese dog, dropped my computer on my foot, discovered I have an abscessed tooth that needs to be pulled, and, last but not least, was scammed today by some hackers who placed a virus on my Apple computer. I'm beyond upset—I am numb. I have just spent the last eleven hours, which I don't have, cleaning up the mess someone made of my laptop with the help of my brother and sister-in-law.

I am beginning to feel like the biblical Job, with everything happening all at once. Even my family and friends are beginning to notice. I have reached into my magic hat and have pulled out all of the tricks I can think of. I have counted my blessings, made a joy list, begged to know why this all was happening to me, got mad, gone to a counselor, and even cried. But problems still seem to keep popping up without any break or warning. I am at my breaking point and have asked my sister-in-law why these things are all happening to me. She explained that although we all naturally try to figure out why as humans, it wouldn't matter, as it wouldn't make any difference anyway. We would still have to deal with the problems. My brother then reminded me of the old Taoist parable of a farmer and son once again, as he usually does when these things happen to me. It goes as follows:

*The Story of the Taoist Farmer,*
written by Dennis Adsit, May 10, 2018

There is a Taoist story of an old farmer who had worked his crops for many years. One day his horse ran away. Upon hearing the news, his neighbors came to visit. "Such bad luck," they said sympathetically.

"Maybe," the farmer replied.

The next morning the horse returned, bringing with it three other wild horses. "How wonderful," the neighbors exclaimed.

"Maybe," replied the old man.

The following day, his son tried to ride one of the untamed horses, was thrown, and broke his leg. The neighbors again came to offer their sympathy for what they called his "misfortune."

"Maybe," answered the farmer.

The day after, military officials came to the village to draft young men into the army. Seeing that the son's leg was broken, they passed him by. The neighbors congratulated the farmer on how well things had turned out.

"Maybe," said the farmer.

I guess we may never know what turn of events all of our problems will play into, maybe something wonderful, as in the farmer's case, or maybe nothing at all.

So, when life seems to dump all over you and you don't know what else to do, follow my example; 1) Take a deep breath 2) Call someone for support (both computer technical support and family in my case). 3) Take care of the problem(s) in front of you. 4) Relax, go to sleep, and reboot!

*Strive for happiness. When your cup runs over, you will have plenty to share with others. Always make being happy a priority. You have a right to happiness, but sometimes you may have to look for it!*

> "The most important thing is to enjoy your life – to be happy – it's all that matters."
> – Audrey Hepburn

This was a lady who certainly knew hard times. When she was young, the Germans invaded and later occupied the Netherlands where she lived, and both she and her mother struggled to survive. Later, after her career as an actress was over, she became a spokesperson for UNICEF. I have never seen a Hepburn movie that didn't make me happy or lighten my spirit, a legacy she would most certainly be proud of.

Today I had to get the last in my series of rabies shots. Because of this, I had to give up a wonderful day of celebrating a friend's daughter's wedding and was in bed most of the day. But yet I chose to make a conscious decision to be happy in spite of my circumstances. You see, we do have *a choice* whether we want to be happy each day in spite of our situations. When my nurse came into my hospital room to give me my shot, I was crying, having just written a particularly touching story in one of my books. When she asked what was wrong, I assured her I was fine and shared what I had written. Soon we were both crying, but these were tender, happy tears.

To pass the time while she gave me my shot, she asked me to tell her about the turn of events that had led me to the hospital that day and about my life. After I had described my life and how I came to be there, I heard myself say, "I have had quite a remarkable life!" with a big smile on my face, surprising even myself. She gave me a hug and said something I will never forget. "I am so glad I came to work today so I could meet you!" I was making it a priority to be happy despite my situation and shared my joy with another. This in turn came back to me. I couldn't help but leave happier than when I arrived.

One of the things I will always remember about *The Oprah Winfrey Show* was her "aha" moments. Well, Oprah, I just had one yesterday. It occurred to me that being happy, once you have found your happiness, is like a strong body or mind; it requires exercise to keep it well. As I was growing up, I thought some people were blessed with happiness and others weren't. But in reality, happiness is like a muscle; protein builds muscle, and dwelling on positive thoughts will help build happy ones. A muscle needs to be exercised to keep it strong, and your days will provide you with plenty of tests to exercise your "happy" muscle. What most people don't do is feed themselves enough on happy, positive, and joyful thoughts. So when they are sad and depressed, they wonder why they got that way. Yes, many times depression and sadness are chemical imbalances, such as post-partum depression and reactions to too much stress. However, many times sadness overtakes us because we let it or don't know how to prevent it. We haven't built up an arsenal of endorphins in our bodies, and when this attack comes, we buckle and sadness wins the battle.

When something happens to bring you down, stop and ask yourself: Am I going to allow this situation to make me miserable and destroy this beautiful day, or can I make a *choice* to be happy? How can I arm myself to fight this daily battle so it will become second nature to me? Decide to be happy and joyful, then stick to this game plan every day. Being joyful and sharing joy with others is like putting money in a secure fund. You will always get a return on your investment. And it's always guaranteed.

*Emotional pain is
much more painful and
harder to deal with
than physical pain.*

The song by Cat Stevens "The First Cut is the Deepest" describes my first experience with love perfectly. I was about twenty-four when I met him, and with a contract for a job already signed in California, my future was pretty much set already for the next year. We spent just about every day together until I left about five months later. I fell head over heels for him but didn't want to make the same mistake I had seen so many others make at my age and marry too young to someone I hardly knew. So when the conversation of engagement came up, I asked him to wait.

What I didn't know was that I was the only one in the relationship who was willing to do so. Nine months later we broke up and I was devastated. My world collapsed, and my heart was shattered. It took me a very long time to get over him. Many years later love took me by surprise again at age fifty, blinding me once more to reality. Four years into the relationship, I was in the same disconcerting situation without a partner.

Both times my feet were knocked out from under me as I was left to begin my life alone again. I cried for months and mourned each man's disappearance as if it were a death. My heart was not only broken, but my already fragile belief in men was dashed as well. I remember thinking I would trade my broken heart for open-heart surgery any day. The physical pain of an operation is finite, and healing can usually be predicted within a few weeks. However, the pain of heartbreak is seemingly never ending.

Not only that, I threw the "woulda, shoulda, couldas" into the mix to make things worse. Both times I wondered if life was worth living. But it was, and it is! Even though both relationships ended with me getting hurt, I wouldn't trade those learning experiences for anything. Growth is never easy, and relationships include some of the hardest knocks in life.

Try not to hold onto past relationships if they are causing pain, and don't be afraid to let go. Healing takes its own course of time, but the sooner you can get back into the dating scene, the sooner you can find what else is waiting for you. I have seen too many individuals hold onto loves well past their expiration date and were later sorry for the lives they missed. Don't let anyone take any additional time from you than they already have!

*Depression is the black hole of life; it will suck you in and crush you into nonexistence. Therefore, always keep a lifeline with you to pull you out.*

*A*nyone who knows anything about black holes knows they are regions of space that have such strong gravitational pulls nothing can escape them. That's what depression feels like while one is in the midst of it. We feel as though we cannot escape its power. All happiness and joy are sucked from life, and we feel utterly helpless. Our strength is gone, and many of us make a tent out of our beds whenever possible and camp out there.

My depression began to take over my life during the second year of my retirement. However, I had been struggling with it for several years already since January 2009. This is still the hardest thing for me to talk or write about. Nothing will set a depression in motion like a broken relationship, stage 4 cancer in a parent, and a major surgery all within two months. However, what put me over the edge was losing my dad four years later, unhappily ending my teaching career, and putting my house up for sale, all within three months. The next year I was waking up at five o'clock to answer calls from schools and driving up to an hour to substitute jobs in order to pay my bills. I was tied to the town I had moved to exclusively to be near work. Without my job, there was no need to be there any longer, and I felt stuck.

I tried to make the most of my first year of retirement by writing, working, and creating artwork—I even took up crocheting! However, I still felt trapped within the vortex of my black hole. The second year I got braces on my teeth as a last-ditch effort to save two of them and came down with shingles at the same time. That was the straw that broke this camel's back. I was more than miserable, I was in pain physically, emotionally, and mentally. Although my shingles were relatively mild, anyone who has had them will tell you how much they itch and burn and how miserable they can make you.

Shortly after this time my fibromyalgia took on a life of its own, and I began to feel more and more sick. This illness affects everyone in different ways, and although I had it for many years already, the stress I was feeling made mine explode. My legs would get shooting and stabbing pains, and my body would feel so weak, as if I had just run a 10-mile race with the burning pain of lactic acid build-up in it. My arms developed raised bumps that would burn, pick, and itch so much that I would wake up bleeding in the morning and my back muscles would be tied in knots. By Thanksgiving, I was ready to give up. Thankfully, my sister-in-law heard my call for help and introduced me to someone who could give me some answers. He, in turn, was able to hand me the lifeline I needed. Through this period of healing, I came to realize I had been focusing so much on what was happening to me and my own pain, I had lost sight of the one thing that could pull me from the blackness that surrounded me: my lifeline to my spiritual life and skills with which to cope. (For those readers who aren't spiritual, always make certain you have another backup plan, such as a good counselor, friend, or an established plan of action.)

Once I figured out what I was missing, I was able to relax more, find and use ways to release my anger, pull myself up to my feet, and stand on them once again. Yes, it was a lot of work; I had weekly assignments, a lot of pain, tears, and junk to shovel through and people to forgive, including myself. I began to get out more, see my friends and neighbors. Then, when the last piece fell into place, I was free of emotional pain, depression, and past trauma. Today I still deal with physical pain on a daily basis, but compared to where I was, I can't help but be grateful to feel alive and free of the past.

*Suicide, attempted suicide, and suicidal thoughts are events we refuse to talk about as a society, but we should.*

In our society, mental illness continues to be a problem people refuse to talk about or even acknowledge.

I am like many others in that I have thought about suicide during the darkest times in my life. Having said this, I can empathize with the unrelenting pain that causes one to contemplate such drastic measures. I have had two such instances in my life: one after my first breakup and the other during my last years of teaching and upon my unplanned retirement. I remember thinking how much I wanted to end things quickly in an accident against a tree or off a cliff. But that's where it stopped for me.

There were three things that kept me from hurting myself. First, it went against my core spiritual belief. I believe that every life is important, and it was wrong to end my own. Second, I remember how hurt I was when our neighbors were killed, and I didn't want to cause my family and friends to suffer that way. Finally, deep down inside, I believed if I would only hold on for another day, things would change. And so I did and my life improved.

*Suicide is a permanent solution to a temporary problem.* Suicide is a reaction to either emotional or physical pain that has become too great to bear. It can also be a result of overwhelming guilt: emotional pain and anger turned inward. Whether the guilt is legitimate or imagined isn't the question. The fact is, when one feels this way, it becomes his or her reality. When pain lasts long enough, it leads an individual down a dark road until one can't tell the difference between right or wrong and no longer cares about anyone or anything, just ridding themselves of their suffering.

If you find yourself in this situation, *please seek help!* Hang on until tomorrow and get counseling. It has helped me tremendously. *Nothing is ever too great to cause you to take your own life.*

*We are so much stronger  
than we could ever imagine!*

We never know how strong we are until we are tested. Just like a rope that holds a great ship by an anchor to keep it from being tossed about at sea in a storm, we are grounded by our inner strength in times of trouble.

Have you ever wondered why some people seem to be stronger than others when faced with a challenge? I believe we all make a conscious decision at some point whether or not to be strong. A good example of this is when my first serious boyfriend and I split up and I was in California, away from family, friends, and security. My job wasn't what I had hoped it would be, I was having financial trouble, and my emotional support was back home in Wisconsin. One of my friends had just died from cancer, and I had just spent two afternoons in a doctor's office, one getting a finger sewn up and one removing an abscess from my mouth. I was miserable.

I could have told myself to be strong until help arrived, which it did shortly thereafter, but I remember telling myself I no longer wanted to be tough, as I was so tired of trying to be. That set the tone for the whole next year. I continued to be miserable and took those around me along with me on my misery-go-round. If only I had known of the challenges to follow in my life, I would have been more patient with these events and with myself.

The next big crisis in dealing with multiple life changing events was my mother's second cancer diagnosis. This time it was stage 4. I didn't tell myself I couldn't deal with the challenges, but, rather, faced them head on. I reached out to my friends, said a lot of prayers, and gave up a teaching job that was already stressing me out. In so doing, I was able to spend more time with my mother and teach on my own terms, substituting in my area.

Looking back, these were both stressful times, but making a conscious choice to be strong allowed me to make healthy decisions ahead of time. Although several years later, when she finally passed away, I developed some stress-related illnesses, I was able to cope with those in a strong, resourceful manner by going to a doctor for medication, getting a lawyer to exercise my rights as a state employee, and taking a vacation to relieve some of my stress.

When you find you are in a storm without an anchor, remember that you are never given more than you can handle. Stand firm and throw your anchor out. Make a conscious decision to be strong and give yourself a break by reaching out to family and friends. Get in touch with your spiritual power and make the changes you can in your life. You may also need to get help from a doctor or counselor to help you through your stressful situation, and that is okay. It doesn't take away from your inner strength, but shows you are smart enough to admit you may just need a little help.

*Tell yourself everything will be okay and reaffirm it, especially when you are in the midst of overwhelming circumstances.*

Many times, in the past nineteen years since my mom's passing, I have longed to feel her arms around me and hear her whisper those magic words in my ear, "Don't worry, honey, everything will be okay!" Unfortunately, unless there are visiting hours in heaven, that will never happen for any of us who have lost our mothers. I do sense her presence and can almost feel those familiar arms around me at times, but, sadly, that isn't the same as her actually being here. Many times my friends and family have tried to comfort me with similar words, and although they help, they still don't have the same power as a mother's comforting words.

There are many times when we must find the strength from within to fight our daily battles. And the only time we will ever believe things will indeed work out is if we convince ourselves they will. *We* can make it so with a little help from our family and friends and from above. These last three months have been some of the most stressful in my life, but I am making it through, and everything will indeed be okay. I'm not just saying this, but I truly believe it will be. I will eventually finish the class in which I am currently enrolled. I will catch up financially, put my fibromyalgia into remission, lose weight, and learn how to control my asthma.

There is one thing we must do after we have found the strength to fight the battles facing us every day, and that is to keep reminding ourselves things really will work out. In that way, if the situation does get worse for a while, as it sometimes does, we won't fall apart. Reinforce this again and again, fifty times a day if you have to. Call a friend or family member and ask them to pray for you. If you aren't spiritual, have a long talk with them over the phone or ask them to come over and chat. The main thing is to hold on to hope, as this too shall pass.

Gather your armies together and fight the good fight. Know that your mom is standing right beside you in spirit as you do, most probably with her arms around you right now, whispering those magic words in your ear.

*You can forgive anything that has happened to you in time.*

> "Bitterness is like cancer. It eats upon the host.
> But anger is like fire. It burns it all clean."
> – Maya Angelou

Forgiveness is required of us and not for those who have wronged us. It is for *US* so that *WE* may move on with our gift of life.

I was young when I first read the book by John Walsh about the kidnapping and murder of his son, Adam. I remember asking myself how this man could have forgiven someone who had brutally murdered his son and still continue to live, much less head up the powerful television show *America's Most Wanted*. I wondered how he found the strength to later testify before Congress on behalf of missing children and victim's rights issues, lobby for a Constitutional Amendment for these same rights, was able to establish the Adam Walsh Child Resource Center, and pursue a host of other efforts. In researching him for this book, I discovered he also wrote a paper on forgiveness. I found it so ironic that a man who had such harm done to someone he loved could forgive such a person.

We are all called to forgive, not just because it is asked of us, but more because it helps *us* to heal. The longer we hold onto pain, the more it will hurt us, *not* the person who has harmed us. Think of pain as an infection or, as Maya Angelou said, a cancer. If you don't take care of it, either by taking medication or having chemotherapy to cure it, or have it excised from your body, you will eventually die. It will overtake your body with its unhealthy cells and kill you. Such is harboring resentment and pain. Most people can't forgive because they don't know how to let go. They can't let go because they don't understand, or they may believe justice must be served before letting go. Many times the problem eats away at them and keeps them from being happy until it destroys their lives, their relationships, and their health.

Forgiveness takes time, but I have found that if you replace your rage and hurt with something more important or use your anger to create, something good will usually come out of it. For me it was coming to an understanding that the people who harmed me had terrible issues of their own. It's up to us to research and discover the circumstances for what has happened in the past, write about it, draw and paint it, or sing about it, then forgive and watch the healing begin.

*Joy is contagious . . . Let others catch some of yours! There is a lot of George Bailey in us all if we just look for it. It IS a wonderful life!*

One of my favorite movies is *It's a Wonderful Life*, with Jimmy Stewart playing the part of George Bailey. It's about a man who is given the gift of seeing how his life has affected those around him. He is reminded of the joy he has given to others, and without him the world would be drastically different. In the end, George realizes what others have seen all along: his life has been a gift, no matter what.

Have you ever been in a room full of people, but one person seemed to outshine the others? That's probably because the person is full of joy and makes it a daily habit of enjoying life to its fullest and making the most out of each situation. Anyone who has met my younger sister would agree she shines. I've always described her to my friends as a bright, shiny, new copper penny, as she just glows. That's because the light inside of her shines! People like to be around her and enjoy her company. She is active in her church and her community, has a nice house, two children, a dog, and a husband who adores her. She also works hard for her money and has gone through the normal problems in life: the buying and selling of houses, illnesses in the family, deaths of parents and friends, and saving for retirement. But throughout her life, she has always remained optimistic, and her glass has always been half full, in spite of her circumstances. I always call her when I need encouragement, as I know her joy is contagious.

Quite recently I went to fill in for my brother at his school as his substitute. Later, people began commenting to him and my sister-in-law how I had changed: that I was joyful and had a great outlook for the future. Since I had begun subbing there, I seem to have caught some of my sister's joy, and now it is *my* time to shine!

*Our subconscious protects us from more situations than we could ever imagine. Never underestimate its creativity!*

Growing up, I knew that something was different about me, that something was missing in my life. It haunted me like a terrible nightmare. Although I could never put my finger on it, I came to accept it as part of my personality, something I had to live with. I knew I had a traumatic first year of school, and that during the same time, my grandmother, whom I adored, had suddenly died. Then another neighborhood boy, whom I loved as only an eight-year-old could, had also moved away. I was a painfully shy girl and kept a lot to myself, something I didn't fully outgrow until I went into teaching.

During my time of healing, a book came out about the neighbor boy across the field who had killed his family. It was a steppingstone for me to get in touch with that part of my life and the people in it. Through a series of coincidences, which I can only attribute to the hand of the Divine, a friend and I were reminiscing over our childhoods when she brought up our first grade teacher. Although I had memories of her treating others in the class badly, I could only remember two incidents involving myself. However, my friend went on to tell me about the many more incidents involving my classmates and myself, all of which I had no memory of. Suddenly everything made sense to me: all of my fears of bullies, anxieties, and the part of me that was missing. My subconscious had protected me from memories which were too painful to face in such an ingenious way . . . it chose to block out that they had even happened!

Our brains use all sorts of creative ways to protect us from what we can't process or handle. My situation is only one. Among some of the others is dissociative identity disorder, in which the brain can't integrate all personalities of a person. There is also obsessive-compulsive disorder (OCD), in which a person develops compulsions that help control anxiety. Our brains can tune out events that are too stressful for us, like it did in my case, and it can make us numb to what is bothering us. And although the reason for blocking out those events had long since become unhealthy for me because they interfered with parts of my life, they did get me through a painful period of childhood.

We all have been given an extremely creative brain. It works in every way possible to help and protect us, in my case even to the point of repressing memories!

*The ghosts of the past are scarier than facing the truth.*

As I mentioned earlier, I grew up with ghosts haunting me. This was particularly true of my early years. During this past year, I reconnected with some of the people who shared those experiences with me. To my surprise, when I learned all of the details involving both situations (the murders and the abusive teacher we had in first grade), I was oddly relieved and found myself feeling incredibly sorry for the two people who caused so much pain to so many. Both had mental issues and must have been in tremendous pain themselves. I immediately felt at peace, and all of the terrifying feelings from my childhood were gone.

Unfortunately, people didn't talk about such things, as mental illness was a taboo part of society. We had no counselors in those days, and the people who are still living don't like to talk about the incident yet. My brother was in the same class with two of the girls, something I just realized this past year, but he has never talked about it with any of us. When I tried to ask him about why he had never mentioned this fact, I got a stern look and he answered, "Some things are just too tragic to talk about!"

Much has changed today, but mental illness is still misunderstood. Wouldn't it have changed so many lives if those events could have been discussed and faced immediately instead of fifty years later? I remember looking into the history of the murders several years ago, going to the local library and looking up old newspaper articles on microfiche. But it wasn't until I could understand the situation surrounding the event that I could successfully release my ghosts.

Although the past can't be changed, we can learn from our mistakes and painful pasts and exorcise all of our ghosts and skeletons from their closets, burying them once and for all by sharing, understanding, and forgiving.

*Leave behind the "what ifs" and "if onlys."*

We have heard of the deadly "should haves," but what about the paralyzing "what ifs" and "if onlys"? If I hadn't done this, then that wouldn't have happened, or if only I hadn't done that, then this wouldn't have happened! These types of thoughts or beliefs can paralyze us, leaving us with self-abusing tendencies, burdening us with needless, painful self-doubt and self-blame. We point the finger back at ourselves as if we were responsible for what happened. Are we omniscient? Certainly not! We can only make decisions based on what we know, use common sense and good judgment, and then follow through with an action. Certainly no one knew on 9/11/2001 the World Trade Center in New York City would become a target. Nor did the people who elected Hitler president know he would turn out to be such a murderous tyrant! It's the same with our daily lives. Did my parents know by moving to our area, we would be exposed to murder and abuse? They say that hindsight is always 20/20. We can't see the next moment, much less into tomorrow. Blaming ourselves only makes the painful process of healing take longer.

    This past New Year's Eve, I got a call from an old boyfriend, my first love, asking me to have coffee. I had always wondered if I had done the right thing as the events played out that led to our split and his eventual marriage to another. So even though it was some thirty years since I'd seen him, I soon discovered our paths on this earth were truly guided beyond anything we can imagine. I had closure, and the "what ifs" and "if onlys" were gone in a flash. Why couldn't I have just trusted I had been on the right path all along? Just like in the situation of "doubting Thomas" in the Bible, oftentimes we need proof to banish our doubts.

    It is very hard to do, but every time you hear a "what if" or an "if only" start to form in your mind, don't let it overtake your thoughts. Repeat to yourself you are only human and not psychic. We don't have control over what happens and aren't the Universal Creator. When we do this enough, it will become a habit and undo the negative pattern of self-blame that often develops. This, in turn, will lead to a happier, healthier you, and give you the freedom to move on.

*Even the worst things in life can work to the good if you only let them. Learn from them and then let them go.*

My life has been a patchwork of highs and lows. I have truly been blessed with what I have been allowed to do and see: I have visited fifteen countries, including two semesters abroad, saw part of Australia's Bicentennial from Sydney Harbor, as well as snorkeled both the Great Barrier Reef and the Reef in Belize. I have been blessed with a wonderful extended family and so much more. However, along with these amazing gifts, I have also had to endure a lot of heartache. Along with the events discussed previously, I have had to deal with my dad's and cousin's cancer diagnoses. (Both of these family members eventually succumbed to the illness.) Many times during my careers, I have had times when money was sparse, and I have struggled financially.

During the past two years, I have posted many "aha" moments on Facebook and shared poems with all of my past mistakes and private struggles. Exposed, those mistakes and battles can't stand a chance against the healing power of honesty and forgiveness. Some of the events of my life are far too personal for me to share in any book, but suffice it to say that I've had my fair share. But without the bad times in which I struggled, I couldn't have written this book to help others. Without my mistakes in travel, I wouldn't be able to help others with their adventures.

If you are experiencing a seriously bad time in your life, don't give up. Please believe there is a plan and you will be able to come out on the other side with something worth holding on to. My tough childhood helped to create a strong will within me. As the oldest girl in a family of five siblings, I was expected to be in charge of my little sister and brother and help with the cooking and household chores. My sister, nine-and-one-half years my junior, became like a surrogate daughter. We remained close as I grew older, and after moving to college, I often invited her to visit me on weekends. We even went on a trip to Jamaica together in 1985, and I later became her daughter's godmother. My responsibility as a child gave me the best relationship with the greatest sister of all time, and we are still very close today. My awful first grade teacher taught me what *not* to do as a teacher and human being. Everything in my life has worked to the good in making me who I am, and I am glad to be me. I am whole and have learned from my experiences, and now I am ready to move on.

*If you don't deal with your problems, they will keep popping up until you do.*

Problems in life are like slow growing cancers that need to be removed. I know this is true, as I have lived it. My problem with my bullying first grade teacher came back to haunt me over and over throughout life with bullying adults. I couldn't stand up for myself and didn't know why I was so afraid. Society calls the ability to stand up for oneself assertiveness. The humorous part about this is that I was advised to attend a class on assertiveness when I first entered college forty years ago. It obviously didn't help because I hadn't gotten to the root of the problem, but was trying to patch it with a Band-Aid instead.

Illnesses are the same; you have to get to what is causing your sickness or you will be medicating the symptoms for the rest of your life. Anyone with illnesses like chronic fatigue syndrome, fibromyalgia, Lyme disease or lupus can tell you how frustrating it is to try to find out what is wrong with you only to discover that no one knows how to fix it. I medicated for several years before they discovered I had fibromyalgia, and I am still looking for a way to treat it instead of patch it.

To deal with problems, one must find the root cause. Are you having financial problems? Ask yourself why. If you are having problems socially, find out what is causing this and create a plan to help overcome it. However, I again must warn you that in dealing with any personal problem, you must be brutally honest with yourself and possibly deal with some unsavory truths. The key is to first admit something is wrong, find the source of the problem, and then a way to fix it. Most people just keep struggling throughout life. It's up to each individual to find a way to fix their problems.

Take a look at the person you are and rip the Band-Aid off one last time. Find the life you have been meant to live by discovering a way to heal yourself and deal with your problems. You will be amazed by how free you will feel.

*There are plenty of others
who want to beat you up.
You don't need to do
it to yourself.*

*Why did I just do that?* I can just hear myself ask. Why did I say that to him? That was so stupid! We beat ourselves up every day with thoughts like these. The worst is when these thoughts blindside us from the past. Pow! And why did you say that twenty years ago? How could you have made such a stupid statement!

Many of us do this to ourselves all of the time. And why? Because we are human and not perfect. But we want to be and many of us expect it of ourselves. We also want to be accepted, so we try to figure out why we do the things we do, and when we can't, we punish ourselves for being human. It becomes a bad habit that is very hard to break. When we punish ourselves, we are actually repeating a punishing thought pattern over and over again, making the connection harder and harder to break in our brains.

I can still remember mistakes I made when I was young. However, fortunately for me, the sting of the moment has turned into the learning experience it was intended to be. We aren't supposed to dwell on the pain of our mistakes but take the lesson along with us and leave the rest behind.

Finally, give yourself a break. You aren't perfect, so stop trying to be! Look at your mistakes, learn from them, and put them behind you.

*Those who are nasty and evil, those who make life unbearable, have their own misery to live through, either now or later. Do not let them steal any more of your joy than they already have by letting their voices take up residence in your head!*

This is an issue most of us struggle with from time to time. There will eventually come a day when we will all run into the nasties of this world, and we may want to strangle them for the pain they cause. After a particularly painful breakup, I decided to send my ex a letter letting him know exactly how I felt and what he had done to me, as I couldn't get him to talk. It wasn't a particularly nasty letter, just factual. I thought it would provide the closure so many had encouraged me to pursue. But after sending it, I wished I hadn't mailed it, but kept it for my own healing.

For those who believe that karma will eventually vindicate you, the thought does provide some comfort. But dwelling on painful memories by thinking those who have wronged you will "get their just rewards" only gives you more time to think of your pain and keeps you from healing. Rather, a better use of your energy might be to work on letting go of your pain by filling your life with more meaningful and useful thoughts and projects. Soon you will find you don't have time to even think of what was done to you, which in turn will allow your heart to heal.

Having said this, I am still trying to get over the pain caused in my last professional job. It hurt me to the core, and I developed PTSD from my last few years there. The last time I went back into the building, I drove away in tears, screaming to myself all the way home. I pray every day for the strength to overcome this pain and rebuild my self-confidence in the workplace. I am getting there. Since that day, I have metamorphosed from an angry person to someone who feels sorry for the people who hurt me. But I am still working on my forgiveness.

Today we live in a terrifying world in which many, including myself, wake up fearful every day. When I think of the hate in our country, I get sick to my stomach, and sleep is hard to find some nights. Those who are at the core of this worry have their own hell to live through, and we don't have to wish any more upon them. However, they are stealing our joy as we worry about the fate of our world. It doesn't help that I believe my Creator is in charge, as I also believe we have all been given a brain to use, as well as a free will.

So what's a person to do? The best we can do is to express these fears and share them with others who are afraid. We can also work against those people causing pain by what we do, in this case fighting fear and hate with love. Loving those who are also struggling can go a great distance in alleviating pain we are struggling with. We can join forces with others to go one step further to put our ideas into action.

There will always be nasties in this world as long as we exist, for we live a flawed existence. Our best hope to overcome these is to do our very best to understand, love, and forgive and to put our best actions into motion to help stop them. Finally, do whatever works to keep those nasties or thoughts of them from setting up camp in your head and heart.

*Don't let limitations hold you back from something you really want. Look at Stephen Hawking, Scott Hamilton, Julie Andrews, and Audrey Hepburn!*

I know of many people who have chosen to let life stop them from doing the things they want to do. Either they have physical limitations, or they let fear stop them. In my thirties, I was desperate to find a husband and wanted a child, as only a woman in her thirties can understand. I would cry and ask my mother why I hadn't found a mate. My mother, bless her soul, gave me some of the best advice I have ever been given by anyone. She said, "Being single isn't the worst thing in the world. Just don't let it stop you from living your life!" I have never forgotten this bit of wisdom and have applied it to a whole list of things.

I have a lot of limitations, just like anyone else. I have a terrible fear of heights, but I have climbed mountains, waterfalls, towers, and bridges; rode to the top of the Eiffel Tower and the Washington Monument; and climbed the Koln Cathedral. I will never jump out of an airplane or parasail, but then I have no desire to do either. I cried at thirty-two when I left by myself for Australia to complete my student teaching because I was afraid, but it turned out to be the best experience of my life, and I will always cherish every moment. I was so shy and soft-spoken as a child, I never even considered being a teacher. But when the time presented itself, I had little problem. I have wanted to travel all of my life, but never had enough money to do as much as I have wanted. Now I am making other people happy by writing about the places I have been blessed to visit in a blog. I also have the time now that I am retired to travel and learn about the places I've only seen in books or on the Web.

My story is not singular in nature. Most people know who Stephen Hawking is. He suffered from a rare form of early-onset, slow-growing ALS, or Lou Gehrig's disease, yet he managed to become one of the greatest minds of our time. Scott Hamilton developed a mysterious illness as a child which began to impede his growth and health. After four years of searching for a cure, his doctor suggested that his parents send him skating in order to give them a break. He took to the sport and as a result of his skating began to recover, eventually becoming one of the most revered male skaters of all time. Later he developed testicular cancer and has now been diagnosed with a third brain tumor, yet he still manages to maintain his positive attitude. He has become a motivational speaker, author, and actor and has graced the world with a whole host of other gifts. Julie Andrews was painfully shy as a child but overcame this to star in numerous movies over the past three generations. And when she lost her ability to sing because of a botched surgery for vocal nodes, she began to write children's stories with her daughter and star in movies that didn't require her to sing like she had in previous movies. Audrey Hepburn grew up in Belgium, but struggled to survive after the Germans invaded the Netherlands. Because of the malnutrition and trauma she experienced during and after World War II, she developed many physical problems. She used this experience and her demure size to portray slight, classy women who always had strength of character in movies. Later she became a spokeswoman for UNICEF to give a voice to children suffering around the world.

Look at what is holding you back and figure out a way to climb over it or use it to your advantage. Remember as you mount your limitations and view your world from atop them, you can see more of everything around you and figure out the best route to follow.

*Never neglect your inner self.
While your looks and figure will fade with
age, your inner spirit will continue
to grow more beautiful.*

Have you ever known anyone who was just plain beautiful? I don't mean blessed with outer beauty, but that special something that attracts everyone? I used to try to figure this out when I was young: what made one person more attractive than others? Like every youngster, I just assumed it was the outer package. But then there were those who broke the rules. So I just became confused. However, as I grew older, I began to see beyond the outer image and looked to what was inside. To my surprise, these average-looking classmates were interesting, loving, and fun to be around. They had taken the time to develop their inner beauty, and although they hadn't neglected the outer one, they had definitely set important priorities.

Although I didn't consider myself particularly attractive in my teens and early twenties because of self-concept issues, I did have a nice figure and could fit into small dresses, even into my early fifties. Now what I wouldn't give to fit into any size under 12! We are never satisfied with what we have, and as we grow older, we must all understand our looks will begin to fade to some degree. If it isn't adding a muffin top, it is seeing something begin to sag, and we are continuously trying to shore these areas up. I gave up trying to plug all of these holes in my dam long, long ago. Now I'm working on my health and my inner self, and that's enough for me.

If you focus on your inner self, you will seldom be disappointed. Your inner self includes your personality, any dreams you may have, how you treat others, developing your world ties, your life purpose, values, code of life, and what you feel passionate about. The list goes on. This isn't something affected by age, with the exception of some illnesses, such as dementia and Alzheimer's. Many of these internal traits are present when we are young; those who were altruistic when young often grow more as they mature, and those who were sweet as children are also usually more so as adults. However, a great deal of growth occurs during life, and the tiny spark we may have had as a child, which might not have shown then, may bloom later.

Continue to work on the traits which make up your core and don't be so concerned with your outside appearance that will someday fade. It is truly a much better investment of your time, energy, and money.

*We can all learn to deal with change and
need not be afraid of challenges
and new situations.*

Change is part of life. We either learn to adapt or we won't make it. We are born, grow during childhood and teens into adulthood, go to college, and get a job. We may meet someone, fall in love, get married, buy a house, raise a family, have grandkids, and retire, possibly have great grandkids, do some of the things that we have been putting off, sell our home, perhaps move into an assisted living community, nursing home, or next to our children, and then slip from our mortal bonds.

We are taught to expect many of these changes throughout our lives so they don't surprise us when they occur. But it's the other events that blindside us and throw our lives out of balance. When I was in ninth grade, my mother told us all that she had to go into the hospital. *Oh great,* I thought, *we are going to have another baby!* However, it turned out she had to have a biopsy done but didn't want us to worry. The next morning my father came home looking very frightened. He proceeded to tell me that Mom had breast cancer, that she was very sick, had surgery to remove the cancer, and almost died in the process. I was told to be brave and take care of the my younger brothers and sister during the morning while he went back to the hospital. I tried to do what my dad had asked, but when I went to school that afternoon, I broke down in tears and had to return home. It took us a long time to adjust as a family.

Retirement was another one of these unexpected times. It was time for the next year's schedule to come out, and the administration had made a big point about us working on new classes in our particular areas to create more interest within our subjects. Our governor had also just done away with seniority in the schools of our state, so it was every man (or woman, in my case) for themselves. Everyone was vying for every student they could get. So when we were sent an e-mail instructing us to go down to the principal's office if we wanted to see our class schedules, I immediately made my way down.

Much to my surprise, I found that my classes as well the the choir director's were cut in half and displayed on a schedule on our principal's desk! He was no where to be found. I was devastated. After putting eighteen years into the education system there and having spent thousands of dollars of my own money to buy additional supplies for my classes, this is how I was told. A month later, after speaking with a financial adviser, I was encouraged to apply for early retirement. I believe his exact words were, "This is a no-brainer." So I had no time to prepare, either emotionally or financially.

Both of these events, and many more than I could recount here, were very hard to accept, but retirement was hardest for me to adjust to, besides the death of my parents. It had not only surprised me, but also left me with little to no self-confidence. I was without a consistent source of income, without an identity, and without a foreseeable future.

Now it's five years later, and although I wished I could have been able to adapt immediately to this change, it has all worked out for the best. I have made some money subbing, met many wonderful people in doing so, was able to heal from past hurts, learned to be strong and confident once more, and studied another trade and two other languages. I have written six books, begun four more, took two trips, moved back to my childhood city, and have been blessed to work for someone who has appreciated my gifts.

Change takes a lot of time and effort to adapt to, even when it is a good change. So be brave, cry if you need to, believe change will work out for the best and open up new areas of life to you.

# Part Two

## Coping Skills: Life's Survival Kit to Deal & Heal

Make an emergency emotional and mental health kit for yourself. I never thought of having such a kit for life's problems, and maybe that's where I have been going wrong. I have a survival package in my car for the winter months, and I carry emergency water if I should travel through a desert region, so why not a list of coping skills for navigating the potholes of life? In this chapter, I have included a number of skills I have learned, either by myself, through counseling, or in researching for this book.

*Validation of feelings is the first step
on the path to healing.*

It takes a lot of courage to share all of your secrets and mistakes with someone else, yet this is exactly what must be done to begin the process of healing. Burying these feelings will never help in getting well, as something or someone will always come along and dig them up, opening wide your wound again. I was amazed by how relieved I was when I first began to discuss what had been bothering me with another person. I soon realized that it was *not* all in my head and I was perfectly normal to feel the way I did. Not only was someone listening to me, but also telling me my feelings were valid as well.

However, it took me a while to find a person I could trust. You can't dump a lifetime of closely guarded worries and secrets on just anyone. By doing so, you are baring your soul and opening yourself up to more hurt. So when I found someone who I felt was trustworthy and able to listen objectively, I opened up. Whether that person is your husband, wife, significant other, counselor, pastor, or best friend, if they listen and can give you the validation and the help you need, you are well on your way to healing.

We all have many different feelings every day: anger, frustration, hurt, love, joy, happiness, tiredness, fear, feeling safe, sadness, hate, feeling cold or hot, and many, many more. Some are inner feelings, and some are physical reactions to our surroundings. But each one of these is a valid feeling, and each one is very real to us.

When I was young, I was always told I was far too sensitive. I was forever being told by someone not to feel a certain way or not to be so silly in feeling as I did. So I grew up not trusting a lot of what I was feeling. We are all given the power of discernment as to what is going on around us. It's what protects us in dangerous situations and helps us to become more attuned to the world and people around us. Because I couldn't trust my feelings, I became very anxious, had panic attacks, developed OCD, and turned a lot of my anxiety inward on myself. As I grew older, people told me I needed to develop a thicker skin. So again, I swallowed my feelings and said very little. I developed anxiety problems and eventually fibromyalgia, my body's reaction to the poison I was swallowing.

But I now know my feelings were—and still are—valid, and I am allowed to be the type of woman I was made to be. That has made all of the difference in the world. If you are feeling hurt, tired, or lonely, it may be your body or subconscious trying to tell you something. Listen to those feelings, and then get someone else to validate them. I am so very grateful I did!

*Learn how to say no. Many people who are people pleasers try to play Superman or Superwoman, trying not to hurt others.*

While growing up, I had a very hard time saying no. I was a people pleaser because I *needed* people to like me. When friends and family asked me to do something extra for them, I just about killed myself doing it. In addition, I had to be the best at what I did. (I still do, unfortunately.) The only thing I was absolutely firm about saying no to was sex and drugs. Grades were the same way. As I got older, there were many more As, until that was all there were. It killed me when I went back to school for my education degree and missed a 4-point GPA by one B. I have never gotten another one since.

When I got into the workforce, it was the same: I couldn't say no. I was always putting my health and my own needs in jeopardy by saying yes. Staying up until three in the morning to complete illustrations for the next day was a common practice in the advertising world during my first career at ShopKo headquarters, and grading papers until 1:00 or 2:00 a.m. became nearly an every night occurrence in education. Needless to say, my health paid the price. I developed chronic migraines and other symptoms of stress.

One of the most stressful times was the summer when two of my siblings were married. I was delighted when I was asked to be maid of honor for my sister's wedding, as I have always adored her, and took on the job with joy. I planned a shower, a bachelorette party, and all of the rest, but also made a lot of the wedding and shower presents myself. When we decided to have my sister's reception at home, I made all of the rolls and breads as well. My mom was busy making her wedding and bridesmaid dresses, as well as my sister's veil, so it was my job to help out.

What would have happened if I had bought some of the shower presents and rolls instead? Probably nothing. I know that my sister would have appreciated them just as much. I would have had a less stressful summer and not have had to stay up the morning of the wedding hemming my dress until 3:00 a.m. Ninety-nine percent of the wedding and reception went off without a hitch. My sister got the wedding she wanted and deserved, and the food was great. Everyone had a wonderful time and everything was perfect. But I ended up lying on the floor for three days trying to relax my back because of my foolishness.

Another occasion was when I decided to have a family art show posthumously to honor my mom. She had always wanted a gallery in which we could all show our work, but she didn't live long enough to see her dream come true. So, we remodeled three rooms in our family home; Dad carpeted all of them and I painted one. I decorated the outside with flowers and shrubs, finished some six drawings and paintings of my own and had them, as well as several of my mother's and my brother's, matted and framed. My younger brother and I hung all of the work and put names next to each one. I bought wine and reception snacks, sent out about a hundred invitations, called the local paper and news station to inform them of the event, and had a friend videotape part of it. I even painted the front of the house at 5:00 a.m. the day of the open house because the paint was uneven due to age!

Can you see a pattern here? It's not that I didn't want to do either of these things. I was the one who pushed for the art gallery, and I would do almost anything for my sister. But no one expected me to try to be superhuman or almost kill myself for them.

In my eighteen years at my last school, my art students went to Washington, D.C., twice, winning two national and over twenty local and state awards during the last ten years of my teaching career. I drove myself crazy, consistently entering my students into several art competitions each year and putting up over three hundred pieces in an annual spring art show. But when classes came to be cut because of budget constraints and dwindling numbers in our school, I still had my job cut in half.

So please give yourself a break, and either say no or cut down your workload if you can. I'm not saying you shouldn't do your best, but don't overdo it either. Most people won't appreciate your extra efforts as much as you do, except special friends and family, and when you die of a stress-related illness or heart attack, your business will probably only mark your passing by sending the traditional flowers!

*Life is not black and white
or all or none; it's all of the shades
of grey in between.*

I grew up in a black-and-white world, as did most of us in our generation. Things were either right or wrong, with no margin for error. I was told, "If you are going to do something, do it well, or not at all" and "If you are going to make a mistake, do it with gusto!" I gave up track my senior year because I had major surgery around Christmas, and I figured if I couldn't perform to the best of my ability, I shouldn't run at all. It was the same with my work in college, and as I got older, I only became more of a perfectionist.

However, things began changing as the world began to challenge my belief system. I grew up in a very conservative area with very strict parents, so I had a narrow view of the world and a very strict code of morality. I believed there was only one way to live my life, and that was beyond reproach; that mistakes were not to be made, there were no grey areas in living, and that the laws and commandments were the same. As I began to study away at college and entered the workforce, I began to question what I had always just accepted. Why are some people born with deformities, I asked myself? They certainly did nothing to deserve this. Why do we, as a human race, always have to use force to get what we want, stealing what we desire, and then being proud of our conquest? What about the Crusades and Hitler's Germany? What about people who didn't conform to my religious belief system? What happens to them? And the biggest question of all: why do people have to suffer so in the world? Many would call this questioning values and maturing, but it just left me in a fugue state. So I did what anyone in my position usually does, I pushed it aside and tried not to think about it. It was the only way I was able to take life drawing courses, study religion, get through college, and learn about Germany where my ancestors came from.

But how do we really grow from a black-and-white or all-or-nothing person to open our minds? My metamorphosis came about slowly, and I am still working on the final product. Getting out and seeing our world firsthand was one of the ways I began to grow. Going through the school of hard knocks was another. Also, I began questioning information and not taking it at face value. I researched it and gave myself a chance to draw *my own* conclusions.

Yes, I am a grey person and proud of it. I fight the good fight along with the rest of the grey people, as well as the black-and-whites on the planet, giving when I can, defending the rights of others, loving those who feel unloved, and supporting those who need a shoulder to cry on. I try not to judge, as I have not walked in someone else's shoes. I realize I'm not all-knowing, so I can't judge according to *my* own life code. I look at the surrounding events before coming to my own conclusion regarding a situation, and I try to take a lesson from my sister's beautiful five-pound Havanese dog: to love unconditionally.

I still question why things are as they are, but I try not to worry about the answers too much anymore, nor do I let them control my life. Those answers are probably not within my understanding, as I am merely human. This has allowed me to relax and not be so judgmental. Someday I am sure we will all understand the answer to all of these questions and much more. We must just be patient.

*Make peace with your past.
Do whatever it takes to forgive
and get beyond it.*

We all have a past: good and bad, right or wrong. But many of us have a hard time living with some of the things we have done or seen. Many of these things can be healed through forgiveness, as mentioned earlier. But how does one get to the point where we can forgive and forget? The truth is, we cannot. We can surely forgive, but unless we develop amnesia, head trauma, or dementia, we are doomed to remember these events for the rest of our lives. So what can we do about past events that are making us miserable or are interfering with our lives? Besides seeing a good counselor who can validate our feelings and teach us skills to deal with such events in the future, we can take some healthy actions.

Remember, we are human and we all make mistakes. That is part of our nature. Mistakes help us learn, grow, and live better and more productive lives to make a difference to those around us. They also help us to find out what we are good at and how to handle everyday situations in our future. We must separate the true mistakes from those we have no control over, such as accidents and misfortunes. Let these go and realize they are not your fault. When no one is at fault, most of us look for someone to blame. We become angry, are deeply hurt, and, many times, lash out at others. Frequently, when there is no one else to blame, many turn their anger inward, which often leads to depression. We need to find a way to stop beating ourselves up, and those we love, over events that are not within our control. This takes time, effort, and perseverance.

The greatest skill given to me to help me dump anger, hate, and hurt was the suggestion to write a letter to everyone who had ever hurt me. So I wrote many letters; some to family members, some to ex-boyfriends, one to the boy who lived next door when I was young, one to my first grade teacher, some to ex-roommates, schoolmates, and others to ex-bosses and miscellaneous abusers. I wrote down every hateful and horrible thing that had been on my mind and called these people every name in the book. I asked them why they had done what they had and why they felt they had the right to hurt me.

When I was done with my little novelettes, I read them over to see if I had missed anything. Then, with one strike of my match, I burned each over my sink. As each was reduced to ashes and was washed down the drain out of sight, I made a mental note they were gone, along with their pain. Afterwards I felt more relieved than I ever could have imagined. No more heavy burden. Later, when I tried to dredge up these painful memories, I immediately remembered my kitchen ceremony and found it much harder to go back to the way it used to be. I also made a promise to myself never to discuss these old hurts unless they related to my factual history. I obviously failed at times, but these moments have become much less with time.

Some of us are not writers, so if you aren't, print the name of the person who hurt you on a piece of paper, think about all he or she has done to you, and then burn it. Or you may want to put your slips of paper in a paper bag or a lunch box and bury them, as if they were dead. Then have a ceremony commemorating their passing and say your goodbyes. Whatever positive steps you can take to leave your past behind are okay.

During this time of healing, I also began to research the events in my life, talking to old friends and schoolmates to fill in the blanks. This was the key to understanding all of the remaining resentment and filled in all of the missing pieces. It was a lot of work and took many tears and time to get through, but I felt so much better when it was done and, for the first time since I was little, whole.

So, if you can, find out why things happened and take care of your resentment in a healthy way. Research those events and look for answers. However horrible, pain subsides, hearts mend, and lives get back to some semblance of normalcy. You will never forget these events and will still remember what has been done to you, but it will be the lesson that will be remembered in the end, instead of the pain.

*Always have a "happy place" on retainer to go to in stressful times.*

We all need a quiet place to go when we are stressed out and need a break, if only in our minds. Mine is floating through a school of sergeant major fishes in a *cenote*, or water hole, in Mexico's Playa de Carmen. I can still see the fish undulating in a single movement, just beyond the touch of my hand. I have never seen such a beautiful scene in my entire life! Before this, it was floating in a boat in Nelligan, New South Wales, Australia, drinking wine and fishing with one of my best friends.

This is a perfect part of my book to be working on today, as I am so stressed that my back and neck burn. We, in America, are in the middle of big political problems, and I am on edge, like so many others. I have put Facebook on hold until the politics die down and I am worried for our country. So I am using what I am writing about today and putting it into action. I begin by taking a few deep breaths, and in my mind's eye I am once again in the *cenote* in Mexico attempting to be one with the sergeant majors. The warm water of the tropics and the sun glistening off of the fish in front of me are taking me away. I feel my body begin to relax once again.

Take a minute to think through your past experiences. What places have you been in which you have felt relaxed and at peace? Is it at home in a certain room? Is it a memory from a trip or vacation? Is it hanging out with a special friend at the beach or in the arms of your mother or husband/wife/partner? We should all have a special place to think about when things get tough that provides peace and security. This is where you will want to go when you are stressed out. Most of us aren't wealthy enough to go overseas every time we are feeling overwhelmed, so memories will have to suffice. If you aren't a visual person, take a photo you have of your special place and study it until you can picture it in your mind, or always keep the photo in your pocket. Then think about it or look at it when you are panicking. This does a lot to calm the mind and parts of your body that react to stress.

So wherever and whenever you have been enchanted by a place, had a vision in a dream, or even created a place in your mind, you can go there when you are stressed. I go to mine quite often in fact. My wonderful friend and former student teaching mentor taught me to do this, and I will be forever in his debt.

*Learn to self-talk. Pay attention to only the positive thoughts and voices in your head. Tell the others to take a hike.*

Let's admit it, we have all heard voices in our heads. You know the ones I mean: the ones that tell us to keep going when we are tired or hurting, to sneak a cookie from the cookie jar when we were kids, or scold us when we think we have done something dumb. Yes, those are the ones I am talking about!

All of us entertain good and bad thoughts from time to time, but it's when the bad ones overstay their welcome that we find ourselves in trouble. Most of the time, they are benign, like melancholy or those that make us blue. But sometimes, when these thoughts camp out, they begin to make us feel sad or depressed. They may remind us of all the mistakes we have made, or all of the bad things that have happened in our lives. They keep spinning their tales of woe and dread, and soon we find ourselves ensnared in their dark webs. Then they begin to invite their friends: fear, self-doubt, and despair. They all pitch their tents in our minds and settle in for the long haul. That's when we find a good housecleaning is in order.

There are several ways to clear out depressing and dark thoughts from our brain, but first we must acknowledge they exist inside of us. We can't fight something if we don't first realize we have a problem. For many of us, our brain has developed a bad habit of *letting* these characters remain as guests, and, like parasites, they are sucking the life out of us. In so doing, they are also making our minds sick, as well as affecting the rest of us, and, as with many bad habits, we have to retrain our brains to deal with them. Mostly this involves evicting them as soon as we have realized that they are there. We can try to bolt the door, but I have found them to be deceitful, and they will eventually fool us into letting them back in.

Our only sure way to change this is to keep reminding these thoughts that they aren't welcome until they get the message. You might also replace them with positive thoughts. This takes time and effort, so you must be patient with yourself. Another technique is to use distractions to help out, such as playing, walking outside, or being with others. Yet another strategy you might use is to compartmentalize your thoughts. Give yourself fifteen minutes each night in which you will acknowledge these bad thoughts—in essence giving them a short guest pass—making it clear you are aware of them but not giving them a green card. If you still can't evict the pests, then give them some art to do or get them involved with a sport so they will leave you alone. Put them into your poems or exercise. All of their energies will be spent on these activities, and they won't bother you as much.

Whatever healthy way you use to free your mind from their control and their presence is perfectly okay. Sweep your attic and clear out all of the dark places. Bring in some bright Christmas lights, regardless of the time of year, put in a few guest rooms and invite all of your positive friends, such as joy, hope, love, and happiness, to stay. Then let the others know unequivocally they aren't welcome anymore and deadbolt the door.

*Practice thinking positively. Begin each day with something uplifting; this will overcome a lot of negative thought and become a positive habit.*

For a long time, I woke up dreading each new day. I felt overloaded with what life had dealt me, and each day was just another reminder of pain and disappointment. Some days I would literally wake up and yell, "I hate my life!" Sometimes, if I could, I would just roll over and go back to sleep so I could forget everything. I hated where I lived, the things I was doing, and a lot of the people around me.

I didn't realize there were plenty of things in my life that were wonderful and that I could change some of those that weren't so nice. Whether a person is spiritual or not, meditation is a great way to begin. Recent research reveals that people who meditate have more positive emotions than those who don't. I am fortunate to be living alone, and my mornings are very quiet. I can meditate while I have coffee or clean. It really doesn't matter what I am doing. And if I keep the television off and stay off of social media, it's easy to focus my mind on the positives if I try.

People who write about positive things have a better outlook as well. I have experienced this while writing this book. Whenever I have focused on the negatives, I have indeed felt them pulling me down, and the reverse is true as well. A lot of people keep a journal to do this. Whenever we write, it's a positive experience, as we are pouring out our thoughts and emotions on paper and can easily see them in front of us. Many times this is when we can act on them.

Lastly, to think more positively, we must set aside some time to play. Which of us does that? Put some time aside to watch your favorite television show, play a video game you like, play with your pet, or join a club and do something physical, like learning to play tennis. All of these lead to a more positive and uplifting day.

Now one of my daily routines is to begin each day with something positive. Whether it's a daily devotional out of a book, an inspirational email message I receive each day, or just walking outside on a crisp morning, these are the things that carry me throughout my day and makes the difference between my cup being half empty or half full. The same things have happened to me—I still have the same physical challenges, the same childhood and adulthood, and the same experiences. But I now see things in a totally different light. I'm so glad to be alive to greet each day and feel very blessed I have all that I do.

*When you find your life
spinning out of control:
stop, look, and listen.*

All of us remember the old phrase "Stop, look, and listen!" when applied to crossing the street. But it can be applied to life when things seem to be out of control as well.

First *STOP* what you are doing. Take some time just for yourself. Feeling out of control usually is a first sign that too much is going on in your life. It might be good things or bad ones. It really doesn't matter too much, as they can both make you a bit crazy.

*LOOK* at your life. What is making you feel as if you are spinning out of control? Make a mental or a written list of things that are happening around you. Have you taken on too much? Are there events or activities you can eliminate from your life? Are there things you have no control over? Can you talk to someone about your problems so you can find a way to deal with them? If you are holding on to hurts or pain, find a way to let them go. Consider going to a counselor, a trusted friend, or a person who has hurt you and discuss your concerns with him or her.

*LISTEN* to your body. It is certainly trying to tell you something, or you wouldn't be feeling the way you are. If you find yourself crying, forgetting things, dealing with headaches or backaches, or unable to concentrate, something is definitely going on in your life. Stress has thrown you a curve ball and knocked your life out of balance. See a counselor, go to a doctor, take a vacation, or divide your day up so you can relax.

The bottom line is to find a way off of the merry-go-round you have gotten yourself onto. They are fun to ride as children, but for adults, they can cause a lot of disorientation, and it can be hard to focus while we are on one.

*Venting frustration is like relieving steam in a pressure cooker: it will keep you from blowing your top.*

I vent, sometimes on Facebook, sometimes to my sister, sometimes to friends, and sometimes to people in my fibromyalgia support group. I tell them how frustrated and angry I am, how much I hurt, and how unfair I find my life at times. Most of the time it has been to my sister though. She has allowed me to vent countless times during the past few years.

If you don't vent your frustration and anger, they can cause all sorts of problems in your life: mental or physical illness, unhappiness, or displaced frustration and anger. I have found joining certain support groups can be of help for various problems. I am in an international fibromyalgia support group on Facebook, which helps immensely. But if you are going to join a support group or vent to friends or family, you must be willing to try what they suggest or at least acknowledge their suggestions. If you don't, they will become tired and frustrated with your complaints and stop listening. You can go online to find support groups, through your church or a doctor. If you know of others who are going through the same problems, you can form your own group.

Exercise in all forms is also a great release. However you choose to use the energy that has been built up by frustration or anger in a positive way, it is good. Anything, from running to sex, is a great expenditure of what has been built up inside. When I was taking tests for my travel course and didn't do as well as I had wanted, I used my anger to fuel my study and resolved to do better on the next test. As I said, any positive approach is worthwhile.

Many people say being angry is nonproductive, or that anger is just destructive. However, I believe all feelings are valid. If someone hurts you physically or emotionally, do you not get hurt and angry? Your feelings are valid. Don't engage people who say they aren't. However, it's what you do with these feelings that's important. To go out and get revenge by planning something to hurt someone who has hurt you is not an acceptable response and solves nothing.

It does nothing to ease your pain and only causes more problems, complicating the matter by causing both you and others pain in the process.

According to the American Psychological Association[1], "Anger is a completely normal, usually healthy, human emotion." These are the four stages to anger, according to Dr. Tim Murphy, a psychologist specializing in adolescent and child anger management. (Murphy, 2001)

1. The Build-up – All of the events adding to a person's anger.
2. The Spark – Like the straw that breaks the camel's back, the spark is something that sets off a person's anger.
3. The Explosion – The point at which a person cannot handle any more stressful events and all of his/her suppressed anger comes pouring out.
4. The Aftermath – After the person has calmed down and can address problems causing the explosion.

Although the above steps were originally applied to children, most adults go through the same stages. If you are in an immediate situation, remember to remain calm, take time to cool off by walking away, whether you are the one who is angry or the one on the receiving end. If you can't walk away, call for help or listen to the other until they have finished venting. When the venting is finished, it is time to talk with the other person.

If you have a long, festering anger where you aren't in any danger to yourself or others, take time to be angry. Tear up pictures of those who have wronged you and have a ceremony to acknowledge that you have moved on. Get rid of past memories that can cause you pain. Most of what festers inside of us about others doesn't matter in the long run anyway.

*If you are struggling with a situation, talk to someone else. Maybe a different perspective is just what you need to help you understand.*

Seek the counsel of others in difficult matters, but then make your own decisions. You're the only one who has to live with them.

Recently I have had to face one of life's challenges. I have fretted about it and cried many tears trying to figure it out. Just when I've thought I have a handle on the situation, another sucker punch hits me from out of nowhere, and I am down for the count. That was, until this morning, when my good friend texted me with a whole different take on the matter. I was floored. I had never thought of the situation in the way she had explained it. It really doesn't matter what I was going through, the point is that she was able to explain it in a new way that I could understand and accept.

So many times in life, we are perplexed by events or situations we find ourselves in. We see things from just one point of view: our own. But when we just take a step back to see events from another angle, we can appreciate them in a whole new light. Before Michelangelo carved his *David* out of a piece of Carrera marble, two other artists who couldn't complete their commissions left behind that very piece of stone. Neither could see the true value in the colossal block of marble or could finish what they had begun. Michelangelo, however, saw the stone from a very different point of view and carved one of the most famous sculptures in the world from it. He was reported to have said, "Every block of stone has a statue inside it and it is the task of the sculptor to discover it." A very different point of view indeed!

I grew up in the same city I moved back to just recently. I was bored and restless as a youngster. I liked going to school because learning was interesting; there were things to do and children to socialize with. I lived out in the country, and our house was built in an area with no electricity or running water when we first moved in. We built our house in the middle of a field atop a hill. The streets were built around our home because we were the first house within one half mile of our neighbors. As we grew older, the joke among my siblings regarding our little city was, "What is the difference between our town and yogurt? Yogurt has more culture!"

There is little doubt that my hometown has done its share of growing through the years. However, having just spent the past thirteen years living in a tiny town along the lake that was a place for retirees, summer tourists, and people who just wanted to relax, I have a brand-new perspective. Although it's a beautiful area, it was much too tiny for a single city-girl like myself to stay for too long. So moving back to my own hometown was much more than a homecoming; it was exhilarating and exciting. There were movie theaters and malls once again to go to and countless things to do. I didn't have to drive an hour to see any of my friends, and when I needed to go grocery shopping, I had more than two stores to frequent. There were roundabouts, overpasses, and people around with whom to visit. Although the city had changed, it hadn't changed as much as I had. That which made me so bored and unhappy when I was young, now brings me great joy and thankfulness. It's just a matter of perspective.

When you find yourself in a situation that causes you to stress out or to be unhappy, it might do you good to get a new outlook. Help out at the senior center or food pantry in your local town, volunteer at a hospital, or go to a third world country to help those less fortunate. I do plan on making a larger move in the future, but if it happens that I don't, I will always remember my little house near the lake that changed my point of view and taught me how to be thankful. Step back, move to your right, or left, or call on a friend as I did. A different point of view might just be what you need to solve your problem and find the masterpiece inside of yourself.

*Learn to love yourself first, then begin the transition of who you are to the person you wish to be.*

Until recently, I couldn't say I actually loved who I was. I didn't even like myself, because I based what I saw only on my circumstances and how others treated me. How silly is that! I saw myself as a single, middle-aged, overweight woman who had never married or had children, been forced to retire early, was struggling with asthma and fibromyalgia, and now couldn't even work full time because of physical limitations! I wasn't focusing on what I was made of inside and had been gifted with: I have a wonderful family, been fortunate to have traveled, taught myself two languages, and have one degree and certificates in both teaching and tourism. I have many loving friends, look young for my age, have been able to continue my writing, am kind and compassionate, have made a difference in many lives, and so much more.

Loving ourselves can help us solve many of our own problems. Take a serious look at yourself. When I was in counseling, my counselor asked me to write down everything I considered good about myself and what I had done in my life. Look at your physical self, your accomplishments, and what you are most proud of. Do you have children that are blessings? Have you bought the house that you wanted for your family or written the book that you wanted to write? Write these things down.

Now, what don't you like about yourself? Are you lazy, too loud, or too quiet? Do you gossip about others? Do you have a poor diet or lack the proper sleep? Maybe you are in between jobs or in one you hate. How many of these things can you change? Now, create a plan that will allow you to reach these goals. Lastly, how do you treat yourself? Are you kind to yourself? How do you talk about yourself? Do you put yourself down or lift yourself up? What can you do to change these habits? Treat yourself to gifts or vacations once in a while. If you are sick, stay home from work or school and rest when you do. When you hurt or are sick, go to the doctor to help yourself feel better.

There are so many reasons why you should love the person you are in spite of any mistakes you may have made. Today I was reminded of how important loving yourself truly is. Someone told me you can't give away something you don't have. If you don't love yourself, how can you love others? Love is something no one can live without. Life is a gift, and so much is still ahead of us wherever we are in life. So appreciate who you are and what you can do, show others kindness and compassion, give to charities, support the lonely and homebound. Give yourself time to change and grow, but love who you are and where you are first. It will show others who need to love themselves how it is done.

*Falling is not failing.
The only real failure is giving up.*

The only time you fail at something is when you give up. When attempting to find a solution to create a light bulb, Thomas Edison is reported to have said, "I haven't failed, I have just found 10,000 ways that won't work." I am still learning this truth. I have a terrible fear of failure, one so powerful that it sometimes stops me in my tracks. But I do the things that frighten me, even if I might procrastinate. I push my way through, even though sometimes I feel like I am swimming through molasses.

I just failed my first test *ever* today. I remember the times I have gotten D's, which weren't very many, but never before have I failed anything. But do you know what? The world has not ended, nor did I explode. I am still getting an A in my class, and in the big scheme of life events it really doesn't matter *at all*. What does matter is that I get up, dust myself off, and try again.

Sometimes the problems we face are in the magnitude of what we are doing, such as becoming a world-class swimmer. Sometimes it is in overcoming obstacles to get somewhere, such as deaf people composing music as Beethoven did, or Bethany Hamilton relearning how to surf after a shark took her arm. Sometimes it's in everyday things like losing weight, finishing a class, or even just finding time every night to read a story to our children. It is also in how we see failure itself.

I have been afraid of failure all of my life, and now that it has happened while taking a test, I see it in a whole new light. Not as something to fear, but something to overcome and learn from: just another obstacle in a whole long line of bumps in the road. I have been over so many hurdles in the past year, I am beginning to feel like I'm back on my high school track team, trying the hurdles for the first time, falling and skinning my knees. But falling over one or many hurdles doesn't make you a failure. It just means you have tried something and didn't do very well the first time through. The real failure would be in giving up.

Yes, it is okay to fail at something. That just means you are living life and not remaining inside the comfort of your safety zone. The whole course of study in tourism I have taken on is the exact opposite of my art teaching degree. It's all about business, computers, and travel, with a lot of world geography thrown in. Polar opposites! I have been scared to death, because I have taken on something new and totally different. But I will eventually succeed, not because I am smart, but because I refuse to give up.

When I was in Australia for the first time, I had the opportunity to go to Ross River Homestead near Alice Springs to ride a dromedary camel in the desert. During the ride, I was bucked off of one. Although I didn't get back on the same camel, I got on another. I wasn't about to let one camel make me afraid of all camels. So when you fail at something, you must remember to pick yourself up, brush yourself off, bandage your knees, and continue to pursue your dreams.

*Learn how to identify and listen to your inner voice, or "gut."*

Growing up, I was always afraid to listen to my inner voice. I have never trusted it for various reasons, and that has gotten me into a world of trouble throughout life. Nothing big, mind you, but I have put myself through many things I didn't need to experience. My inner voice was very confused because it was always fearful. Most of my friends would be surprised to know this, and a good many of the big decisions in my life have come with a lot of thought and hard work.

When I was young, I suffered terribly from anxiety, panic attacks, and obsessive-compulsive disorder, as I have mentioned earlier. We didn't know what I had back then, we just knew it interfered with my life. I used to wash my hands until they were rough and red because of my anxiety. I would walk halfway to grade school and run home crying because of my fear. As I grew older, I grew out of the OCD, but never my anxiety. I have learned to live life and deal with it, but it's still a big part of who I am. I'm just learning to trust my inner voice. Mine is usually a soft, quiet voice telling me what I must do in troubled times. But other times I don't have anything to guide my way.

When decision-making, how can you tell if it is fear or your gut telling you not to do something? According to Marie Forleo, professional life coach, motivational speaker, author, and web television host, one way to tell is to listen to what your body is telling you to do. Does the thought of your present course of action cause you to stand proudly, throw your shoulders back, and embrace what you plan to do? Do you get really excited, or does it cause your body and movement to withdraw? Do you feel a sense of dread, or does your head start to shake no? You can also ask yourself what the best and worst case scenarios would be if you were to follow through with your plans. Lastly, Marie suggests taking your plans out for a test drive, as I did recently this past summer to see if living in Florida was right for me. I stayed at a relative's house for two months while she and her husband were away. By doing so, I had a test run of how it would be to live in the Sunshine State. It was not for me.

Another way you can know whether it's fear or your gut telling you something is a good or bad idea is to gather good friends around you and tell them what you are planning. Fortunately, our body language can tell us what our brains cannot. If you begin to look sad or depressed or like you are sick, your body will let your friends know this may not be a good decision. Ask your friends to tell you how you looked as you were talking. Good friends will want you to be happy and will let you know.

This is different from trusting your feelings. We all have these. The feeling I am talking about is that deep-down, gut feeling you get that will tell you when something is amiss. You know the one I am talking about; that gnawing, deep-down feeling that won't leave you alone. Those feelings send up a red flag and ask you to listen. Many times they will save you from needless pain and suffering when they are heeded.

Common sense tells us not to do certain things, like driving in the wrong part of Milwaukee or New York at night or standing too close to a drop-off, but our "gut," that little inner voice, will also give us great instruction. Listen to it. Learn to hear it when it talks to you.

*Make a joy list. You can go back and look at it when you are having one of "those" days or weeks.*

This is one of those times in my life when I am trying to sift through a lot of garbage and figure out what my next step is. I am afraid to move, to be honest, even if I knew what that step was. I'm anxious and I hurt because of my age and illness. But the worst thing is I have forgotten to be grateful for my many blessings and to remember them daily.

Every person's joy list is a little different. For you it might be being a mom or grandmother, or having a great husband or partner, or just being healthy. Look at your life. What do you have in your life that truly makes you light up with joy and happiness? Some of mine include: being able to close the door on my past and move on, having the time now to explore my life, having the greatest circle of friends and family in the world. I could go on and on.

Make your list and go over it regularly. Add or subtract items as they come into or leave your life. Write them down on a post-it and place them anywhere you look regularly, such as your bathroom mirror, your refrigerator, or on the side of your laptop. Looking at these joys regularly will reinforce a positive outlook, which will be there for you in times of need.

Count your blessings and write them down for you to look at. You will get your mind off of the events and situations that aren't so pleasant in life and begin to see how truly blessed your life is!

*Find a counselor, pastor, or psychologist you trust, who fits your needs and personality. Some of the best come without degrees, just a lot of experience.*

One of the best things I have ever done for myself was to find myself a good counselor. But it wasn't the first time I had tried to find one who could help me with the challenges I was struggling with. According to the American Counseling Association, counseling is, "Providing guidance to help people navigate life's challenges." However, not all people are the same, and their needs are very individualized. Many people believe the same as Michael J. "Crocodile" Dundee did when reporter Sue Charlton tried to explain why people in America go to see a psychiatrist.

> *Sue Charlton:* People go to a psychiatrist to talk about their problems. She (Dorothy Wainwright, a family friend) just needed to unload them. You know, bring them out in the open.
> *Michael J. "Crocodile" Dundee:* Hasn't she got any mates?
> *Sue Charlton:* You're right. I guess we could all use more mates. I suppose you don't have any shrinks at Walkabout Creek.
> *Michael J. "Crocodile" Dundee:* Nah. Back there, if you got a problem, you tell Wally. And he tells everyone in town . . . brings it out in the open . . . no more problem.

But it's not as simple as that. We all have a complex web of events interwoven in our lives, events that either help us to live a normal and productive life or hinder our efforts. I had been to several counselors and had gotten many points of view, but no one really fit well enough or could tell me what I needed to hear before. They didn't listen or give me exercises to help me heal. Instead, one wanted me to be strong and "pull myself up by my bootstraps," while another gave me a book on burnout. They didn't spend the time to hear me out and get to the root of my distress. They all tried to put "bandages" on my wounds instead of giving me the skills to deal with them to help them heal.

It wasn't until I found a person who listened *and validated* my feelings that I began to see what was wrong and how to correct it. As I said before, validation of feelings is the first step in healing. It takes a lot to open up and tell your secrets to a total stranger. So many of us wait until we are hanging by the last thread to start looking. A good counselor is insightful and will also give you exercises with each visit to help you heal and become all you can be. They will also step away when they believe you have healed enough to handle life on your own.

But you need one who will fit with *you*. Some of us need tough love and some need a gentle hand. Others need someone to empathize and some need a counselor who is energetic and a cheerleader. Whoever you need, you will know when you find him or her. All I can say is to keep looking until you find one who fits. I know I have found the best person for me.

*Do not label yourself based on your shortcomings or the mistakes you may have made.*

I have made many mistakes in my life and have a lot of shortcomings. But just because I have made mistakes, does that mean I am one? Certainly not! I am a pretty amazing person, and you are as well.

In 2003, I chaperoned a group of French students from our school on a trip to France. I was very rushed in preparing for my trip, as we left just after school was out. I had my grades to finish, my yearbook to finalize, and my room to clean. Because of this, I got very little sleep for several days. While in France, I began to make silly decisions and hurt myself by doing things like falling down a hill and stairs, and catching my hand in a Metro door. Later, some of the adults I knew began to tease me about being clumsy until I finally set them straight. Just because the situation caused me to have some accidents didn't make me clumsy. I was simply stressed and tired.

So, too, are some of the situations in your life. Don't look at yourself through your past mistakes or let anyone else either. Never allow anyone to get into your head with statements like, "You're clumsy, you're fat, or you're lazy." If you have ever been in trouble with the law, had to go on disability, or have been let go from a job, that doesn't mean you are lazy or a troublemaker. It just means, that for whatever reason, you found yourself in an unpleasant situation for a while. You either needed some help to get through that time or needed to find a better fit for your life's work.

So please don't label yourself! We all have so many great qualities that are just bubbling up inside of us. And if others can't see them, that is their problem, not ours!

*Learn how to delegate.*

People who are perfectionists are not normally good at delegating. They are usually meticulous about how things are done and generally don't like other people doing their work because it's usually not done to their satisfaction. Unfortunately, I'm one of those people. I would make a terrible boss because I have a hard time delegating. However, I'm learning.

Those of us who suffer from this "condition" take on much more than we need to. We think we're the only ones who can get things done right. Perhaps this is true, perhaps not, but we certainly make our lives much harder because of it. Perhaps this may be the right way to run things at work, but at home, others who wish to help could do many tasks to contribute. I have always been a go-getter and have always taken on more than humanly possible. (My sister will quickly agree with this.) I definitely have a type A personality. But when teaching, while my load got terribly heavy during art contest season and the annual art show, there were times when I enlisted the students to help me mat and hang the artwork. I had to be very specific with how I wanted things done and be willing to make some compromises so I didn't go crazy. I did eventually learn to delegate in the end out of necessity.

Another approach we have employed at our family gatherings for quite some time now is to ask everyone to bring something to the event. However, we agree ahead of time what each will bring. This reduces the cost, the overlap, and the workload on the host and allows them to enjoy the celebration as well. But again, one must learn how to ask for help and have a plan in mind.

Whether it is out of necessity or as a result of careful planning, delegating will result in a less stressful life and allow us to be more productive and enjoy our life with a lighter load.

*Go for a time-out.*

There are times when we all need some time away from our work. While I was working on my tourism and travel degree, I would get so tired from studying and trying to figure out the computer program, I would not be able to cram one more item into my head. So I would take a little time away from my work, or a *time-out*. When I came back, I would be refreshed and able to tackle the problem with a fresh outlook. Sometimes I drove to my sister's house to get away, sometimes it was just fifteen minutes to clean house, other times I went for a short walk outside.

When I went to college for my first degree, I had already learned how to somewhat balance my life as a student. All of the students on the wing of my dorm went out on Friday nights. We would spend the rest of our nights studying in our rooms or the neighboring study hall. That was my time away from my studies, or my *time-out*. I remember the few times that I visited friends on weekends or drove home, but those times weren't often. Now I find I need more immediate time-outs, so I write poetry, answer emails or Facebook messages, or go out for coffee. Even little time-outs can bring the same effect as large ones, save on time and the cost of vacations. In editing this book for example, I usually work on two or three pages, do some housework or eat lunch, then go back to editing. It helps me to focus better, minimizes my problems from sitting too long, and I still get everything done needing my attention.

What can you do for a time-out? Can you call a friend and go for a cup of coffee to get out of the house? Do you like to go for rides on your bicycle? Can you put on some music or take a short nap to rejuvenate? Would you like to join a bridge club or poker club? Or does your refrigerator or basement need a good cleaning? All of these can act as time away from a bigger chore.

Allow a good time out to relax, refocus, and get more done in the process. You will thank yourself at the end of the day.

*Be mindful and live
in the present.*

This advice doesn't fit my life very well, as I am a dreamer. Like John Lennon said, many of us in this world are. This is not to take away from our dream life, but when we dream all of the time, we miss what is happening in the present. Also, if we don't pay enough attention to our surroundings, it can get us in trouble.

There is a time and a place for everything. When you are eating, be mindful of what you are eating. Pay attention, and you will eat more slowly, enjoy your food more, and eat less. When you are driving, drive and don't have your mind on something else. Although we all allow our minds to wander from time to time, this can be dangerous. When you are on a trip, don't you try to soak in everything you can? Life should be like that. Drink in every bit of green you can on the first day of spring. Enjoy every moment of your weekend with your kids or grandkids. When you go for a walk, notice all of the sounds, smells, and colors around you.

Be mindful of your family as well, and don't take them for granted. My counselor told me there was a study done some time ago of men who had survived having been shot down behind enemy lines during wartime. They found the people who came out of the situation the most often were surfers. What does this have to do with mindfulness? It's because surfers not only have to balance every part of their body to ride waves, but they also have to pay attention to every bit of their surroundings as well. They have learned the skill of being mindful of the present.

I am certain many people wish they had a second chance at seeing their children as they grew, being young themselves, or being on that once-in-a-lifetime trip again. We never know when something will be taken away or how fast life is going until it is too late, or it's gone. We only have one life to live, so enjoy the moment while it's yours. Leave the daydreaming for times when you are alone in a safe place or when you don't need your attention to be focused on life.

*Fill your life with beauty,
hope, joy, and love.*

I tend to reflect the people and my surroundings in my life, and I believe many others do as well. If I am around peaceful things, I tend to feel tranquil, if I am around happy people, I tend to be happy, but if I surround myself with things that are sad and people who are negative, I find myself reflecting their energy too.

No one ever chooses to fill their lives with negativity and sadness, but we sometimes find ourselves in those situations anyway. It's like the fable of the boiling frog. If you put a frog in boiling water, it will jump out, but if you slowly turn up the heat, it may cook to death. So it is with us. We find ourselves in situations that may be good for us at the onset, but as time goes by, they may become toxic. Most of us realize what is happening, but we may feel powerless to do anything about it; we may need to stick it out or may feel trapped in a situation.

Three of the biggest of these are living situations, marriages, and jobs. It's somewhat easy to break a friendship that causes us grief or find a new job if we have only been at the present one for a short time, but marriages, careers, and houses you have invested money and years in are much harder to end or give up. We have to consider all sorts of things in these situations. However, what is more important than mental and emotional health? There is really nothing, with the exception of physical health. And that too can be affected by these situations if we aren't careful.

I lived in my last town for thirteen years, the last seven of which I was completely miserable. Something that had been a blessing once had turned into something I had completely outgrown. I'm now in a place where I can enjoy the seasons, have my apartment looked after when I'm gone, and don't have to spend time and money on the upkeep. Moving into a new apartment in a bigger town was a win-win solution for me. I have reconnected with old friends and let go of some I had outgrown. I have filled my life with beauty and joy in what I do and have even changed careers at age sixty. I'm not saying this was easy; it was one of the scariest and hardest things I have ever done. But it was very healthy, and I am SOOOO much happier.

So, if you find yourself in a similar situation, sit down and take an inventory of your life. Find the relationships that fill you with joy, places that fit your needs, and jobs that will bring you pleasure while earning a living. Whatever you decide to do, fill your life with beauty, hope, joy, and love. You will not only reflect those traits, but you will also embody them and live a life you will truly enjoy.

# Part Three

It's All About You

*You can and do make a difference in more lives than you realize!*

You may never know when something you have done will make a difference in someone else's life. While I was growing up, the little boy down the road would come to our house to find that my mom had freshly baked cookies for him every morning. He still mentions it to this day. Our grade school organized a drive for my kindergarten teacher who lost her house in a fire, and she still talks about that kindness. I had several openly gay students in my high school classes while teaching, and I always encouraged them to be the best they could be and not to let other people get them down. They became some of my biggest supporters.

You may never know the people you are affecting. I'm always surprised by the little things that are remembered. I was told a story by one of my brother's co-workers the other day. My brother, who is also an art teacher, has been teaching in the same school district for thirty-two years and does all sorts of very unique and interesting things with his kids. He writes stories and songs for them, plays the ukulele, and many more things than I can mention here, and he does it all in the name of teaching and creativity. One day some of his art students were in another class when they started humming one of his songs. Suddenly a group of five broke out singing! They weren't only learning art, but music in a room where wonderful memories were being created. What a legacy!

I also have many friends who work in soup kitchens, some friends who take their vacations in third world countries to help the people there, and many others who raise funds for the less fortunate. It really doesn't matter how big or small something is, the fact is that your life touches others in ways you can't begin to imagine.

Take a look at how you affect those around you. Perhaps you have a chance to make a big splash, or maybe you just want to venture out in your neighborhood or city. Whatever you do, find something close to your heart that you feel strongly about. Whether you are showing kindness and acceptance to someone who isn't getting enough in their life, listening to someone who is having problems, doing something extra for someone while doing your job, or just asking someone how their day is and giving them a smile, it's all about making a difference in the world around you and in so doing your own as well.

*It's just as important
to take care of yourself
as someone else.*

When was the last time you really spent time taking care of you? Caring for yourself is part of loving who you are. Unfortunately, many past generations have not. They considered it more important to care for others in their lives and generally put themselves last. You might remember your mom or your grandmother waiting on everyone and eating last or staying up until all hours of the night to sew a new holiday dress for Easter Sunday service. What they didn't realize was in their selflessness, they were teaching the next generation how *not* to care for themselves. I am not trying to take away from anyone who is giving, but it's important not to do so continuously at the expense of your own health.

Stop and think: What will a child or spouse remember, your time with them or how much you do for them? Then, what does sleep deprivation, lack of food, and not enough down time do to you? It is a recipe for disaster and future health issues. That doesn't help your loved ones or yourself. It only serves to shorten and diminish your quality of life. And what does it say about what you think of yourself? So many of us remember the Golden Rule when it comes to others, but totally forget it when applied to ourselves. Mothers are notorious for putting themselves last in almost all situations: making meals, getting enough sleep, buying clothing, and the list goes on. Many jobs also zap the life out of people, especially public service or caretaking jobs such as nursing, doctoring, teaching, police work, and those working in nursing homes.

Mothers and fathers, please make your children do some of the work around the house. They live with you as well. It will help build their work ethic for later in life and make them learn that things in life are not free. (Although I am not a parent, teaching both younger children and those in high school has taught me much in this area.) Mothers, eat with your family and don't be their servant. My mother wouldn't sit down until everyone was served on Sundays and holidays. Don't you think your family would rather have you with them to share special days than to see you nervously flitting about? And by all means, have another life! Stay connected to the community, church, and friends. God forbid, if something should happen to any part of your life, you will have a support system and something to fall back on. Take time to relax and enjoy life. It goes by in the blink of an eye!

*You are so much more
than your job or career.*

Unfortunately, many of us define ourselves by what we do: a mother, a teacher, a doctor, a husband or wife rather than by who we are. Then if something unexpectedly happens to the things that define us, we are left feeling lost, without a path to follow.

That is exactly what happened to me in my last career. I spent so much time teaching and all of the duties that went along with the job that I completely lost myself. When my position was suddenly cut in half and I was forced to retire, I didn't know who I was any longer, as there was nothing left of me. I forgot I was supposed to have fun and play, be a good friend, and have interests of my own. I got so caught up with being a teacher, I forgot how to just be me.

Just think of all the hats each one of us wears every day. When I was challenged to write all of these down by my counselor, I came up with three pages! A mother is also a caretaker, nurse, problem solver; a dad is a provider, role model, big buddy, chauffeur, etc. We are all people with other jobs and interests besides our careers.

One of my young students saw me in the grocery store after my first year of teaching in the public school system. When he saw I was buying potatoes, he asked me if I was going to make a sculpture when I mashed them! We often find that we similarly view our lives within very narrow parameters; that we can only be one person or that our job defines us. But if we seriously look at our lives, we are so much more. We are writers, bicyclists, photographers, cooks, party planners, gardeners . . . and the list goes on for miles.

Using a paper and pen, write down all of the skills you are blessed with and the many people you are every day. Spare nothing. After you have completed your list, take a good look at what a complex person you are. Remember to keep this list handy in case of emergency. If something should happen to any part of your life, it will remind you it was only part of who you are, and this will help you to move forward.

*Not everyone will like you . . . end of story. The reverse is true as well, and that is okay.*

When I was young I learned one of Aesop's Fables about a man, his son and their donkey. It goes as follows:

The Man, the Boy, and the Donkey

A man and his son were once going with their donkey to market. As they were walking along by its side a countryman passed them and said: "You fools, what is a Donkey for but to ride upon?"

So the Man put the Boy on the Donkey and they went on their way. But soon they passed a group of men, one of whom said: "See that lazy youngster, he lets his father walk while he rides."

So the Man ordered his Boy to get off, and got on himself. But they hadn't gone far when they passed two women, one of whom said to the other: "Shame on that lazy lout to let his poor little son trudge along."

Well, the Man didn't know what to do, but at last he took his Boy up before him on the Donkey. By this time they had come to the town, and the passers-by began to jeer and point at them. The Man stopped and asked what they were scoffing at. The men said: "Aren't you ashamed of yourself for overloading that poor Donkey of yours—you and your hulking son?"

The Man and Boy got off and tried to think what to do. They thought and they thought, till at last they cut down a pole, tied the Donkey's feet to it, and raised the pole and the Donkey to their shoulders. They went along amid the laughter of all who met them till they came to Market Bridge, when the Donkey, getting one of his feet loose, kicked out and caused the Boy to drop his end of the pole.

In the struggle the Donkey fell over the bridge, and his forefeet being tied together he was drowned.

"That will teach you," said an old man who had followed them: "PLEASE ALL, AND YOU WILL PLEASE NONE."

I used to *need* everyone to like me, no matter who they were. Why did I need the nasties of the world to like me, or the loud and obnoxious? Now I cannot for the life of me figure out why!

I worked with someone a few years ago that I absolutely couldn't stomach. He was arrogant, deceitful, chose favorites, was a bully, and liked to micromanage and play games with his subordinates. It's okay that I didn't like him and that he didn't like me. He was as far away from my belief system as you could possibly get. As I began to like myself, I began to understand he was just one of the sad people of this world I didn't have room for in my life.

Everyone will run into people in this world who will rub them the wrong way from time to time. It may be their sense of humor, how they treat others, one of their habits, their personal hygiene, their arrogance, their lack of open-mindedness, or many other reasons. All of the other people in the world have similar sets of standards. They may not be able to tolerate the amount of schooling you have received, or your lack of education, the sound of your voice, or the way you handle yourself in public. Just like you, they are entitled to their own likes and dislikes. It is nothing you have done wrong. It's what makes you who you are. Please don't think you have to change who you are to please these people, as you will become a chameleon, always changing to meet others' standards and never developing the real you.

Be the best person you can be, and you will attract those who will make you feel comfortable, as well as those who *you* will like and those who like you for the person who you have grown to be.

*Let your voice be heard. We all have our own special stories to tell. Share yours with the world. You may never know how many it may touch.*

This book is *my* story. You can find me in and between the lines on each of its pages and in my future books as well. They contain my successes and my failures, my fears, and my confidences. But it is *my* story and *mine* alone. In these pages, you will find me without any armor to cover my scars or shield to protect me. Within these pages, there is nowhere for me to hide.

Michelangelo told his story in his *Pietà*, his *David*, and many other pieces of work. Mikhail Baryshnikov and Anna Pavlova gave us unrivaled ballet to enjoy. Danny Kaye and Lucille Ball gave us comedy to fill our lives with laughter for many generations. Meryl Streep and Anthony Hopkins have given us many characters in movies that have moved us all. Songs such as "Stairway to Heaven" by Jimmy Page and Led Zeppelin and "Hallelujah" by Leonard Cohen are sung again and again for us to enjoy. And all of us figure skating fans surely will never forget the beauty and grace of Jayne Torvill and Christopher Dean gliding across the ice as they danced to *Bolero*.

You have your story to tell as well. Just think, no one has had a life exactly like yours. You have had a unique upbringing; you have chosen your own classes while in school and jobs when you graduated. You have your own likes and dislikes, hobbies, friends, childhood, and the list goes on. In a world of over seven billion people, you are totally unique among all of them.

It's not enough that your voice be heard, but it is very important to pass on the skills and knowledge that you have acquired while on this earth as well. This voice of yours and your story can be expressed in so many ways: in government, singing, writing songs, stories or poems, artwork, acting, comedy, and so many more. If you want to tell your story in a certain way, but don't have the skills, find someone who can transcribe it. But give a gift to the world for others to remember you by.

Along with this book, I have shared my story through poetry and artwork. My poetry and some of my artwork and photography can be found in a future book, *Love Songs of the Heart*. Before this book was finished, my poetry had over 417,000 readers on hellopoetry.com. It is scary to tell your story to all; to bare your soul to the billions of people in the world; to let others know you have fears, insecurities, phobias, and dark secrets such as abuses and failed relationships in your life. You may worry about what others are thinking.

However, as for myself, I know it's more important for me to share my story and help others than to worry about my pride and what others may think. I am telling my story so that others may know they are not alone and show them what they may do to help themselves.

Tell your story, however humble or grand, simple or flamboyant, cautious or adventurous it may be. Shout it out so the whole world may benefit. It's one of the only things that is truly your own. Be brave and share your triumphs and failures. Turn your lemons into someone else's lemonade and make a difference.

*You should define your limits. Those who are respectful will listen to you and follow your wishes.*

If you are a yes person like I was, you will have problems defining your limits too. When you are a people pleaser, you certainly don't want to hurt others' feelings or disappoint anyone. But if you think about it, you are disappointing the most important person: yourself. And you deserve to be heard too.

I was told the story when I was young of a couple who stayed too long at a neighbor's house. The husband of the household finally said to his wife, "Come on, honey, let's go to bed. The neighbors have to go home!" Most of us have friends or family members who intrude into our lives. Two great examples of these are pets and children. Sometimes they intrude into our personal and sex life as well. Many people don't mind this intrusion, but teaching kids to always knock on a closed door goes a long way toward general politeness and respecting personal space. I call my sister almost every other day, but I always try to ask if it's a good time to talk so I am respectful and always welcome.

If someone is exceeding your time or spatial limits, please let them know. Most probably, they don't even realize they are intruding, and if they do, they are just being rude. You really don't want this type of person around you anyway. If you know someone is going to visit you each week, set a time convenient for both of you. If you know someone is a person who touches or hugs, and it makes you uncomfortable, it's your job to tell him or her about your comfort level. That is part of who both of you are. They need to know your boundaries and not hear about it second hand from someone else. But eventually you will have to sit the other person down and define your boundaries, and they will probably wonder why it took you so long.

I have a friend who I had lost touch with for fifty years and recently found on Facebook. He would spend hours texting me, as he wanted to catch up. Even though I was excited to find him again, it was a very busy time of my life, and I began to resent his intrusion. Finally I told him I was busy, and I needed time to finish the work I was doing. I asked if he would mind catching up at a future date. I am certain he understood, and I got my coursework done.

You see, it's about having respect for yourself and your needs too. You have a life, and you are just as important as everyone else. So when that dog or cat intrudes into your love life, kennel them for an hour or so. It won't hurt them. If you are busy when someone calls, tell them how much they mean to you, but that you are busy and will get back to them as soon as you can. Your relationship with yourself and your friend will be blessed.

*Being selfish is sometimes okay.
It's not the same as being self-centered.*

My brother and I try to keep up the German we learned in high school and use it whenever we can, even if it is *nur ein kleines bisschen* (only a little bit). But he taught me something the other day he had never shared with me before.

When my mother was sick the first time, she changed. She became happier, took better care of herself, and spent more time on herself. She also began to spend money on herself and even left items of clothing unpressed. (Gasp!) She began to use phrases such as, "You are on your own, honey" and began to go out to breakfast with my dad more on the weekends. She told me later that cancer had taught her how to live her life.

Now, many years later as we sat at a recent family party, my brother told me the story of how my mother had shared with him another of life's little insights. She had told him it was okay to be selfish sometimes. Such a concept was foreign to me, but yet it made a lot of sense. She had learned by almost losing her life to keep some of her time and resources for herself.

Many times, throughout the years, I have made excuses not to do things with people because I was exhausted, and later felt guilty because I thought I was "being selfish." But it appears sometimes we must be "selfish" in order to remain healthy or sane, to say no when we are overwhelmed, or just have some "me" time. We shouldn't have to make excuses to friends and family. They will understand, as they get sick and tired too!

So, *vielen Dank, mein Bruder* (thank you very much my brother) for passing on Mom's special wisdom to me and those reading this book, and for helping her to continue to live on in our lives and memories!

*Don't make promises or resolutions to yourself you don't intend to keep. (In other words, don't lie to yourself.) You will just end up frustrated and unhappy with who you have become.*

I have given up making New Year's resolutions and promises to myself, as I fail just as much as I succeed. I tell myself instead I am going to *try* to do something, not promise. (Yes, I know I am going against a basic premise of Yoda!) When I do make promises to myself and other people, I generally have a plan for how I intend to accomplish them, but that is where I stop.

I have spent far too many nights trying to walk on my treadmill without much success because of my illness. I have also made promises in the past to put more money away for retirement and travel, only to have something come up to deplete my resources, such as needing new tires or paying for medical expenses not covered by insurance. So when it comes to promises, I tell myself I will try hard to make it happen, but if reality sets in, I'll forgo it and am not disappointed.

A good example was this past year. I wanted to go to Belize to snorkel in the worst way, but with my newly diagnosed asthma, fibromyalgia flare-up, and money shortage, I could not make it happen. So I went down to check out Florida instead. I had a wonderful time on the beach shelling, investigated a possible living situation, and met some relatives I had never met before. It was a good compromise. I saved money, didn't put my health in danger, and found a possible place to live in the future.

How do you feel when you make promises to yourself that you cannot keep? I, for one, feel frustrated and sometimes angry with myself. Be honest and don't break the promises you make to yourself. You will like yourself much better if you do!

*You don't need any excuse to feel good about yourself.*

Growing up I felt very different from other kids. I often felt out of place among my peers and never felt like I fit in. Interestingly enough, I always believed I truly deserved to be normal like everyone else seemed to be. So without knowing it, I began to use my abilities to be noticed and feel accepted. When I was very young, I used skills that I was good at, like Double Dutch jump rope, to fit in.

Later it was my running ability. I discovered in sixth grade I could run faster than all of the other kids in my class, even the boys! I couldn't wait to join track in high school, and at the beginning of every year, I would ask to join the varsity track team until they finally allowed me in as a freshman. Later my ability of choice became grades and drawing. I began to get nothing less than As. Oh, I had to work very hard, but that didn't matter. I needed to be recognized. I also became known for my art around the area. Years passed, and I began a job in illustration. But my body began to hurt from all of the sitting and bending over a desk, and it wasn't enjoyable any longer.

Looking back, I was always trying to substitute abilities for ways to fit in and feel accepted. Unfortunately, what I didn't realize, like so many other children with self-concept issues, was that I really didn't need anything to make me feel good about myself. I was okay just the way I was. I just had to make myself believe it. I was confusing being accepted for who I was with being accepted for something I was good at. Now, I don't need any excuse to feel good about who I am. I am fine just as I am: a woman who has been blessed with a very interesting and rewarding life. I can enjoy my life as I am. If I don't fit in, it's *NOT* because of something *I* am lacking, but something else altogether.

What excuse do you need for feeling good about yourself? Is

it hosting social events, playing in a band, or being the head of something? Before getting involved, have a heart-to-heart with yourself and ask why you are doing what you do. Are you doing something because it allows you to express your inner self, have fun, or help others? If you are doing something for yourself or to help those around you, then you are on course, but if you find you are in a situation in which you need something outside of yourself to feel good about the person you are, then I would suggest you rethink your plan. I remind those who are reading this you are good enough by yourself!

*Don't be so focused on yourself and your troubles that you don't see the big picture.*

Being focused on ourselves and our problems is like looking at ourselves in a mirror all day. It keeps us from seeing what is happening in the world around us and spending time enjoying friends and family. We cannot grow or see the changes around us when we focus on the past, often keeping us in a prison of toxic thought. Without being able to look around, we miss out on many of the opportunities and adventures life has to offer. We all need change and challenge in order to remain healthy. Looking at our troubles doesn't allow us to do either.

When we focus on problems, we tend to become obsessed with them, forming a cycle in our minds and deepening that neural pathway with each time we think of them. Perhaps a better use of our attention would be to figure out how to solve our problems instead of treading water. Rather than focusing on what is wrong, we might ask ourselves what we can do about it, then use that plan to take action. We will then be moving toward a constructive end to those problems and not lose sight of the wonders around us.

But some people are not good problem-solvers and cannot figure things out right away. When this happens, experts say one thing that can be done is to shift your focus to something that doesn't take brainpower, such as cleaning out your refrigerator or playing a game. It gives your brain a break and allows it to process your situation. You can also take a break from your circumstances by trying a stress reducer such as yoga or meditation. Another way to get your mind off of your problems is to exercise them away by walking, jogging, or some other form of physical exercise.

So figure out how to solve your problems, and if you cannot, try one of the suggestions above. They will help you to forget about the troubles that remain and make you a happier person.

*You don't have to be everything to everyone!*

My mother WAS Supermom. She was everything to everybody. There wasn't anything she couldn't do with the exception of swim. She was active in the PTA at our grade school, volunteered at school and church, taught Sunday school, was a Girl and Boy Scout leader. She knit mittens and slippers for all of us, made all of our clothes as well as coats, made rugs, and had a business to alter clothing. She crocheted doilies and made bread as well as fresh cookies for our lunches. She could paint, draw, and designed and helped build the house we grew up in. She kept journals and wrote poetry, kept a garden, canned every year, made jelly and jam, stretching our budget to feed five growing kids. As I said, she was Supermom. However, this set the bar much too high for all of us to follow.

I am a very good illustrator, artist, and teacher. I enjoy writing, I can snorkel, bake, and am a good cook. I can organize parties, set up art shows, crochet, speak German and communicate in Italian, understand some French, and have traveled by myself world-wide. When I was younger, I ran, biked, water and snow skied, ice and roller skated, climbed mountains, did counted cross stitch, sewed my own clothes, threw pottery, bought a house by myself, gardened, canned, and still found time for a career. But I couldn't have raised a brood of kids and found time for these things too. I cannot even fathom how my mom did it. However, she did pay a hefty price with her health in the end.

Two days ago I had a Fourth of July party at my new apartment for my extended family. And I went overboard as usual. I had three meat choices, corn on the cob, a fruit salad, two cheese choices, chips, crackers, dip, shrimp, potatoes, beans, and salsa dip, besides what everyone else brought, and two pies with whipped cream (brought by my sister-in-law and brother). Then we had beer, mixed drinks, and after-dinner drinks with coffee. Afterward, when I was left with over half the food, I began to question if I had even learned anything from my mother. I was following the same path, but instead, I was trying to play Super Sister.

Since then, I have decided that I am starting a new tradition of underplaying holidays. I have decided to pick and choose the best for me from now on and not try to be everything to everyone. I will continue to be the best teacher (on occasion), sister, and person I can be. I will continue to travel and write, and I will continue to try to be the best aunt around, just not to the extreme and not to the detriment of my health.

P.S. I am still relearning this a year later, but at least *I am trying!*

*Ask for what you want in life. You don't have to depend on someone else to tell you what you need.*

Many of us go from one support system in life to another, never asking ourselves what *we* want from our lives. We have our family to support us as children, our school system to teach us the necessities of education, maybe college or technical school for a career or job, a husband or wife for marriage, then children to rear. Our kids move out, we retire, and then we sometimes find ourselves asking where *we disappeared* in the midst of all of this and what we really want out of the rest of our lives? I believe this is where midlife crises begin, when we realize there was no "me" in the equation for all of those years.

My sister does something I think everyone should do who is married: She goes out on a date night with her husband every so often. That way, neither of them gets lost along the path in life. She spends time with her children, her dog, her friends and husband, and sets aside time for herself. She knows what she needs and never forgets to ask herself what she wants out of life. She created a business years ago because she wanted to stay home with her children as they were growing up. Now, eighteen years later, she is once again adjusting her work situation to accommodate her changing needs. Kudos to her for her courage!

Listen to what your body, mind, and heart are telling you. Are you doing work that is too heavy for you? Do you injure yourself on the job? Do you dread going into work? Do you dream about doing something else? Is your job or activity something that you really enjoy doing or have you outgrown it? Sit down with yourself and ask yourself if you are on the right path or if you need to retune your inner GPS. Are you happy with how your life is going, or would you like to try something else? What are your dreams? Have you made plans to achieve them? What do you truly want for your body, mind, and spirit?

I truly thought I was too old to make a change and find a different path. However, I find I am just beginning. I now have an account in my bank in which I save to go on vacation (no matter how small) and still grab for every ring that passes by me. And there are many that do. Won't you join me in grabbing one for yourself?!

*We should be ourselves. We shouldn't feel we have to apologize to anyone for the people we are. We have been created as unique individuals with gifts and talents no one else has.*

My friend Christine and I have different natural gifts: She has been blessed with a once-in-a-lifetime voice that rivals such greats as Ella Fitzgerald and Etta James, and I have been given the gift of drawing and painting what I see. I cannot carry a tune for the life of me, and she cannot draw. (Or so she says.) I would give anything to sing like she does: to move people to tears while singing "Hallelujah" or make a room go silent when singing in harmony with another.

I sometimes take what I have been blessed with for granted, as it comes second nature to me. Growing up, I didn't appreciate all of my special gifts and often wished I could be like the other girls around me: those girls with natural gifts of gab, those who were able to perform in front of groups, play guitar, ice skate, or those who were popular. I dreamt one day of becoming something other than a "skinny-mini" and grow into the proper body parts, preferably before I was out of college.

Now, looking back, I have tried out all of those things in life: I have a guitar, which I don't play anymore; a pair of ice skates that remind me of the hours and hours of practicing pursuing my childhood dream. I have never been popular unless you count some students I took under my wing while teaching and, unfortunately, like most others, I have more than grown into those body parts I wished for as a young adult. Why do we always wish for that which we don't have?

Embrace your gifts while you have them. Give thanks for the ones you have. Though they may be different than what you might have wished for, they are still blessings. You shouldn't be embarrassed that you are skinnier than everyone else, can memorize a classic poem in kindergarten, be able to run faster than everyone in your class, or even that you are shy and reserved while others are boisterous and loud. Each gift will be used in its own time. One day when your gifts are gone, when you can't do the things you once did, you can say you lived your *own* life and were your *own* person, and used the gifts given to you well.

"Today you are You that is truer than true,
There is no one alive who is Youer than you!"
– Dr. Seuss

*Learn to laugh at yourself;
it helps lighten your load
as well as your spirit.*

Laughter always helps to lighten the load and laughing at oneself will always go a long way to make an awkward situation less stressful. I remember one particular time I was teaching in front of the class. Someone had moved a chair from its place and left it nearby earlier in the class period. I wasn't paying attention and upon backing up, I fell backwards over it. Luckily my training in skating clicked in immediately, and I tucked and rolled to the floor. After the students asked me if I was all right, they commented on how gracefully I fell. We all had a nice laugh, and I couldn't help joining in, as it *WAS* funny.

Most of us are far too serious about ourselves, which is a standard in most of our society. One of the things I love most about the Brits and the Aussies is their ability to be self-deprecating. They are able to poke fun at themselves and their problems and to be a bit, if not a LOT, irreverent. Two famous people in U.S. history who chose to laugh at themselves and their problems were Barack Obama and Bill Clinton. Both of them had their fair share of problems during their terms in office.

The more we can laugh at embarrassing or stressful situations we find ourselves in, the better it is for our health. When we laugh, the stress hormones in our bodies are decreased and the immune cells and antibodies that fight infection are increased, helping us fight disease. Laughter also releases endorphins, helping us to feel good, and it can even help with pain.

So when someone comments about your looks, your shortcomings, or something they might think will irritate you, turn what they say or do into a joke and laugh at it. It will catch those trying to make you uncomfortable off guard and let them know you know how to handle them. If you can't laugh at yourself, life will continue to be harder than necessary. Make those endorphins flow and give your health and your happiness a boost.

*It is okay to follow your own dreams. Don't feel like you have to fulfill anyone else's.*

Growing up, half of me felt compelled to fulfill my mother's dream of being an artist, as she wasn't allowed to accept the art scholarship she'd been given when graduating from high school. The other half of me knew I was a gifted illustrator from grade school on. So I worked hard to get good grades in high school and in college. But once I was out and in the real work world, I soon discovered what an unpredictable career art can be for an illustrator. Four years into my career, I was out of a job when the company I was with decided to use photography instead of my illustration skills. So I went back to school to get a teaching degree with the encouragement of my family, believing a teaching career would be much more stable and a way for me to still use my gift in art.

Flash forward twenty-nine years, and we find ourselves in a new state of affairs, one without a seniority system for teachers and other public employees. Once again, finding myself with half a job and in a state with no unions, I have been given the fabulous opportunity to follow another dream. This dream had been there all along, though I was probably the last to realize it and had been preparing for it all of my life: I bought my small house in order to travel, saved in order to do so, bought travel books and magazines, and read novels like *The Da Vinci Code, Angels & Demons*, and *The Thorn Birds* for their adventure and settings. I had been dreaming about traveling since seeing the African Watusi dancers on *National Geographic* as a child of five! So why should this new dream be such a surprise to me?

I am now following many of *my* dreams. My bucket list becomes longer with every passing month as I keep adding new things I see and learn about. Granted, there are those that are no longer possible, but that's okay too. I have been given so many other things to take their place. As I see it now, the sky is the limit. We don't have to be satisfied with following the dreams of others; it's up to us to choose. Research new places, new interests, and new dreams, and keep learning, as you never know where your inspiration or your next dream may come from. One of my favorite quotes by Norman Vincent Peale is, "Shoot for the moon. Even if you miss, you'll land among the stars!" Wherever you are in life, aim high!

*Be the leading lady or
man of your own life.
Be your own hero.*

*The Holiday*, one of my favorite movies, is about two ladies who have just had their hearts broken by the men in their lives and have decided to exchange houses for the Christmas Holidays. In one scene of the movie, Iris is sitting across the table from her new, temporary neighbor, Arthur Abbott, who is a retired screenwriter. He has just finished explaining to her in very clear terms that she has been behaving like a best friend in her relationship when she is definitely a leading lady. Her reply was, "You're supposed to be the leading lady in your own life, for God's sake!"

This is so true. And I have always played the best friend in life. I'm sure many of us see ourselves in Iris or Cameron Diaz's character, Amanda Woods. That is why the movie was such a success. (That and because Jude Law is so doggone cute!) We go through our lives struggling with our confidence, and when we see others who are confident, we often think they are arrogant. There is a difference between arrogance and self-confidence. Confidence *is believing in yourself*, which is a healthy way to be. Arrogance, however, *is knowing* something about yourself and letting others know that you know it too.

Being your own leading lady or man comes down to putting yourself first from time to time, knowing what you want and going after it. It's not a matter of being selfish or rude, but of not allowing yourself to be second best. And that, dear readers, begins with a good self-concept and confidence in yourself. Too often women and people who are shy, unique, or different-looking than others are taught by society they are second-class citizens and not privy to the blessings the stars of the world have. Well, I have a clue for you: we are all blessed and should play that starring role in our lives. In spite of what men say about women, or women say about men, we are all only separated by a gene. Different races have the same genetic background and being unique is often a gift we haven't opened.

Growing up on an American Indian reservation, I knew many Native Americans throughout life. One I will never forget I met through my brother in college. He was a strikingly handsome man with an amazing gift in art. Yet he struggled with his heritage because of the burden our society placed upon him. He has done twice as much as most people in his lifetime, and yet our world tends to judge people like him. He, like others in the local tribe, struggled with society's perception of the Native American and had to prove himself over and over again by overachieving because of this.

We need to work at overcoming society's attitudes toward us and build our self-concepts and confidence. Once your confidence is established, you can start to bloom. And with time, you will come to love yourself. When you treat yourself well, so will others. You will begin to be your own hero because of who you believe in, who you are, and who you have become. I now have the starring role in my own life, and that's a great place for me to be.

*You can redefine yourself and have a do-over! You are never too old to learn or change.*

Five years ago, I had no idea I would be the author of this book, have my travel and tourism certificate, be working on a travel blog, or be writing another nine books. I was an art teacher and loved travel and photography. That was who I was. I was *"too old"* to go into a new area. I was fifty-eight when I finally realized I might have a new chance at life. However, before that, I was quite certain I was at the end of my career and life, and I had nothing more to offer. I would just substitute teach until I, too, melted away into that large ocean of retirees not to be heard from again. How absurd!

I was one-and-one-half years into retirement and had nearly finished the book we all want to write. Physically I was limited because of age and illness and was emotionally spent from a stressful career and all of the life-changing events that had recently happened. I really didn't know what to do until my sister asked me to stay at her house to look after her children and dog while she and her husband went on vacation. I began to think: *I deserve a vacation too!* I had retired with no big send-off to mark twenty some years in teaching, so I was going to give myself one.

I didn't even have to think twice about where I wanted to go. Years before, I had promised myself that I would go back to see Italy when I was older and had the money. So I began to plan the trip. In so doing, I went to the local AAA office in our area where I ran into a friend from a previous job. We talked about travel, and I told her that I was interested in a travel career. She introduced me to the manager of the branch, and he told me a little about the business. Between the two of them, I learned how and what to do to begin travel school. When I called the local travel agency that was sponsoring the schooling, I was stunned to find out I was speaking with another fellow retired workmate from my first job in teaching. That cinched it. I was not too old! And if my old workmate could do it, so could I!

I have since learned Italian and now am 70% proficient in reading the language and have my travel certificate. I have discovered through all of this that I love to learn different languages, and when I am finished with Italian, I will brush up on my German and try my hand at Spanish. Who would have guessed even two years ago that I would be doing this and loving it? So those of you who think that you are too old to follow your dreams and learn new things, think again! Follow in the footsteps of Grandma Moses (Anna Mary Robertson Moses), Julia Child, and Harlan (Colonel) Sanders who all began their dreams later in life!

*Reward yourself when you accomplish your goals.*

Some time ago I finished my travel course after over a year of study. I also finished with the A I thought was going to elude me. Even though I didn't have the finances to give myself the trip I deserved, I still took myself out to celebrate. This book has taken nearly five years of writing, researching, and editing on my part. It was a much bigger enterprise than I had first anticipated. However, being nearly finished feels fabulous, and I want to shout it from the mountaintops and give myself the reward I deserve.

When we work to accomplish a goal and do it with style, we deserve to be rewarded. If you are like me and live alone, there is no one around to surprise us with a night out or a special gift. Although many of us can't afford to do so in grand style, we should always treat ourselves to something that makes us feel as special as we are when we accomplish something. My goal was large, but there are also many in our lives that are much smaller, such as losing ten pounds, saving up to buy a new television, or perhaps just keeping your house clean for a whole week. If your goal is met, let people know! Call a friend or friends and go out for a celebration on the town. If you shed the ten pounds that you wished to lose, go out and buy that dress you have wanted to fit into!

However you go about giving yourself a pat on the back, always let yourself know you are appreciated, even if it is just with you. I went out with a friend and shared the occasion of earning my travel degree over a champagne brunch. However, if she hadn't been around, I still would have taken myself out, as I am important. Just remember how you treat yourself is how others will treat you, therefore, be kind to yourself for the special person you are!

*Always remember what you are worth.
Many men and women have given their lives
so you can live yours. Believe in yourself!*

Just like loving yourself, no one will ever believe in you if you don't believe in yourself.

Many of us do not realize our own worth, either as humans or as Americans. The truth is that countless people have given their lives for us in wars, so we may have the freedoms we do in America. Yet many of us, especially women, tend to allow others to treat us badly. We put up with verbal and emotional abuse, both in relationships and in the workplace, and then we wonder why we feel so bad. Worse yet, we begin to believe we deserve to be treated as such.

I recently watched a video on Facebook one of my friends posted about the practice of Conscious Discipline and how bullies and victims are created. I realized I was watching myself. I had been molded by my circumstances growing up to behave like a victim but was not aware of it. Although I have always been very strong and didn't fall totally within that category, there was enough for me to recognize myself when I saw the video.

I have discovered that for belief in yourself to begin, you must lift yourself up rather than put yourself down. You must never allow others to put you down either. Surround yourself with kind and supportive people and feed yourself on good and positive ideas, thoughts, and healthy food. You may not be the perfect person, but then who is? We all have a great deal of growing to do no matter where we are on our life paths. And if you are just beginning your journey, you must start somewhere. It is a building block for each new step in our lives. Successful people usually are those who believe in themselves and have a firm understanding of who they are and what they can do. Do not let anyone tell you that you are any different!

Remember what you are worth, treat yourself as the special person you are, and surround yourself with people who believe in you too. You will see your belief in yourself grow as you do!

*Take some time off from work
when you feel you need to.*

Thank heavens my mother understood we all need some time off from school once in a while and didn't push hard when I said I didn't feel well. Truth be told, I wasn't always physically sick, I just needed a mental health day once in a while.

A lot of us push ourselves far too hard for our bodies or emotional selves to handle. Whether in high school, college, grad school, at work, or as a parent, such hard work takes a toll on both our physical and mental health. Most teachers I know don't want to take off of school because it takes far too much work to prepare for someone else. But there comes a time when even the most dedicated employees have to take a break. Secretly most teachers pray for a snow day in the north just to get some down time! During the thirteen months I went back to school to get my travel agent certificate, I spent most of my days studying. However, I found that a little afternoon break actually helped me to concentrate better and refreshed me so I could put in the twelve or thirteen hours a day needed to finish my work. Sometimes we need an hour's rest, sometimes a day, and sometimes a week to catch our breath. It just depends on the load we carry.

I have an acquaintance who refuses to put her work down, even on vacation. I have told her several times this could affect her physical, not to mention her mental health, but she refuses to listen. She keeps plodding along, feeling she must do what she is doing and defending her position. My dad had a great job, and after my mother became sick with cancer the first time, it allowed him to successfully separate his work and home life. I can only remember him bringing his work home once, and it only meant dropping off some samples at a plant at night. He made it a priority to separate his work and his home life. It was the only way for his PTSD, our large family, and my mother's needs to work in harmony.

Take the time and give yourself the break you need, whether it is an hour or a month. You will be a better parent, spouse, and employee if you do.

*Make sure to set aside some quiet
time each day for yourself.*

We all need quiet time each day: some time when we don't have someone bombarding us with noise pollution. Depending on our lives and jobs, most of us have to create this time for ourselves. I'm not talking about once in a while, but EVERY DAY.

Why is quiet time so important for us? For one thing, it helps us regenerate brain cells. A 2013 study on mice found that two hours of quiet time a day helped mice develop new brain cells in the hippocampus, according to an article published in the journal *Brain, Structure, and Function*. (2015) It also helps to restore our mental resources, relieves stress and tension, and taps into our "default mode" network of our brain. The default part of our brain allows us to daydream and to think creatively. But in order to do this, we must break free from the noise pollution in our society. Is it any wonder that Henry David Thoreau spent so much time in nature, as did young Delacroix and Keats?

When I was teaching, having quiet time for myself was very important because my job involved so much noise. Being an art teacher is a creative endeavor, so I always encouraged talking and problem-solving in class. Coming home to a quiet house was non-negotiable for me. But I am single and without children. How does one schedule quiet time when living with a family? The solution may mean getting up early or going to bed an hour after everyone else. I like to have my quiet time in the morning as it helps prepare me for the day ahead. One can also use it as a devotional or meditation time to help create a positive mindset for the day.

However you wish to use your time is up to you. Maybe you have a book that you want to finish, read the paper for the day, or just catch up on email—it's your choice. But make it a priority to schedule some noise-free time each day so your nerves, your ears, and your brain can rest and rejuvenate.

*Be your own advocate.
Sometimes you have to toot
your own horn.*

There are many times we have to learn to toot our own horns in life. Whether or not this is fair, it's still true. By doing so, one is not being boastful or conceited. It is what it is: just being your own best advocate and bringing attention to what you have done or what you stand for.

When I was teaching art in the public school system, there were very few besides myself to toot my art horn. As in most schools, they were all about football, basketball, and the core classes. Few people among the staff, with the exception of a very special school counselor and a few parents who knew how important the arts are in today's world, were in my corner. But more often than not, I found I had to go down to the office and round up my principal to have him see what was going on in my department, to look at the amazing artwork my students had produced. Most of the time when these students won an award at state or on the national stage, I had to write my own morning announcement congratulating them. As I said, whether this was fair isn't the issue, it just is what it is: a fact.

Another area I am working on lately is being my own advocate for fibromyalgia. I no longer sit and listen to what the doctors say as gospel, but do my own research. I probably know more than most of them about the subject, and I am protecting myself while holding the medical field accountable, as well as tooting my own horn for my cause. In so doing, I am helping others. I have begun a group called Project Health on my Facebook where I post anything I can find with new research; information about the nutritional benefits of certain foods, spices and oils; and breakthroughs in illnesses such as fibromyalgia and cancer, wellness, and many more health-related items.

In the work world, being your own advocate might mean

the difference between having a position and not. Now that I am finished with my travel course and this book, it is time for me to search for or create a job, and I will need to advocate for myself. Prospective employers or merchants don't know what I have to offer unless I tell them. Just like male birds during the mating season, I will need to strut my stuff. I have collected a number of skills in my teaching career that can be viewed as experience in the market; I have chaperoned trips, I also have photography skills, writing skills, and can manage a classroom, I had an art history minor in college, am well-traveled, and I understand Italian and German. However, unless I speak up, all they will see on my resume is art teacher, illustrator, and a travel counseling certificate. The same thing applies to dating. If you are a shy, introverted person and not able or willing to share what you are like inside, no one else will know what you have to offer. Why do you think the loud people in your high school or college classes got the dates? They were the ones who let themselves be known and tooted their own horn and advertised. However, when you toot your horn, you don't always have to *tell* others what you are like if you *act* it. Let others know how beautiful you are inside by how you treat others or how gifted you are at something by how you use your blessings. My brother always says, "Show me, don't just tell me!"

However you advocate for yourself, make certain you get your audience in your corner and play your horn like no other.

*Do something that makes you happy
or brings you joy daily.*

How many of us actually do this? I'm not just referring to major events such as vacations or day trips, but small things too.

Like many other things in life, we tend to get caught up in our busy days and often find we cut out things like exercise, quiet times, and doing something to make us happy. This doesn't have to be. No matter how busy or financially strapped we are, we can spare five or ten minutes for something that gives us pleasure each day. As I mentioned earlier, while studying for my travel class, I would work up to twelve or thirteen hours a day. But even on the busiest of days, I still took time to call someone. This gave me joy because I was connecting with a friend or family member. It didn't cost me anything extra, other than the time.

In the past two weeks since finishing up my studies, I have treated myself to a day trip up to the nearest art community to see the fall colors, an afternoon picking apples, and a day of preparing Halloween-themed food for a product party I was giving. Each made me happy and didn't require much other than time. You may receive joy from giving, such as volunteering or babysitting the neighbor's child, reading ten minutes of a book, going through a drive-through for a cup of cappuccino, or just watching a late-night movie. If you enjoy nature, go out for a walk. If you are active, go for a bike ride. Whatever it is, do something daily that brings you joy.

Please don't wait as I did and have to be retaught how to be happy. Being happy should be one of our inalienable rights. Nurture happiness in your soul and you'll be "happy" you did!

*Live your life on your own terms, not on the terms of others. You are the only one who will have to answer for your todays.*

Many of us live our lives by the standards of our society, community, friends, or family. We go about our lives doing what we *think* we are supposed to do and leave what we really want to do behind with our dreams. Many times we ask what others would do and follow their dreams instead of our own.

Parents are fantastic for guiding us when we are young. As we get older and marry or live with a partner, our spouses and significant others do the same with their suggestions, again mainly out of concern and love. But in truth, they aren't living our lives, *we are*. In the end, we are the only ones who will have to answer for our mistakes and successes, not them. You have to choose, and choose early if you can, how you want to live your life, and make certain you can pay for the consequences of your actions. I have many friends with beautiful huge houses who choose to work hard for their lodgings, but I have chosen to travel. I have friends who will not go near foreign food, but I love it. I choose to make my life about family, friends, creativity, travel, and helping those around me. Others love the life that an all-encompassing job brings with all of its frills and the things they can afford to collect in life. We all make our own choices.

Make all of your choices based on the person you are and who you want to become. This means physical, mental, emotional, spiritual, and every other part of your life you have some control over. If you want to live a healthy life and eventually try out for the Olympics, you will want to eat right, work out, and practice daily to work toward that goal. If you want to write the Great American Novel, then you will need to study writing, practice daily and then dive into the deep end. But don't let others influence your decisions. If you ask for guidance or others offer their expertise, then listen, glean what you can from their suggestions, and do what you need to do for yourself. You are only given a certain amount of time on this planet, and if you allow someone to turn you into something you are not, you will most likely be miserable.

The best parents, partners, and friends will want you to live a happy and healthy life, not just to follow in their footsteps or become rich. Although they might be giving you advice with the best of intentions, they aren't you and will not live your tomorrows. So get to know yourself well enough to know what it is that you want, count the costs, and then take the leap!

*Discover what your purpose is on earth.*

All of us search for our purpose in life. Some of us find it early, and some search their entire lives and find it later on. But I have discovered that until you find your purpose, you are unsettled and restless.

I have finally discovered my purpose in life; it is to help other people, more specifically, help others through my writing and mentoring. I know that beyond any doubt. And when I combine this with my passions, I have found my work and life have become a joy. I am okay with the fact I don't have children or a partner, or that I am no longer a professional teacher, because I am happy with who I am and what I do. I have grown and have become the person I need to be in order to fulfill my life's purpose. But without all of my trials, I wouldn't have been able to do so.

I recently watched a small documentary film *The Sacred Science*, which talked about ancient medicine and the shamans who still use it in the Peruvian rainforest. In this film, a small group of people traveled there in an attempt to find a cure for their illnesses. These people spoke of the journey they were on and how blessed they felt to have had time to have gotten to know themselves. Like them, I had struggled to find the woman inside and embrace my life, good and bad, for far too long. I had been distracted by the business of life and never bothered to find a peaceful place to listen to the quiet voice inside that for years had told me to stop and heed its call. Only by my own journey of becoming ill could I have found my purpose and ultimately become not only happy but incredibly joyful as well. My life is not what I thought it would be, and even now it is constantly evolving. But it's so much more than I could have imagined, and I feel incredibly blessed.

If you were to ask me how to do this in your own life, I would have to say I haven't a clue! However, in researching for this book,

I found an article called, "How to Read the 3 Signs Telling You Your Purpose in Life" in *The Entrepreneur*, that really spoke to me. This article suggested every time I thought I had found my calling in life, I had missed something very important. It was because I was only focusing on what I loved and what I was good at. In this article, Tor Constantino interviewed another author and blogger, Jeff Goins, and suggested there are three areas you must consider:

Listen to your life – You must first discover who you are.

Accidental apprenticeships – We don't realize our life purpose by ourselves, there are many people and situations that mold us into what we need to be to become successful.

Prep for painful practice – We only make it to our goal through painful practice.

After this we must ask ourselves these three questions to find out where the first three areas intersect.

What do I love?

What am I good at?

What does the world need?

I hadn't discovered who I was or asked myself what the world needed. Now that I am familiar with my strengths and weaknesses and my inner most workings, I can ask the last question, "What does the world need?"

Open your minds and heart to what is happening to you and embrace yourselves and your road in life. Learn who you are and then listen to what you love and what the world could use. Then hold on dearly for an incredible ride.

*Learn how to be your own best friend.*

Not everyone is lucky enough to have the wonderful friends I do. I have truly been blessed. But it hasn't always been so. I grew up with few friends and felt like an outsider most of the time. But I have since learned that if we want to have loving friends surrounding us, we must learn how to be our own best friend first.

Loving who you are begins with discovering who you are and embracing that person, whoever you may be. It involves learning about the gifts you have, what your dreams are, and treating yourself as someone you really love. I didn't understand this principle until quite recently. I had been treating myself as someone I really didn't know and saw myself only as others who had hurt me throughout my life saw: someone who didn't deserve any better.

Ask yourself: how would you treat a best friend you love dearly and what would you do for them? Among other things I do for those I love is send little notes, either by snail mail or by text. When they are sick or struggling, I let them know they are in my thoughts. And when they do something amazing, I give them a pat on the back or help them celebrate. So too, you should do the same for yourself. When you are tired after a particularly long day at work, put your feet up, make a nice cup of your favorite tea, and read a book or take a nice soak in essential oils and Epsom salts. Clean any negative thoughts about yourself out of your head as well. You are what you believe you are. If you can change your thoughts and keep practicing this, you will find that you actually may start liking yourself better and can be a better friend to yourself. As you begin to do this, you will begin to attract people who will notice the difference.

Tomorrow is my sixty-first birthday and when I wake up in the morning, I plan to spend the whole day doing things I like. If I feel like I want to spend the whole day napping or watching movies on Netflix, I can. If I decide to spend the day writing or shopping at the local consignment shops, I feel I have earned that right and don't have to explain myself to anyone. I have learned to be my own best friend, and you should as well.

*Set realistic goals for yourself. Whatever may be realistic for someone else may not be right for you.*

We are all very different. When you set goals, make certain they fit you. Some people dream huge dreams and reach them, some dream small. Your goals should be whatever is right for you.

When New Year's comes around, I'm always amused by how many people set huge goals for the upcoming year: goals to lose weight, pay off debts, or go on a long-awaited cruise. These people establish their goals but don't consider what will have to be done to see them to fruition. If you are on a doctor's plan to lose sixty pounds, it might be realistic. However, most people don't consider the exercise, time needed to prepare healthy food, or how much effort it takes to lose one pound, much less sixty! If you have come into an inheritance or find a better-paying job, you may be able to pay off your debt in a year. But you have to take into consideration how long it took you to accumulate this debt and what you need to spend from your income in order to pay it off. If I said I wished to become a mountain climber at age sixty, it wouldn't be very realistic, but doing it in my twenties when I was strong and young was a different situation.

Make your goals fit you. Consider all factors that are pertinent. How much time do I need to spend to make my dreams come true? How much money will it take? How much effort do I have to put into it? Am I physically able to make this dream a reality? Whatever it is, there are a myriad of variables to consider. Whatever your dream, make sure it's your size.

*You shouldn't have to settle for anything in life. Not ANYTHING!*

People *settle* all of the time in life and then wonder why they are so unhappy. Consider what a miracle life truly is. Think of everything that has to happen correctly in order for a person even to be born! Doesn't such a miracle deserve the best life has to offer?

This comes with a caveat, however. If you decide you are not going to settle in life, with that decision comes a lot of hard work and self-discipline. This is especially true in your education, marriage, really anything you do or own. How hard are you willing to work to get the things you want? Someone once told me they knew they could get As in school but didn't want to work that hard to earn them. To them, a B wasn't settling but compromising to get other things in life they wanted. They wanted a life along with high school and college. For those who are dreaming of a family, are you prepared to get up late at night, run to the doctor with sick kids, and give up some of your own desires to save money for their education? If you aren't, then perhaps children aren't for you. Your way of settling would be to live someone else's life instead of your own.

As I have gone through life, I have noticed a pattern emerge when accepting some things. I noticed this when selecting men, jobs, housing, and how I allowed others to treat me. As I have already stated, I had been trained by life to settle for less than what I deserved. Afterwards when I was disappointed, I blamed myself rather than considering it might be a problem with how I saw myself. I thought I was just too sensitive or too picky. So as I went out into the world, I settled for less in my relationships, always thinking there was something wrong with me; I stuck out jobs in some of the most toxic environments possible for the same reason.

The truth is, we all deserve the best we can get in life. Yes, it takes effort and patience, like working very hard to get good grades or crawling through drainage pipes on construction jobs to have enough money for a semester abroad in college. But if we don't want to settle, we must work for it. You may have to patiently sift through a lot of junk to find the right place to live or the right job. And you may have to "kiss a lot of toads" to find the right guy, but it's worth it in the end. So if you are in a job, relationship, or town you can't tolerate any longer, you have two choices; either seek the counseling needed to adjust to what you have or cut your losses and move on. Always remember, though, you deserve the best, so hang on until yours comes along.

*If you aren't happy with the person you are, you will never be happy with someone else either. And the reverse is true as well.*

Growing up and during most of my adult life, I was a very unhappy person. I was always told by others to be something other than who I was: I wasn't the right type of girl, I was too quiet, too messy, too scared, too clumsy, or I had to be better at what I was doing. I began to believe I was an inadequate person and never quite knew why I wasn't comfortable with who I was or those around me.

I have recently learned that if you are happy with who you are and what you are doing, it absolutely shines through! You begin to draw others to you who see that inner glow. But getting there is the secret. In counseling, I was asked to make two lists, one for the things I liked about myself and the other for things I didn't. What I found was there were far more characteristics I liked about myself than not, and those I didn't like were either thoughts, behaviors, or physical attributes that I could either work on or weren't important in the grand scheme of things. I had once again zeroed in on just the negatives in my life, as many of us do. Once I understood the person I was, I could appreciate the wonderful lady inside.

If you don't like yourself, you are always looking to be someone you are not. And unless you are fortunate to find friends who are willing to see beyond your lack of self-confidence, you will continue to push people away. Which type of person attracts you the most; a person who is comfortable with themselves and happy with who they are or a person who is uncomfortable and withdrawn? The answer is obvious to me. Everyone would rather be around someone who makes their time together comfortable and fun.

If you don't like the person you are, either see a counselor who will help you to find the person hidden inside or make lists, like I did. Once you see the many facets of yourself, start chipping away at those that can be changed and embrace what you like. It will make you much happier and attract those who will truly appreciate the person you are!

# Part Four

## The Body Beautiful: Your Physical Health

*The heavens and nature brought you into the world unclothed. You and your body are nothing to be ashamed of. Whatever your form or shape, you are alive and beautiful!*

Growing up, I was a gangly, skinny little thing, weighing all of sixty-nine pounds at 4'11" in sixth grade. I was embarrassed by my skinny arms and my scrawny legs and couldn't wait to grow into adult body parts. I waited and waited, and even at my twenty-fifth year high school reunion, I was still a size 4. Now what I wouldn't give to have some of that little body back!

The point is that we are never really satisfied with the bodies we have been given. We are led to believe we should mold our bodies to be like those in the tabloids. The problem is the people in those magazines on the newspaper stands are Photoshopped beyond recognition, and we are all sucked into believing that is how they actually look. The truth is very few people look as beautiful as supermodels do. I know I will never have the body I had in my twenties, and that is perfectly okay with me.

However, as long as we are healthy, can walk from one place to another, and aren't in pain, we should be grateful. So many people hide themselves, or parts of themselves because they aren't perfect. They have scars on their bodies from various surgeries or varicose veins in their legs or a mid-life bulge around their middle. But those are life's battle scars, and we should be proud of those we carry. Nothing else should ever matter.

So the next time you are on a beach or on the deck of a cruise ship, be thankful that you can afford to take the trip and that your legs can carry you around. Think of the beautiful children you now have that were traded for your young figure or for the scars that tell your life story. Your body is still only a house for what is inside, and beyond a healthy discipline, make that your priority and forget the rest!

*It is so important to learn how to deal with physical pain in life. Dealing with illness is difficult, but not impossible.*

I was, as my doctor put it, "healthy as a horse" while growing up. He would end each appointment by smiling at my mother and telling her I was a healthy little girl, with an unspoken "be grateful."

My mother wasn't so fortunate. She grew up having all of the normal childhood illnesses along with scarlet fever twice, anemia, and a serious staph infection. At forty-two, she was diagnosed with breast cancer, and after surgery and radiation, the cancer went into remission for twenty years. But at sixty-one, while I was teaching, she became sick again, but this time it was terminal. My body reacted horribly to the six years she was sick, and soon after she passed away I was diagnosed with fibromyalgia. Nearly five years ago my dad succumbed to mesothelioma, a form of lung cancer. So when I suddenly developed adult-onset asthma and my fibromyalgia suddenly flared, I wasn't terribly surprised, and quite recently I discovered I have arthritis in nearly every joint and pinched nerves in my spine. I am in pain almost every day. Mind you, it isn't the pain of a migraine or appendicitis, but an ache that never lets up.

Sometimes when the pain is bad, I find myself in bed, and other times I hardly know it's there. But all of these problems seem to flare up at the very worst times, like a child getting sick on the day of a vacation. I long for the healthy little girl I once was. But no matter what, I will always remember the pain both parents endured as they fought cancer and the problems of chemotherapy before they died, and it gives me courage to push through my struggles.

To help yourself mentally and emotionally handle similar situations, look to the many others who have it worse than you: those without food, water, medical treatment, pain medication; those who can't walk, see, hear, have cancer, AIDS, cerebral palsy, Alzheimer's, and myriads of other problems, and you may find it easier to deal with your struggles. Also, there are hundreds of support groups that can provide emotional support if family and friends aren't present. I have found two such groups I am a member of: one on Facebook and one on the Internet. They provide comfort when I am especially frustrated or angry with my conditions.

I cannot speak for those reading this, but only for myself. I am using both conventional and alternative medicines to help me control my conditions and deal with their symptoms. I have spent thousands of dollars on medicines, and although they helped for many of the everyday illnesses, they haven't even begun to touch my fibromyalgia pain, and they come with a truckload of side effects. So last winter when I was so miserable, I began to search for alternatives. I found that for me, a combination of healthy foods, enzymes, exercise, and medicine are helping. Although I still cannot work, I am feeling better. I don't spend my days in tears or angry any longer, and the pain is more manageable if I don't overdo it. At least I can work on writing from home and am hoping this will help others deal with their pain and illnesses while sharing a part of myself that counts.

My suggestion to each one who is reading this book is to keep searching for what works for you and to be your own advocate. Do whatever you can, within reason, to become pain free, but count the costs as well. I hope one day to become pain and medicine free, despite what the doctors say, and I won't stop until I am! Join me and never give up!

*Don't be afraid to go to a doctor or counselor. Both are healers.*

I have seen more than my fair share of doctors and counselors in my life. Some of them have been very good and others have left a lot to be desired. I have had some listen to me and others yell at me. Some I have found through trial and error and some have been recommended. However, I have never given up until I found someone that could meet *my* needs. Just as we all have preferences with regard to food and friends, we all have special needs and preferences regarding doctors or counselors.

Some people may be afraid to go to a doctor for various reasons, so they don't even try. However, this is sometimes a way for us to hide when we are afraid and don't want to face the possibility there might be something wrong with us. Most of us have families and friends who love us, so it is our responsibility to take care of our health and ourselves so we may live long and healthy lives.

For me, my criteria for finding a good doctor includes the following requirements: experience, good listening skills, acceptance, understanding, good diagnostic skills, and a willingness to work with me to find a way to manage my illness and possibly someday cure it. I have stopped going to doctors without recommendations, as I have been disappointed too many times. As for a counselor, I believe I have found the very best. He not only listens and validates my feelings, but also gives me skills so I can deal with my problems. That is a good counselor! Although I don't see him anymore except on rare occasions, I know he is always there just a phone call away to listen and help.

There are many things to try outside of traditional medicine. According to medicinenet.com, complementary medicine is "a group of diagnostic and therapeutic medicines that are used in conjunction with conventional ones." Alternative therapies, in contrast, are used in place of other medicines. The following is a list of these medicines and therapies; acupuncture, Alexander technique, aromatherapy, Ayurveda (Ayurvedic medicine), biofeedback, chiropractic medicine, diet therapy, herbalism, holistic nursing, homeopathy, hypnosis, massage therapy, meditation, naturopathy, nutritional therapy, osteopathic manipulative therapy (OMT), Qi gong (internal and external Qiging), reflexology, Reiki, spiritual healing, Tai Chi, traditional Chinese Medicine (TCM), and yoga.

I have only tried a handful of these myself: aromatherapy, massage, chiropractic, meditation, Reiki, biofeedback, diet therapy, holistic nursing, and yoga. For me, the most effective has been using diet therapy, chiropractic, biofeedback, and holistic nursing. I continue to use chiropractic once or twice a month when my back begins to hurt, and although I have been to many chiropractors, my present one is by far the best. The doctors used biofeedback on me when I injured my shoulders and needed therapy to improve mobility. However, many people have benefitted from the others. I know many people who regularly practice yoga and swear by it, several who regularly get massages to relax, and others who have tried acupuncture and love it. My current holistic nurse is using diet and enzyme therapy to help me recover my health.

Whatever you use is personal to *you*, and it's up to you to fill your needs. But whatever you do, make certain you see someone and do something when you need help in healing.

*Laugh whenever you can.
A good belly laugh is contagious
and relieves a great deal of stress.*

Many of the great comedians from my childhood have since gone off to the great stage in the sky, but they can be found on the Internet. One night my sister was replaying a skit she had seen on Facebook with Dana Carvey on the *Carroll Burnett Show*. Many know it simply as the Dentist Chair Skit. If you have ever seen this, you can appreciate that when we started to laugh, we couldn't stop, and before we knew it, we were in tears, could hardly breathe, and were nearly on the floor. Many of the episodes of *The Big Bang Theory* on television have the same effect on me.

What is it about a hearty belly laugh that makes us feel so good? Medical reports say that it relaxes us and releases endorphins, which help us feel good and even help with pain. Belly laughing helps us to burn calories, protects our health, and may also help us to live longer. Dick Van Dyke is over ninety years old and still acts like a man half his age. I believe it's partly because of his ability to laugh and be a child. An excerpt from the song, "I Love to Laugh," from the movie *Mary Poppins*, which he starred in sums it up perfectly:

> I love to laugh
> Loud and long and clear
> We love to laugh
> So everybody can hear
> The more you laugh
> The more you fill with glee
> And the more the glee
> The more we're a merrier we . . .

This is especially true when it comes to our daily lives. When we can laugh, we are replacing an unhealthy, stress-filled emotion with a healthy one. On New Year's Eve my sister, her family, and I went to a mutual friend's house and played a game called Crimes

Against Humanity. It is a very silly and sometimes very sassy game, but I haven't laughed that hard in years. Why is it that we often find it so hard to relax enough to let go or need an excuse like New Years to laugh?

What can we do to laugh more often every day? We can spend more time with funny and entertaining people. We can also listen to television comedy episodes from years ago: Johnny Carson, the Chuckles the Clown episode from *The Mary Tyler Moore Show*, *The Court Jester* with Danny Kaye, Laurel and Hardy, and I can go on. If you are having a particularly hard day, have them on "speed dial" on your smart phone, and when taking a break at work, listen to one. Learn to see the humor in situations that you get yourself into. This will really go a long way in diminishing your stress.

Do whatever you can to lessen your anxiety, improve your health, and feel good by having a good laugh.

*Save some energy for yourself.*

I was an art teacher for over twenty years, and still teach summer school. As I watch the students' little bodies running around the playground and going to and from their classes, I am still amazed at their overabundance of energy. I believe I would most certainly become a billionaire if I could ever find a way to harness that energy and bottle it for sale!

We all think we have an unlimited supply of energy, but in reality, our energy begins to dwindle as we grow older or we deal with illness. I was so active as a child few people could keep up with me. I will always remember the first day of kindergarten, being so proud that I beat my older brother home from school. The only time I stayed in one place was when I was sleeping, eating, or searching for fossils in our driveway. Now that I am older, I am beginning to think I used up all of that energy when I was young! Now the only time I have some left is if I take a siesta in the afternoon, sleep until noon, or fill myself up with caffeine until I am flying like a kite.

We all need to slow down a bit and save some of our precious energy to do some of the things we need to do *for ourselves* in life. Many of us say we will sleep when we are dead, but then again, isn't that a self-fulfilling prophesy? We all have our own lives to live and need energy to get through our days too. Women are notorious for spending all of their energy on others and then not having anything at the end of the day for themselves. They often do everything, from being a mom for their children to doctoring and chauffeuring. I have been doing this all of my life, and even though I have never been an official mom, I now am squeaking out barely enough energy to get through my days.

One thing I have noticed that people like myself tend to do is refuse to delegate. I go into many homes and see the parents killing themselves while their children play on Gameboys or sit in front of the television. If you have a husband or children, train them early to help you with folding the wash, doing dishes, and cleaning their rooms. They live with you and should behave as such. You are not their slave. You might use their allowance as part of their payment for each thing they do. If you are a teacher, make certain your kids either clean up their messes right away or stay in for recess to do it. If you are on a committee, make certain everyone does their fair share. In this way, you have some of that precious energy at the end of the day to do something for yourself besides falling into bed!

Another thing that you can do is to rest in between jobs. When I am having an especially hard day, I may do a few small jobs, then sit down and do something different while relaxing. When I have my energy back, I attack my work once again.

However you do it, you must rebuild your energy reserves or save some for yourself to make it through your day. And be aware: the European tradition of napping after lunch is a proven option as well!

*If you have health issues,
become an expert about your problem.*

I have had fibromyalgia for nearly twenty years now and have become somewhat of an expert on the illiness, as have many others I am sure. Doctors are far more knowledgeable about the subject then they once were, but no one has equivocally solved the problem of what causes it or which medicines or treatments work best. Perhaps it is like cancer, working differently in each one of us. All I know is that I am beginning to have some success with how I feel. I use a combination of healthy foods, good rest, exercise, enzymes, and medication.

Extreme temperatures, such as very hot and cold, and changes in barometric pressure tend to give me flare-ups. These are somewhat of a cross between having arthritis in your muscles and feeling the burn after running a race. My energy is low and I am tired a lot from fighting pain. I have stabbing pains in my legs, my back aches most of the time, and my arms get such bad rashes that I sometimes wake up bleeding in the morning from scratching. I occasionally have tendonitis in my elbows, and I have developed asthma along with sleep apnea. This all makes it hard to exercise, which is not good for this condition, as most people who have it are well aware.

In addition, I have major problems with digestion if I eat incorrectly. My brain used to be very sharp, but now I have to write everything down, as I forget because of the "brain-fog" that is part of the illness. When I study, I have to work twice as hard. I do know that this illness tends to run in families, and mostly in women. When my doctor suggests a change in medications, I am always prepared, and if I'm not, I ask for time to research the new drug. (I not only rely on test trials but on people's experiences as well.)

Breast cancer is another disease I have researched, as it not only runs in our family, but gallops. My mom died of it, as did three of her aunts, and a young cousin. So I get annual checkups and keep myself abreast of any new research there is on the subject. Five of my friends have had to go through treatment for breast cancer as well, one having just passed this last July. Heaven knows something has to be done about the Big C.

Because both of these conditions seem to be genetic and partially a result of inflammation in the body, I do the best I can now to keep myself as healthy as I can by staying gluten and sugar free. I try to avoid red meat, whole milk, and other fatty foods. If I want to fill up on something at home, I either juice with organic vegetables and fruit or have frozen grapes. (They are like tiny popsicles!) I use inflammation-reducing enzymes provided by one of my health care professionals as well as turmeric, cinnamon, garlic, and ginger regularly to help fight the pain of inflammation. I do regular stretching exercises for my back and take baths in Epsom salts to help ease the pain as well. I have also begun to use essential oils topically and in an infuser to help heal my body.

I have become a member of several informational blogs for fibro fighters that have medical evidence to back them up. Presently I am reading, *What Your Doctor May Not Tell You About Fibromyalgia: The Revolutionary Treatment That Can Reverse the Disease,* by Dr. R. Paul St. Amand, *Eating Well For Optimum Health*, by Andrew Weil, M.D., and *Medical Medium*, by Anthony William, to learn more about what doctors and others say about the disease. As a result of my research, I have created a group on my Facebook called Project Health on which I occasionally post interesting articles about health-related topics. As many friends and two of my sisters-in-law suffer from fibromyalgia, I would say there is a lot at stake. Hopefully this will help all of the other people I know with problems such as this, type 2 diabetes, thyroid disease, and other inflammatory conditions.

Once again, become your own advocate: read, study up on your illness, and bring attention to your cause. Don't be afraid to find people and doctors to support you either. The very least you will do is make a difference for yourself. Just maybe one of us armchair doctors will be able to connect the dots one day for these diseases or more!

*If you don't want to take
care of yourself for you,
do it for those who love you.*

Many times in life we may find we are either too busy to take care of ourselves properly or are too depressed to do a good job. I found myself in both of these spots during the past two years; too busy and too blue. Both my brother and sister-in-law have given me a lot of support during the time I struggled with this, but when I told them I would repay them, they just replied, "The way you can pay us back is just to get healthy."

That is how most of our friends and family feel when we are either physically or emotionally sick. They just want to see us get well. They know that money is only relative, and getting better takes time and effort, and because they love us, they want to see us happy. Many times our lives get so out of balance we pay for it in our eating habits, our weight, our muscle tone, and our emotional and mental health. When we are down in a hole and cannot find a way to dig ourselves out, we tend to remain there. However, most of us have family and friends who love us and will help, much of the time without even asking. Heed their suggestions; if I hadn't done so, I would still be at the bottom of that pit, or perhaps not even here!

So when you are thinking only of yourself, add those who love you into the equation. If you have children, take care of yourself for them, if not for you. If you don't, do it for your significant other, if not him or her, for your extended family and friends. They all love you and want to see a happy, healthy, and productive *you,* so you can enjoy this great gift we call life.

*When you are dealing with health issues, keep a healthy, positive attitude. It will give you one less thing to worry about and help you to live each day joyfully.*

I have been dealing with health issues for some time now, most brought on by stress but some genetic. Though mine are not life threatening, they are limiting, painful, and need attending to. Sometimes because they do involve pain and keep me from doing what I want, I get irritable and frustrated. All can be very debilitating so I try to manage them, for the most part. But when I do too much, which is often, I pay for it dearly. I get frustrated, then angry and down. Not depressed, thankfully, but I'm not dancing around either. That is when I put my "sunshine committee" into action. I throw open the curtains, put on some uplifting music, make some soothing tea for myself, and call my sister to see if she is available to talk.

If I am some place where I can't do these things, such as running errands or grocery shopping, I take some ibuprofen, set my sights on getting home as soon as possible, count my blessings, and thank my lucky stars I don't have cancer. You see, we can always find someone else who has it worse off than us. I have found the only thing you do by allowing yourself to be down is to give yourself something else to worry about.

Perhaps you would feel better at a friend's house or in your bed phoning a friend for support. If you are like me and are having a bad day, then your house isn't up for company either. We now have Facebook with free talk time for family and friends who might be scattered around the world. Smart phones also have FaceTime on which we can all talk face-to-face if we need to. But it's up to us to let others know our needs, our frustrations, and our struggles. If you do choose to go it alone, you will need to have an arsenal of blues-busters at your fingertips like me. Do anything you can to change your thought patterns. Soon, by doing so, you will develop a good habit of healthy thoughts, which will lead to a happier life.

So if your health issues begin to get the best of you, don't let those issues get you down. Pull out all of the stops when you begin to go down that path. Put on "Here Comes the Sun," open up a frozen Mai Tai, immerse yourself in a travel magazine or a good book, and let yourself think happy thoughts!

*Get outside more and become one with Mother Nature once again.*

Young people don't usually have to be told to go outside and play. It's in their blood. Many are outside at the crack of dawn, playing in the sand with their toys or a number of other things. If you give them a backyard swimming pool, then you have summer long entertainment; in the winter, give them an inner tube and a hill and you have a day filled with fun. They enjoy all sorts of activity, from bike riding and camping on the weekend to climbing monkey bars at school.

One of the things we forget to do as we get older is to be connected to nature and the outdoors. I know I can no longer lie in a sleeping bag on the ground in front of a campfire. (I wouldn't be able to move the next morning if I tried!) Nor can I go for the twenty-mile bike rides or the eight-mile walks I used to take. But there are activities we seniors can still do. We can walk along the shoreline and beachcomb for miles, take nature walks along bike trails with friends, and pick flowers in spring. Other activities we can enjoy include: bird watching, walking dogs, photography, gardening, picnicking in a park, listening to free summer concerts, snorkeling, and the list goes on.

When I was younger, I was always engaged in activities such as camping, swimming, cross country and downhill skiing, ice skating, biking, fishing, mountain trekking, hiking, walking, running, tobogganing, sledding, cherry and apple picking, crawdad fishing, lying in the sun, and building sandcastles, snowmen, and snow forts. I was active OUTSIDE. Have you forgotten how much fun it is to sit on the dock and fish for the day? And when you were done, pull off your clothing and leaving only your swimsuit on, jump into the water to cool off?

It really doesn't matter what you do, it just matters that you *do it*. I remember my aged grandfather with Parkinson's disease; even though he could barely move, he managed to get outside and sit in a chair and enjoy a beautiful day and go on his daily walk around the block. We have bodies that use blood to transport oxygen to our cells and need vitamin D from the sun. However, many of us have forgotten that exercise and being outside isn't so much about the *action* but about a way to get more oxygen and vitamin D to our cells so we *stay* healthy.

So while your neighbor sits in his house and your kids are on their laptops, grab your dog and take a spin around the block. Or better yet, take your family for a camping trip and enjoy the sun and fresh air.

# Part Five

Wise Quotes
& Old Sayings

*Read Desiderata and take it to heart.*

The following is a poem by Max Ehrmann written in 1927 but was really brought into the public eye when Les Crane recorded it in 1971. His recording is both a vocal recitation and song that fit so well in the '60s and '70s, with the period's songs about love and the universe. I have always thought this poem carried a special wisdom that is timeless.

*Desiderata*

> Go placidly amid the noise and haste,
> and remember what peace there may be in silence.
> As far as possible without surrender
> be on good terms with all persons.
> Speak your truth quietly and clearly;
> and listen to others,
> even the dull and the ignorant;
> they too have their story.
>
> Avoid loud and aggressive persons,
> they are vexations to the spirit.
> If you compare yourself with others,
> you may become vain and bitter;
> for always there will be greater and lesser persons than yourself.
> Enjoy your achievements as well as your plans.
>
> Keep interested in your own career, however humble;
> it is a real possession in the changing fortunes of time.
> Exercise caution in your business affairs;
> for the world is full of trickery.
> But let this not blind you to what virtue there is;
> many persons strive for high ideals;
> and everywhere life is full of heroism.

Be yourself.
Especially, do not feign affection.
Neither be cynical about love;
for in the face of all aridity and disenchantment
it is as perennial as the grass.

Take kindly the counsel of the years,
gracefully surrendering the things of youth.
Nurture strength of spirit to shield you in sudden misfortune.
But do not distress yourself with dark imaginings.
Many fears are born of fatigue and loneliness.
Beyond a wholesome discipline,
be gentle with yourself.

You are a child of the universe,
no less than the trees and the stars;
you have a right to be here.
And whether or not it is clear to you,
no doubt the universe is unfolding as it should.

Therefore be at peace with God,
whatever you conceive Him to be,
and whatever your labors and aspirations,
in the noisy confusion of life keep peace with your soul.

With all its sham, drudgery, and broken dreams,
it is still a beautiful world.
Be cheerful.
Strive to be happy.

© Max Ehrmann 1927

Desiderata speaks to people of all ages and all walks of life with a wisdom that few pieces of written work can rival. It is an inspired piece of poetry that needs to be taken out of its drawer and dusted off more often and shared with those around the world. Everyone can learn something from its special wisdom!

Thank you so much, Max Ehrmann, for your gift to the world!

*Never allow ANYONE to make you feel bad about yourself.*

Eleanor Roosevelt once said, "No one can make you feel inferior without your consent."

The first time I ever heard this quote was when I saw the movie *The Princess Diaries* for the first time. When Joe quoted Eleanor Roosevelt, it made me think of how many times I had given that control to another person and the countless times I had found myself hurting. That being said, I still had no clue as to how to stop from being hurt. Once someone has hurt you, it cannot be undone, so I wasn't certain I quite understood.

However, I was looking at the situation from the wrong point of view; I was seeing it as if it had already happened and not how it could be prevented. The answer requires you to believe in yourself more than in another person's words and not allow them to hurt you in the first place. For example, someone may say that you are a poor artist, but if you believe in yourself and have had many compliments on your work, what should one person's opinion matter? A friend doesn't try to bring another friend down but builds them up instead.

Remember, only small people put others down—those people who are insecure about themselves and their world. You must ask yourself: do I respect this person and are they knowledgeable in regard to what they are talking about, or are they just insecure? When you have decided where this person stands, then you can decide as to what to do next.

Finally, with regard to the wisdom Mrs. Roosevelt shared with us: anyone who hurts your feelings intentionally and makes you feel bad about yourself doesn't deserve to be called a friend, period. Clean house beginning with this person, then start to add people who treat you as a friend should, by supporting you and making you feel good about yourself.

*The old saying,
"Look for the silver lining"
is all well and good, but why not
go for the gold ring instead?*

My sister is the queen of finding silver linings. She can always find something good in just about anything. I think she picked this up from my mother, as she was known for her positive thinking. I grew up just the opposite. People used to say my middle name should have been Murphy's Law, as anything that could go wrong often happened to me. I have been bucked off of a camel, lost my wallet in the ocean while ocean fishing, got lost in the subways of Paris, lost my passport on a train in Germany, had to hitchhike back from Oberammergau to Munich in Germany because the trains were no longer running that day, got stranded at the Florence train station because of a train strike, and had to pitch a tent and sleep under the stars in Moorea, Tahiti, because the local hostel hadn't opened yet. Also, I am always hurting myself. These all make for great adventure stories, but at the time they are happening, they aren't always pleasant.

However, that's all beginning to change. I have begun to see that as you think, so you are. I was beginning to believe what people were saying about me: that I invited trouble and had begun to accept it. But what does this say again about my self-image? Now when things begin to happen, I think about what I should be learning from my situation or talk to friends to get an objective opinion. Usually these types of situations happen because I am just over-tired, worn out, or don't know when to quit.

We all need to reach for the gold—the best in life—and remind ourselves we are worth it. My sister's dog Bella had a stroke from which she has mostly recovered, but it encouraged the family to get another puppy. That is the silver lining: a beautiful new member of the family to love and a little sister for Bella to play with. My last relationship and subsequent breakup left me with four wonderful vacations I will never forget and two beautiful friends I will keep for life. All golden treasures!

As you can see, when you look for the good in what has happened, don't just settle for the silver, but look instead for the gold. Gold is the color and symbol of everything sacred and pure. So go for the gold and grab the golden ring. It has always been more prized than silver anyway. If you have to put all of your eggs into one basket, make sure they are golden!

*"Good things come to people who wait, but better things come to those who go out and get them."*
— *Anonymous*

"Patience is a virtue", a quote we all know, is from the poem *Piers Plowman*. We need patience to wait for good things to come along. Sometimes they come into our lives all by themselves and fall right in our laps. However, much of the time we have to go out and actively search for these ourselves, and much of the time this requires a lot of hard work.

Many times we are inspired to do things in life. But these works would never get done if we didn't take the time and put in the effort to do them. Look at how long Pope Julius II had to wait for the Sistine Chapel ceiling to be finished? He waited four long years for Michelangelo to finish this backbreaking job. But he first had to find the right artist to paint the huge fresco. What would have happened if he hadn't invested either the time or effort to find the perfect person and "convince" Michelangelo to do it and keep him on task? We wouldn't have this awe-inspiring work to enjoy today. I could have wished for years and years for degrees in travel and teaching, but if I hadn't worked to pursue them, I would still be wishing and hoping.

What would you like to see happen? Again, you must first decide what it is and create a workable plan on how to reach your goal. That is the easy part. Next comes the hard work and persistence to see it through. This usually involves money, time, patience, and long hours. How badly do you want your dream? How hard are you willing to work in order to see it come to fruition? These are some of the important questions you must ask yourself. I know I'm making this sound much easier than it is, but the truth is that good things usually come as a result of hard work, pure and simple. The person who coined the saying on the previous page was trying to tell us to get up and get going to make these things happen in our lives.

So the next time you think something good will just fall into your lap unexpectedly, although it might, it's more likely you will have to work hard to get it. The result will be much better and sweeter in the end when you do!

*Leave your footprint on the world.*
*Let the world sing a song of you.*

*"If I know a song of Africa, of the giraffe and the African new moon lying on her back, of the plows in the fields and the sweaty faces of the coffee pickers, does Africa know a song of me? Will the air over the plain quiver with a color that I have had on, or the children invent a game in which my name is, or the full moon throw a shadow over the gravel of the drive that was like me, or will the eagles of the Ngong Hills look out for me?"*
– Karen Blixen (Isak Dinesen) (1937)

I remember the first time I saw the movie *Out of Africa*. I was amazed by the beauty of the land and the incredible story of Karen Blixen. Her life and struggles struck a chord with me, and I felt a kinship to her. But there was one part in the movie that stood out, and that was this elegant quote. Years later, when I read her book, I noticed this quote had been written word for word into the movie's script. "If I know a song of Africa . . ."

Does the world have a song of you? How will you leave your mark on the world? Most will leave their legacy with their children. But what about those like myself who have not been so blessed? Look at Michelangelo (Buonarroti) and Leonardo da Vinci who had no children but left behind unimaginable artwork for us to enjoy. There are poets like Emily Dickinson and Robert Louis Stevenson who painted pictures with words, along with writers like Isaac Bashevis Singer. There are the superhumans who have seemingly done the impossible, such as climbed Mount Everest, competed in the Olympics, walked in space or on the moon. Some people have become great teachers, humanitarians, foster parents, big brothers or sisters, worked in government, and have even become presidents.

I ask again: Does the world have a song of you, and what are you planning to leave as your legacy? Can I hear your song in the trees or do others sing a song of you? How are you going to use this beautiful gift of life you have been given? What is your color, can you tell me?

*"What counts is not necessarily the size of the dog in the fight—it's the size of the fight in the dog."*
*– Dwight D. Eisenhower*

My sister is a peanut, having been dubbed Miss Short by her senior high school class: she is all of 4'10 ½". My mother was pretty tiny as well at 5'2". (But then, I am no giant at 5'3" either.) But when my mom walked into a room, people took notice. It had nothing to do with her size; it was all about her confidence and presence. Someone once told me my mother was like a colorfully dressed Jackie O. She was elegant, beautiful, and intelligent, and when she meant business, well, you had better get out of her way. My sister is a bit more relaxed but still has that shiny countenance. She breezes into a room and you can just feel her presence. They are and were great women, both living their beliefs and sharing their love with others.

My sister told me many years ago of her chance meeting with Mary Lou Retton, who most of you will remember as a gold medal gymnast from the 1980s. Retton was a keynote speaker at the convention that my sister and her husband were attending. She is also a tiny person, measuring 4'9½", but every inch packed full of strength and energy. I always think of that tiny gymnast as a powerhouse of tenacity and toughness. Much of the time, those of us who are small develop personalities or presences that overcome any shortcomings. Some have done this as Ms. Retton did, some as my sister does, some as my mom, and some like Dustin Hoffman, 5'6", Al Pacino, 5'7", and Salma Hayek, 5'2", all television and film stars who are much bigger than life, and all amazing people at any size.

My sister's new dog is all of five pounds dripping wet. Lola still looks like a puppy even at one-and-one-half years. She is so small she can still hide under the couch. However, when some other, bigger dog steps into her territory, which usually includes food or myself, she acts like a dog ten times her size! She doesn't back down and has a mean growl, enough to make most dogs retreat.

My fight doesn't come with looks or toughness, but with perseverance. My fight isn't big because of my size, but because of stubbornness: the length of time I'm willing to fight on and how I set my jaw to hang on.

So when you see one of us "little people," remember the quote by Eisenhower and don't misjudge us. We have much more practice at fighting to stand up for ourselves and walking tall.

*The old expression, "the squeaky wheel gets the grease," is true, so squeak away!*

We all have to squeak when we have needs or when the going gets too tough, instead of keeping it inside. Squeaking lets others know we need support, someone needs to listen to who we are, what we are doing, or someone needs to help us fix something in our lives.

I have been tried to the limits of my patience during the past few weeks, but the final nail in the coffin came when I got a text from my class advisor last week. I had been working on an online class for the past year and now with only two weeks before the deadline, I found out I had five *more* parts to finish. These were not in the book, but online, so I had missed them totally. I panicked, calling a family member nearly in tears. I thought with so little time left, I couldn't do much about it anyway. Not so fast . . . I hadn't counted on the magic of my sister-in-law and her amazing sense of business and accomplishing the seemingly impossible. She helped me to draft a letter, which I had in front of me when I made the call to the school the next Monday morning. I must have made eleven or twelve calls, most leaving the same voice message every ½ hour. By the end of the morning, I had everything worked out; I had the extra computer time, the extra time to finish my course, and my sanity…I *was* the squeaky wheel.

Many times we just let things happen to us because we think it is just the way things are or maybe that's what we deserve and we don't have a say in the matter. But this summer I have had many lessons on how to squeak and how to stand up for myself. By nature, I avoid confrontation like the plague and hate anything to do with fighting, arguing, or debating. I have always been so afraid to hurt others or stir the pot. But in so doing, I have allowed people to walk all over me most of my life. (I have the tread marks on my back to prove it!) Not any more, as I am learning from the very best.

So, the next time you need a little help or just need someone to listen, throw out the grease and squeak until you are heard.

*"Work smarter, not harder."*
*– Allan F. Mogensen*

*A*t one point in my life I was a high school and middle school teacher, the VP of the Northeast Wisconsin Art Education Association, I entered my students into three yearly competitions, exhibited approximately 300 pieces of student artwork in a yearly exhibition, completed a yearbook annually for our school, met one of my students in Washington D.C. to support her while she received a national award at our nation's capital, was teaching adult art classes one night a week, completed and entered my own work into art shows, and all of this time trying to carry on a long distance relationship, and oh, yes, I was taking classes to recertify my teaching license. My significant other and I even took a trip to the Dominican Republic, and I hosted a friend from Australia who visited me for two weeks.

Looking back, I wasn't working smarter or less, only more and more each year. It was like I was on a non-stop adrenalin rush, collapsing into bed before I could even turn off the light sometimes and crying while driving between events and in the shower because I was so miserable and tired. There are so many things I could have done to lighten my load . . . I could have said no to the vice presidency when it was offered to me. Most of my students were in high school and could have helped me more with matting and labeling artwork for their annual art show. I didn't have to enter my students or myself into any art competitions for that matter. And my students could have been more responsible with cleaning up the art room and helping me with the yearbook. I could have said no to one of the trips when my girlfriend decided to visit, or even said no to the meeting we had for the WAEA in the north of nowhere in Wisconsin.

It's all about delegation: making others responsible for their own lives and knowing when to say no. No wonder I got so burned out and finally couldn't function any longer. These skills were already discussed but are big parts of "working smarter, not harder." Another way to do this is to get organized. This saves a lot of time. Don't make extra work for yourself by putting off work or avoiding it. Things have a way of piling up when you aren't looking. If you can double-book activities, do so. For example, if you have to go out to pick up something at a store, try to do something else while you are out. Don't spread it out, unless you are physically unable. There may be more ways for you to lighten your load, such as having your family pitch in or trade a skill you have for something you don't care to do; trade shoveling for cleaning, or gardening for plumbing. This will make it more pleasurable for you at least.

However you do it, make your load easier so that you can begin to enjoy life a bit more. You will ask yourself why you didn't start sooner. I know I did!

*"Youth is not a time of life; it is a state of mind. People grow old only by deserting their ideals and by outgrowing the consciousness of youth. Years wrinkle the skin, but to give up enthusiasm wrinkles the soul...You are as old as your doubt, your fear, your despair. The way to keep young is to keep your faith young. Keep your self-confidence young. Keep your hope young."*

*– Dr. L.F. Phelan (Vincent Egoro)*

I have heard the expression "You are only as young as you feel" for most of my life but haven't really internalized it until recently. Last year I was feeling as old as an eighty-year-old retiree and as drained as a bottle of Gatorade after a football game. I was filled with doubt, fear, and despair. I always said I was glad that I didn't look my age, but inside I felt used up and thrown out. I had lost my zest and enthusiasm for life along with my hope and belief things would work out. I had almost given up.

Thankfully, I have caught my second wind. I am healing inside and out. Physical problems that once kept me in bed are now more manageable. I no longer feel like I am too old, and the wrinkles in my soul are slowly being ironed out by proper care, love, and support. Unfortunately, we live in a society where age is not always respected, and even though it's against the law to discriminate, prejudice is rampant. Those of you who don't think it will happen to you, well, think again. We get tossed out by bosses, mates, and when we do try to find new jobs, we are either too experienced or too expensive. It all takes a toll on our mental and emotional selves.

Some of the things you can do to stay young at heart is to associate with the youth of the world, such as to socialize with those you know at work or on Facebook. Another way to remain young is to keep up with the latest technology, television shows, movies, and music. Try to get out to get more fresh air, drive with your sunroof open, travel, and go to more outings to socialize. Always look at the bright side of life, be spontaneous, and never believe you are too old to take on new challenges. Yet another is to do something extra just for yourself, such as having a glass of wine, taking up something new, or wearing bright clothing.

We must all find new places to be productive, appreciated, and loved when we find we are no longer appreciated where we are. I have found a new city, am working on my health, and, once that is established, hope to travel again. I have new dreams and goals, and I haven't felt this inspired since I was nineteen and in college for the first time. Both my hope and my faith have been restored, and I am out to conquer the world. (Well, at least my little corner.) I have no idea if it will be through travel or my books, but it really doesn't matter, as I feel good about myself. My self-confidence is growing, and I am working on a sign for my door that says doubt, fear, and despair: not welcome!

Make certain that you keep your heart young and your faith in yourself strong so you retain your zest for life. You, as well as those around you, will be glad you did!

"Self-confidence is the most attractive quality a person can have. How can anyone see how awesome you are if you cannot see it for yourself?"
– Unknown

When I was young, I couldn't help but wonder what the popular girls had that I didn't. I looked at them and tried to analyze their appearance, the way they treated others, and their skills. However, in many cases they were similar to me. How then, did they earn their popularity? I was clueless! But I realized as I grew older that it was often because they had loads of self-confidence (or appeared to) and I had very little.

I have wondered my entire life how one develops self-confidence? Are you born with it? Do you have to consciously work at it? Does it come with life experiences? Do our parents help to instill it? What I now know is that it is all of the above. Everyone is born with a certain personality. We are the product of genetics, our experiences, and how our parents bring us up. When we get out into the world and are lacking self-confidence because of any one of these things, it is up to us to turn things around. This requires a lot of hard work and stepping out of our comfort zones.

Recently I reconnected with a group of girls I had known in high school. They were some of the lucky few who were in the spotlight during my teenage years, "the golden girls," going out with the cool guys and to school dances. Much to my surprise, many had just as many fears as I did about themselves but had developed an outer appearance of self-confidence. Others already knew what value they had in this world and had already developed this quality.

If you are shy like I was, try to work on the areas in which you are having problems. If you are trying to overcome life experiences from your childhood, have a friend help you or go see a good counselor and work through these problems together. If you had parents who made mistakes in raising you, by all means see someone to resolve those issues. It doesn't mean you love your parents any less, it just means you love yourself and your life more.

Work to fill yourself with self-confidence and appreciate the person you were created to be. Be yourself and let others see your true nature and how awesome you are!

*Take some time to smell the peonies.*

Most quotes tell you to stop and smell the roses, but few people listen. So I am telling you to slow down and smell the peonies, because they bloom for such a short time. And such is life. You are here for an instant, a veritable blink of an eye, and then you are gone. Peonies have beautiful, full, delicate flowers when in full bloom, and their smell is intoxicating. However, they don't last very long and their many petals brown quickly and fall from the flower heads as they age. They aren't at all like roses, which bloom all summer long. Once peonies are gone, they are gone for the year. So if you are too busy for those few days they are in bloom, you will miss their fragrant beauty until next year.

Living is all about stopping along the way to enjoy life's little moments. We all get so caught up in trying to get too many things done we forget it's all about the journey and adventure along the way. We work ourselves to death to save for our kid's college educations, our houses, retirement, and we are gone before we have a chance to really relax, enjoy the grandkids, and see the world. What about life's journey?

This year, autumn came swiftly, in a matter of a few days, and the trees were painted with color. I decided it was time for me to enjoy every season of life and not just put up with the cold that is our Wisconsin winters. I went out for several outings and took in the beauty. It was as though I had never seen the fall colors before, as they left me breathless. Door County's colors were even more so. For those who are not from the Midwest United States, Door County is the thumb of Wisconsin and is known for its arts community, beautiful harbors, and fall colors. I am beginning to be appreciative of the little things given me in life.

Try to savor each moment, however small or insignificant. If I had just one thing to tell myself back when I was just beginning this adult journey, it would be to not work so blooming hard! (Pardon the pun.) I would also tell myself to enjoy life's journey and try to make each step a pleasant adventure. Stop and smell each flower as it comes along, and don't be afraid to pick some to brighten your life as well!

*The grass is NOT always greener.*

Someone once said the grass may be greener on the other side of the fence, but it is only because of all the manure that has been spread so thick on it! Many people aren't satisfied with their lives and are constantly looking over the proverbial fence at their neighbors' yards. Everything looks so much better from that point of view: relationships, houses, children, possessions, pets, anything you can imagine. But we don't see what goes on behind that façade, what others have to do or go through to make it look so appealing.

Please don't try to tend someone else's grass, as chances are you won't like what you find. We are all given our share of blessings and problems, some more than others, that's true. It just has to do with your perspective on events and how you see things. I don't live in a terribly fancy apartment, but compared to my old house I just moved from, it is bigger, cleaner, newer, and closer to everything; to me it's like a resort. My perspective is different than if someone moved here from a million-dollar house. My life would appear different to someone from a third world country as well. But consider this: some of the happiest people in the world live in Africa in the middle of nowhere, according to studies. And people who have a lot of money aren't necessarily the happiest.

I had the opportunity to spend some time with someone this past year that I thought had it all; she has a husband, children and a nice home. I was extremely surprised to find the grass was just as green on my side, maybe even greener! We have no idea what is going on behind closed doors or behind the smiles that people put on when they go out. Nor can we guess which are the little white lies people tell to keep others from finding out what is really going on in their lives. When I was young, I read a story called "The Necklace" by Guy de Maupassant, a short story that has always stayed with me. It's about a woman who was envious of another's lifestyle. She borrows another person's necklace to fit in with the rich, loses it, and spends the rest of her life paying for her envy and what she believes other people have.

Looking at our neighbors and what they have only serves to make us envious and unhappy. It is trying to be something we are not. Again, count your blessings, work for what is right for *you,* and remember to tend to your own lawn!

*"Being single is not the worst thing in the world, but don't let it stop you from living your life."*
*– Mom*

As I mentioned earlier in this book, my mother gave me this bit of advice in my thirties when I was feeling down because I hadn't found someone to share my life with. I remember exactly where I was and what I was doing when she told me this, so it was something that has really stuck with me. But when you really think of it, it's so true. It's not the worst thing . . . there are thousands of other things that could happen that could be so much worse. I don't have to go into detail and give examples; there are plenty around the world that come to mind. But it's the last portion of these words of advice that made such a difference in *my* life. I have never let it get in the way of me living my life. The only part of life I haven't experienced, that other people may have, is to experience childbirth and raise my own children. However, I knew at an early age how very hard it was to raise these little beings, and I wasn't going to do it by myself.

One evening at one of our ladies' nights out last summer, we happened to be talking about being single versus being married. One of my married friends said to me, "So many married women would be jealous of you!" That started me thinking of the many lifestyle differences I am blessed with that married people don't have. I have been able to grab more brass rings (excuse me, golden rings) than most people have and seen more of the world than any two people. I can come and go as I like and can spend my money as I please. And if I get too hungry for love, I just have to visit with my sister's little Havanese dog Lola and I get all of the love I can possibly handle.

For those of you who are "wishin' and hopin'" for that right man or woman to come into your life, or child to be born . . . Think of how much you would have to sacrifice to have a good relationship or child. Perhaps you are supposed to adopt a child that is in need or become a foster parent. Maybe you would be miserable in a relationship and need to be open to different experiences like travel or advancing your education. Perhaps you have a dream that is hiding in the back of your brain. Who knows why, but I do know while looking for that brass ring in all the wrong places, you may just miss the gold ring waiting for you along life's path.

# Part Six

Daily Living Skills
to Make Life Easier

*De-clutter your life.
It will give you room
to move and grow.
Throw out anything that
doesn't bring you joy,
isn't beautiful,
or can't be used.*

I have just spent nearly six months throwing out or giving away half of the items I have ever owned. Moving makes you do that, especially when downsizing from a house to an apartment. And I still have more to go. It has made me take stock of the rest of my life: my family heirlooms, memorabilia, travel treasures, social media friends, memories, and my life in general. I have literally cleaned house, both physically and mentally. I discovered how much junk I had collected over the past forty years, and even though one of my friends told me to be ruthless in throwing things out, I moved over fifty boxes to my new apartment.

As I began to put items into their new places, I discovered there was not nearly room for it all. So I began to go through everything again after the move, pitching some, giving most away, having a rummage sale for others, and sharing family heirlooms with the next generation. It's amazing how clean and refreshing a new de-cluttered apartment can feel!

Collections are just *things*. Everyone has items they treasure. These are things we will never let go of: pictures of family, certain special gifts, mementos from trips, items from your parents, grandparents, or great-grandparents. We all have our share. I'm not talking about these items, as these are what we store in our cedar chests and pass down to the next generation. What I am talking about are the items like clothing, knick-knacks, old Christmas cards and letters from years ago, gifts that we no longer use, and the like. These items make it hard for us to move from place to place and cause a sensory overload while we are living in an apartment or house. But many of us still go to rummage sales and Goodwill stores and shop for the latest trends.

The emotional baggage we hang on to is much heavier. It keeps us from living our lives fully so we can be happy and grow. We hold onto these items as if they were treasured memories from the past, although they are all but. So why not get rid of them like cleaning house? Pitch all of the resentment of an ex-spouse, ex-boss, or even family members. Throw them out like you do on spring cleaning day. Throwing them out means that they are *gone*. You wouldn't go digging through the dump for items tossed, would you? So please don't keep digging these items up and rehashing old trash.

My life is now free from most junk, physical and emotional, and I can't remember feeling so free and unburdened. Tomorrow is brimming with new adventure and everything good awaits me. Henry David Thoreau said it very well when he wrote the following: "Our life is frittered away by detail . . . simplify, simplify."

*Make a daily list of things to do. It will free your mind, and at the end of a long day it will do your heart good to see how much you have accomplished.*

Do you all feel like I do when I first get up in the morning? My mind is clear and focused, and I am ready to take on my work. But as I get going, things begin to crowd my mind: things I need to do, people I need to see, bills that need to be paid, this person to call, that errand to run, and medication to pick up. It never seems to end.

As I go through a normal day, I make a list of things to do. Actually, I have a ready-made list of things I must do every day, but then add on the items that come up. My everyday list includes things like taking medication, stretching or exercise, writing or working on my travel blog, eating a healthy breakfast, lunch, and dinner etc. The additional items include things like paying bills, attending family get-togethers, visiting relatives and friends.

In periods of time that are unusual, such as studying to complete a course, or for travel, I make a list every night, and what I don't get done that day, I put at the top of tomorrow's list of things to do. That way everything gets done and my mind doesn't keep going at night. I actually learned this skill from my sister, as she has been making lists ever since I can remember.

I also have a pocket calendar that goes everywhere with me. I have had it for about a year, and it is literally falling apart. I put all of my doctor appointments in it, my substitute teaching days and which schools they are at, as well as my outings with friends and family. If I had to remember all of this with all of the other things I am doing, I would go crazy. There are just too many things to remember, so I write everything down, simple as that. If I get a call, like I did today for a future sub job, I can quickly look to see if my schedule is clear and write it down right away. When I go out with my girlfriends once a month, I can write the date and the place down and forget about it until it appears within sight in my datebook.

I know so many people who try to keep all of this in their heads.

I just have one question: Why? Why, when it is so much easier to keep track of dates, plans, trips, meetings, and appointments in a place you can refer back to. My sister has a wall calendar and uses colored marker to differentiate between events for each family member and herself. She has done it this way for years. I know many men and women who are now using their smart phones to keep track of their meetings and events. I haven't used that yet, as I like to have my calendar in front of me. Many of the new smart phones have apps that will even warn you when an event or meeting is coming up.

However you do it is entirely up to you. But do yourself a favor and free up your mind for other, more important pursuits, such as relaxing, enjoying life, and falling to sleep before 1:00 a.m.!

*Don't try to micromanage your life.
When you try to manage everything, you
relinquish the joy of surprise.*

"It's ok to be surprised by life, that's the fun!" This is a quote from possibly my all-time favorite television show, *Castle*. I love the way the writers have created the relationship between the father Richard and his daughter Alexis. They are clever and witty, playful, and funny, and above all kind and loving. But what Alexis said is so very true. We do give up a lot when we try to manage everything and know exactly what is going to happen, and yet some of us never learn.

When I was a young girl, I was just like every other child, persistent and, sometimes, just a pest. One year I saw an advertisement for a stamp book on TV, which I decided I wanted for Christmas. It was a book about the animals around the world and information about them. I must have really pestered my mother about getting it for me, because one day she sat me down on the stairs and pulled out what was meant to be my Christmas present from a drawer and handed it to me saying, "Here you go!"

I can still remember the feeling of hurt and disappointment at not being able to be surprised at Christmas. I tried to convince her to put it back in the drawer and promised I'd forget about it, but I had spoiled the surprise. That was the day I learned the lesson about not trying to control everything and not knowing everything that was going to happen. That was the day I found out just how much it cost to relinquish the joy of surprise. I have never made that same mistake again. My mother truly knew how to teach a lesson and make it stick.

When I went to Australia the first time to student teach, I was very surprised because I didn't have the time or resources to research it ahead of time. I happened to land just a few days before their Bicentennial and was able to participate in all of the festivities. I hadn't researched about the school I was teaching at, but it was to become my best teaching experience to date. And the lifelong friends I made there are more like my family. Best surprise ever!

Too many people micromanage their lives and their workplaces, making everyone unhappy. When was the last time you were surprised by life? Do you need to know everything that is going to happen to you? Then tell me, how much you are willing to give up to control everything!

# Part Seven

## Learning & Growing

*Although it's important to have a daily plan of attack, it is also important to have future goals and backup plans.*

They really messed up when they put together business education and family and consumer economics back when I was in high school. All I can remember learning was how to write a check, do my taxes, and the three S's: *sewing, the science of food preparation,* and *sex.* We should have been taught many more practical things along with these that would have helped prepare us for life, such as how to plan for the future, about our financial health from college on, and how to prepare a will and funeral.

When I retired, I didn't have a plan to follow. We had never been taught how to plan ahead as children in our family, and the only thing talked about as adults in education was retirement at age sixty-two and saving in a tax-deferred investment account. So when retirement from education hit me in the face suddenly in my later fifties, I had some savings to fall back on financially, but certainly no plans for what to do in my immediate or future life. My retirement fund helped, but it was not enough to live on by far, even in my little house. It has taken me nearly five years to regain my footing. If only I could have had an alternative plan. I could have saved myself so much stress and heartache. But would've, should've, could've . . .

I cannot stress how important it is to have future goals and backup plans in place for all seasons of your life, as you never know what is right around the corner. It's part of the Boy Scout motto: Be prepared! It allows one to feel secure and less stressed if something should happen.

Now I have plans for everything: the near future, a one-year plan, a five-year plan, a ten-year plan, a bucket list, and funeral plans. I have a daily list of things to do and blanks on it for things that come up and need to be done. The truth is we are never given more than this moment, but the past few years have taught me we must have alternative routes in life in case we find a detour in our road. So for all of you back road travelers, this is for you.

*It's okay to make mistakes.
They are part of learning and growing.
Learn from them, forgive yourself,
and then move on.*

We all make mistakes. We are only human and aren't meant to be perfect. However, many of us treat ourselves as if we expect ourselves to be. Then, when we do make blunders, we use these memories to punish ourselves over and over again. Some of these miscalculations may be small, like forgetting someone's name that we have known for years, and some may be much more serious, perhaps landing us in jail. But whatever our transgressions, we are bound to make mistakes and learn throughout our lives.

I remember when I was in Germany for my semester abroad, I went out with some friends to celebrate the end of the term. I must have put my passport in my regular pants pocket instead of the one with Velcro on it that I had for safekeeping. The next morning when I found that it was gone, I began to panic. I blamed myself for being so thoughtless and believed I had simply lost it. Months later, my passport was mailed back to me in the U.S. from an area that I had never been in, so I most probably had been the victim of a pickpocket. Someone must have found it and sent it back to me. Learning this helped lessen the self-recrimination, but not by much.

Forgiving the child inside of ourselves is one of the hardest things that we must do in life. We carry some of the pain around, and when it surfaces, we use ourselves as punching bags again and again. The cycle seems never ending. But remember that we should be able to forgive ourselves just as we forgive others. That does *not* give us permission to make mistakes on purpose! But when we do make one and ask for forgiveness, we need to learn how to let go and get on with life.

So when you make mistakes or remember those that have happened in the past, please do not dwell on them. Use them as learning tools, not as self-abusing memories. Work on forgiving yourself and then forget them. When they pop up again, as they are certain to do, tell them that they are not welcome in your mind and memory. Love yourself enough to let go of the past. You will be surprised at how free you will feel.

*We are all evolving,
learning, and growing,
becoming the people we were
meant to become.*

We never stop learning, evolving, growing, and changing. When we do, we cease to exist. When I was young, I was a shy, emotional, painfully quiet girl. I was a skinny, gangly tomboy who used to hide in my mother's skirts and cried whenever anyone so much as looked at me cross-eyed. I spent my summers making sand forts and climbing trees.

I am still pretty quiet, but man, am I a strong woman. It takes a lot to scare me or make me cry. I'm no longer skinny and can no longer climb trees, but that is just the outer layer, my shell. What really defines me is what lies deep down inside. Forty years ago I couldn't imagine doing anything else except for art. That evolved into teaching art, and that has evolved into photography, travel, and writing. Who would have guessed?! It's all about our growth inside that matters. I am no longer afraid of the bullies of the world and being without someone to protect me.

One day in the future I will have evolved into someone else I have yet to meet. I will have reached most of the goals I have set for myself and will be off on another adventure on a different path. As I write this, I am reminded of a song from back in the seventies by the Australian vocalist Helen Reddy, "I Am Woman":

> ...Oh yes, I am wise
> But its wisdom born of pain
> Yes, I've paid the price
> But look how much I gained
> If I have to, I can do anything
> I am strong
> (Strong)
> I am invincible
> (Invincible)
> I am woman

And so it is. We are strong, and whether we are men or women, we will survive and evolve. Just give us the time to grow.

*Given the right situation, care, and soil, you will bloom!*

With all due respect to the author of the expression "Bloom where you are planted," Saint Francis de Sales, probably never was planted in the Sahara or had to try to grow on Mount Everest. Sydney, Australia, is the most beautiful city in the world by my standards, but to a person who loves and flourishes in the wild outdoors like Canada or out West, it would constitute a desert. For me, living in a town of less than 100,000 without an arts community, places to go, or things to do, is just as bad.

The fact of the matter is many of us find ourselves in situations like this every day. We find ourselves in the wrong relationship, the wrong city, a job that doesn't fit, or a wrong housing situation, and we are miserable. But uproot us and replant us in the right relationship, the right city where loved ones are near, in the right job where people appreciate us, or in the right living conditions and we will glow! The right situation provides us with the nourishment, understanding, and appreciation we all need in a job or relationship.

It's important to find a comfortable place to live and grow. If we are not happy where we are, it may become necessary to find some place that will make us happy. As I said before, I moved back to the city where I grew up, a city of over 100,000 from a town of just over 3,000. Many of the people who grow up in small towns love the close-knit community where everyone knows everyone else. However, I have longed for everything a big city has to offer all of my life.

Again, if we are put in a job in which we need to have finesse and we are all thumbs, we will not be happy. Common sense tells us if we are an intellectual and in a relationship with someone who does not value education or growth, we will become miserable and soon leave. But find someone who shares our values and goals, and we will shine. If we fill our lives with people who support us in our work, then we will grow beyond what anyone could have ever guessed. Again, all of this means that you must get to know yourself, what you like, and what you want out of your life. If you need something, go out and find it so you can bloom. Don't settle for anything less. Keep looking until you find that job, that relationship, that town, or that sunlight. From someone who is two thirds of the way through the planting season of life, its best to find them first than try to transplant yourself later.

So if you must bloom where you are planted, be it your first attempt or your tenth, choose a place that has nutritional soil, a job that will provide you with sun for learning, and people around you to shower you with love, and you will grow to reach your full potential and bloom!

*Retirement is not the end of life, just a closed door and a window opened to another adventure.*

At the end of 2012, I found myself in an unplanned retirement. I literally had to decide overnight what to do after eighteen years of working at my job. So without anything but a Tax Deferred Retirement Account that I had been smart enough to put aside and my Employee Trust Fund from our school, I was out of work. I hit the road job hunting, running full tilt. But after countless applications and many interviews, I realized that was not going to happen, at least not in my area. One year of substitute teaching went by, then another as I fell further and further into a serious depression.

What I didn't realize was that I was making a common mistake by focusing on only my former career. I was just looking in one direction, and that was in the past. I was terribly hurt when my position was cut in half and I had to leave something I had put so much of my life and effort into. Not only that, but I was exhausted and burned out by years of pushing myself so hard. And, unfortunately, having tunnel vision, I couldn't see myself doing anything else.

One morning when I was crying out for someone to tell me what I should do with the rest of my life, a light went off in my head. *Travel career.* What, a travel career? But I knew in an instant this was what I was meant to focus my attention on. I had studied German in high school, had some French in grade school, and was in the process of studying Italian for an upcoming trip. My minor in college had been art history, during which I studied the major art attractions all around the world. Not only that, I had made it a priority to travel as much as I could during life. It fit perfectly.

Then, that night, a friend texted me on Facebook out of the blue suggesting that I should be a travel agent, that I would be perfect for it. What a wonderful confirmation! Whether or not I will ever get a job in travel is yet to be seen, but it gave me direction during a very dark time in my life and opened the window to a beautiful segue into the future.

Before you find yourself in my situation, it's wise to begin planning your retirement even if it is ten years until you plan to leave the workforce. Choose another way to make a living, start taking courses for a new future, and make certain it is secure. Remember, I hadn't planned to retire in the near future either. If retirement is already upon you, and it's not what you had envisioned, try not to be discouraged. Look for the open window and begin to put the pieces of your life back together. Seek out other options or careers or even consider relocating. Don't limit yourself, as you never know what may be just down the road.

Now that the chapter on education is finished in my life and I am not so focused on the past, I am seeing all sorts of windows opening up for me. My house is a veritable greenhouse of open windows, and I am taking my time going through each until I find the right one for me.

*Our journeys, just like the skills we learn in life, begin with small steps.*

I always tell my students when learning to draw, they must take bite-sized bits. I compare drawing to learning the game of basketball; first you must learn to hold the ball, then to dribble it, then to dribble and run, then dribble, run, and pass, and so on. You must add a little bit to what you already know, then build and expand on that.

Big journeys are just like this as they begin with small actions. First you must decide what to do or where to go and then set yourself in motion, deciding what you need to do to get it done. There is an old saying that you can't steer a parked car. So too, unless you put your foot forward, you are not going to get anywhere. Lao Tzu, the famous philosopher, said it this way, "The journey of a thousand miles begins with one step."

But where to begin, therein lies the problem. Five years ago I was stuck in life, not knowing what to do. I had no purpose and could not see any future for myself. I even went to the local technical college and had a skill survey done. However, everything pointed to education, and after a quarter of a century in that field, that was in the past. When I recognized I needed to see a counselor to help me move on, that was my first step. My life had been put on hold for that very reason. Gratefully I was able to work through a lot of the problems I had been carrying with me from childhood.

During this time, I decided to pursue another dream. This gave me purpose for the time that I was healing emotionally. Although I have learned a great deal and I have regained much of my self-confidence, I am now working on my health. My sister calls these "baby steps." And so they are. Each of these areas needed attending to before going on to the next part of my life: small steps on my journey.

Figure out where you are and where you want to go. Then figure out a way to get there. You may do this by talking with friends, family, a counselor, completing an interest inventory, or any number of other ways. But however you do it, make certain that you take one step at a time.

*Out of the most painful times in life comes the most growth.*

> "All progress takes place outside the comfort zone."
> – Michael John Bobek

One of the things I was asked to do during my time in counseling was to make a calendar of all the significant events in my life. Positive events were to be put on one side of a time line and negative on the other. Once this was done, I was able to see what was going on in my life and what changes occurred during these times. The biggest thing this did for me was to make me realize the pain I had during these times was not just imagined but was very real. I also realized that out of this time came the most growth in my life. I was challenged to mature, deal with situations in creative ways, and become responsible for my own life, as well as others. I learned skills such as how to be sensitive to those around me, how to deal with illness, death, loss, and disappointment—things we all must learn to live an effective life.

Those times helped me to become a strong woman, one who is resourceful and creative in facing the challenges of life. I have learned how not to give up when my strength seemed to be all but gone, how to help others when they are in trouble, and how to make the world a better place by my being here. Yes, I have stopped along the way to have my share of pity parties, but they didn't last long, as I realized they were getting me nowhere fast.

The first thing we all want to do when we encounter serious problems is to run away from them or avoid them altogether. This is a very natural thing to do. I have tried unsuccessfully to run away from certain situations in my life, but they always seemed to follow me like the bullies they were, until I found my strength, turned around, and confronted them. We all ask ourselves the same question: Why me? Why did this have to happen to me?

But in truth, the pain and anxiety we feel is a type of growing pain. We are being stretched into a bigger and better version of ourselves. I used to think it was just plain stupid when someone would tell me that. However, it is so true. If we embrace our problems, learn from the lessons they were meant to teach, leave the pain behind, and then move on, the problems will be gone and they will leave us alone.

When I was in kindergarten, an older boy chased me home saying he had a knife. Whether or not it was true is not the question. He was bullying me. I had two choices, either shut up about it because I was scared, or face the person the next day. So I told adults as I had been instructed and faced him in the hallway the next morning. He never bothered me again.

We speak about teachable moments in education. But in life everything is a teachable moment. *Every single moment* we are here is a moment of learning. Some of the lessons are pleasant and some are very difficult. During the easy lessons, we tend to put our feet up and coast. But when times get hard, we dig in our heels and put our minds and bodies into action. It's then we grow and get things done. Look at your life and what you have learned during the tough times. Do you see any correlation?

So when times get hard and you begin to ask, "Why me?", look instead at what can be learned, then go out with a friend, have some chocolate ice cream, and celebrate the lesson learned.

*Traveling makes us realize how little we know and how small our world truly is. Traveling is the classroom for learning about different cultures, languages, traditions, and adventure. Never shortchange your education. See the world!*

Did you know that the world's smallest nation is Vatican City? Did you know that a sloppy joe in Australian slang is a sweatshirt, and the word *amici* is "friends" in Italian? Everyone's world is small when they are young. I remember meeting a young man in my first year of college from Chicago and thinking the city was so far away. As I grew older, I began to add cities, states, and then countries to the places I visited.

No amount of introduction to culture and language can prepare you for your first trip abroad. It is like going to a different planet. Even the countries that have the same languages can have so many different colloquialisms, foods, and customs you may just as well have traveled to Mars. We, as Americans, often have an arrogant reputation overseas. And from what I have seen, it is well deserved. We tend to think everyone speaks English around the world and the cuisine in other countries is like that in America. When I was in Germany as a junior in college, there were people in our group who would seek out McDonald's and miss the wonderful cuisine of the German culture. I was so confused!

I thought if you wanted to eat what is in America and speak English, you should save your money and stay home. This, people, is half of the fun! I learned the Italian language to go to Italy because I thought I should, and I had a ball! While in Australia, I fell in love with the people and immersed myself in the culture, cuisine, and nationalism. I learned the words to their national anthem and became familiar with many colloquialisms, even memorizing "The Man from Snowy River" just because I thought it would be fun to recite to my niece and nephews. I began making baked lamb dinner and Pavlova dessert regularly, and still do. What I got out of my experience was a group of lifelong friends that are more like family, countless memories, and endless adventures.

So don't sell yourself short when you travel. Get out of your world and venture out a bit. Experience the culture, learn the language, taste the food, and go to art museums, church services, concerts, historical buildings, and cultural heritage centers. Experience the people and their country firsthand.

*Life is all about learning lessons and passing tests.*

Sorry kids, but if you think school is out when you graduate, you are in for a rude awakening. Living is *all* about learning in the *school of life*. Like I have said many times, the day you stop learning is the day you cease to exist. And who knows, we probably haven't even begun the real lessons on this planet!

So those of us who don't like to learn are in for a big surprise. Most of us have to learn how to parent, cook, bake, do dishes, learn a trade to earn money, change a tire, drive, travel, garden, take care of a household, balance a checkbook, do our taxes, and many more skills. Then we have to turn around and teach our own children how to do these things! Some of these experiences are enjoyable, such as learning to skate or snorkel, and some most of us hate to do, such as taxes or cleaning the toilet. But like it or not, these things must be done on a regular basis.

Book learning is really not what life is all about, although schooling gives us power and opens many doors for our future employment. It's the school of hard knocks and having common sense that make the biggest difference in life. Many people I know can't function in life but are extremely intelligent. Recently my life lessons have been in the area of health, trying to figure out how to deal with my illness and the complications that go along with it. I have been researching everything I can get my hands on to help myself and those I love who also suffer from fibromyalgia and similar conditions. Each day has been a test in both patience and endurance as I struggle against the fatigue and pain. But I am passing the tests and am raising my grade as I go.

Lessons in life are hard to accept at times and sometimes nearly impossible. What does one learn from watching a child or spouse die, as a few of my friends have had to suffer through this past year? What can one learn from seeing a parent die of cancer or slowly slip away due to Alzheimer's and what can be gained from being in constant pain?

I don't know the answer to these questions for other people. I can only answer for myself. For me, everything that I am and will be has come out of the lessons I have learned in life, both good and bad. I wouldn't be writing this book without all of these experiences, and that is enough for me. Each of us has to ask and answer this question for ourselves. If we need extra help to get us through to where we can see the lessons and move on, there are counselors. The point is, that no matter what the lessons and tests are in life, we can all find something to learn from a situation, even if it's just to teach us not to do something again.

We should all learn from lessons as part of the school of life if we are to grow. Fighting against life's lessons is like swimming upstream against the current: it doesn't get us anywhere. I encourage all to join me as I float along: learning, passing each test, and moving on.

# Part Eight

## Habits & Behaviors

*Never use the past as an excuse,
but rather use it as a strength to stand on.*

Our past makes us what we are today, and it is part of our lives. However, we should never use it as an excuse. I have heard people say things like, "I have had such a rough childhood, therefore I can't do this" or "I am bad because of what happened to me in my life." Yes, I understand we may have had a difficult time in life, but that doesn't give us any excuse to behave badly ourselves. We may have seen unspeakable horrors, but that doesn't give us any right to carry those on to the next generation. Look at the survivors of the Holocaust. They did not go out and torture or kill others, but worked their whole lives to forgive.

Try not to exploit your history as an excuse to behave badly or avoid opportunities in life. It's not okay to use your past as an excuse to avoid things because they frighten you or cause you anxiety. I would never jump out of an airplane, not because of my fear of heights, but just because it doesn't interest me in the least. However, I have stood on the bridge behind Neuschwanstein Castle, which is VERY high, and have climbed down the Untersberg Mountain, both are tests for those of us who are fear-of-heights-challenged. And although it took me some time to overcome the anxiety I developed as a child, it will never stop me from moving to other states in the USA or from traveling all over the world.

Look at your problems and fears as *challenges* or as puzzles needing to be solved. Life is always challenging us to see what we can do with our pasts. Learn from them and move on. I have an old friend who is afraid to drive across town. How limiting is that! I am terrified of the Marquette Interchange in Milwaukee because of the height, but I have driven across it to get where I wanted to go. So it is with life. We all have pasts that challenge us in various ways. They make us afraid of situations and try to put limits on our lives. It's up to us to break through those barriers to a life of wonderful memories and adventure, full of the freedoms we were meant to have. Use these problems as steppingstones to stand on rather than burdens that hang around your neck. if you use your problems to stand on rather than weigh you down, you are that much closer to your dreams!

Make your choice to work on your past so it doesn't become a burden, but the lesson intended. And never, ever let it be used as an excuse or stop you from reaching one of your dreams!

*Practice courage. It gets easier with time, just like any other discipline. Have the courage to follow your own hopes, dreams, and heart.*

> "All our dreams can come true
> if we have the courage to pursue them . . ."
> – Walt Disney

Although Disney was a huge success later in his adult life, his early twenties were not so lucrative. He opened his own studio in 1922 with the help of a number of friends and animators. However, because of the huge staff and salaries, the business went into debt and he was forced to declare bankruptcy. I can't imagine such a quote coming from a person who had failed in his first attempt at his dream. But because he didn't give up, he went on to share his vision with the world. Think of how different our planet would be if he had!

I am not so courageous. Like many of us, I have been shot down far too many times to *feel* confident about myself. But maybe that's the secret, going beyond the *feeling* of confidence. The previous quote by Walt Disney does not include his fears or apprehensions. Those were probably shared with only his family and closest friends. I am still pursuing my dreams, and although they have evolved along the way, I still struggle with some of the obstacles in my path. We all need practice in developing courage: working through challenges, allowing for growth and change, fighting through fear, but not giving up.

Courage is defined in the Oxford Dictionary as "The ability to do something that frightens one; bravery . . ." Following your dreams isn't always easy—sometimes it's downright scary. I will never forget my first trip to Australia. It is nine thousand miles away from my home and nearly a day of travel. I was alone, didn't know anyone in the country I was going to, and had committed myself to a semester of student teaching in the town of Gosford. I was thirty-two, and as I was sitting on the tarmac ready to take off for Los Angeles, the first leg of my journey, I began to tear up. The elderly gentleman sitting next to me quickly asked me what was wrong and if I was all right. He then proceeded to ask me where I was going and for how long. When I answered him, I believe I remember him agreeing it was a long way to be going alone. And so it was.

But it was one of the best decisions I have ever made. I loved it there and made many lifetime friends, some like family. Now I am departing on another dream, one of a travel writer and author. I love both and am as passionate about them as I am about photography and snorkeling. Once again, I am scared to death. I am taking a huge chance in so many ways: financially, with my time, and emotionally. But I am screwing up my courage and following my heart and my dreams. They will lead me down the right path to happiness and fulfillment. I am so certain this is the road I am supposed to be on that I will never quit, and maybe that's courage too, having such conviction in your dreams you would swim through molasses to get to where they are.

I went out for coffee with a friend the other day, and during our time together, she made a comment that evoked my immediate response. She couldn't believe someone as quiet and shy as me could travel all over the world by myself . . . Without hesitation, I replied, "Quietness is not courage." And so I found myself affirming I had the courage within to pursue my dreams. Who would have guessed! I encourage you to find your own courage within and take it out for a drive every day. Practice so that it can grow, and when it is needed, you will have the skill to overcome your trepidation and find your own dreams.

*Be honorable and live your life with integrity. Make certain to take the high road whenever possible.*

> "The greatness of a man is not in how much wealth he acquires, but in his integrity and his ability to affect those around him positively."
> – Bob Marley

Unfortunately in today's world, people who are honorable and live their lives with integrity can't always be found. I believe it is up to each individual to make that decision to choose those character traits on a daily basis. I have found that with a lot of people, when push comes to shove, they will cover their own backsides. But that isn't how it has to be. I also know many honorable people who live by the Golden Rule. We all have to make that choice, and what we choose makes us who we are.

My mother was a great role model and instilled in us how to live and showed us how to do so by *how she lived*. She would stand up for herself, but I never heard her swear or treat others with disrespect. She was always there for those around her to help out in times of illness, death, or for those who didn't have anything. She was always moving, but when she would sit down, she would use her time to make items for herself and others using her skills in crocheting or knitting. And she was always there with a batch of cookies when the neighborhood kids came to play. When she said she would do something for others, it would get done. She was a faithful wife and mother and was married to my dad for forty-five years. As for me, I couldn't even come close to living that type of life, as I have made my share of mistakes. However, I have tried to learn from these and continue to live the best life I know how.

We live in a country in which the bottom line is the almighty dollar, and many don't remember what integrity is. So how does one live a life of integrity anyway? It means to live above your problems and situations. How can we do this? We must all learn to make good choices and develop good habits, lift others up rather than bring them down, and keep our promises whenever possible. None of us is perfect, as I have said earlier, but when we can, and when a situation presents itself, we should all try to follow these rules. By taking the high road, we can feel good about the person we are, whoever we may be.

How do you want to live life? Do you want to have a life full of things you don't want to remember or have others remember, or do you want to be able to hold your head high and live a remarkable one? It is really your choice.

*Expect and demand respect.
It isn't in the U.S. Constitution
but should be!*

We all need respect to live our lives well and feel good about ourselves. Unfortunately, we don't always get it, whether we are men OR women. This is the one thing that will anger me quicker than anything else, *disrespect*. We live in a world where too many adults don't practice it, and children aren't always taught it when they are young. They, in turn, grow up to be disrespectful adults, and the cycle continues.

Businesses and organizations contain some of the worst offenders, in my experience. With my recent move, I used a national moving company. While moving, they broke furniture and some of my frames and lied about having brought everything up from my basement. When I reported the incidents, they refused to pick up the remaining boxes without being paid extra and refused to pay for their damages. Needless to say, I was very upset. I couldn't replace all of the damaged items, as it would have cost me several hundred dollars, but what really made me angry was how I was treated.

Another example was in my old school district when one of the management personnel treated me disrespectfully by yelling at me in front of class and fellow staff for something that wasn't my fault: the kid's behavior. I had a large class of notorious students and needed help one day. What I got instead was disrespect. Two of the kids in the class, bless their hearts, went down to the office following one incident and confronted my superior for how he treated me and for "being so disrespectful." Even they knew that this was wrong!

My mother always told us the story of when she was young and was working retail. The manager of a small local business was trying to bully her one day for something and told her that, "girls like her were a dime a dozen." She calmly reached into her pocket, pulled out a dime and gave it to him saying, "Here is your dime, now go find your dozen!" and walked out. Later that same manager called her, begging her to come back. She, of course, told him no. He had to hire three people to fill her shoes. Expect and demand respect.

We are all humans, whether young or old, handicapped or gifted, skinny or overweight, ill or well, dark or light, and we should be given the same amount of respect. All of us are part of the same human family, so please follow the Golden Rule and respect one another and demand that same respect from others!

*Know when to say when. The difference between giving up and knowing when to quit is in knowing when you have had enough!*

There comes a time in everyone's life when you know it's time to call it quits with someone or something. You say, enough is enough, I give, you send up the white flag of surrender, and move on. However, not everyone has the instinct at which time to do this. I am one of those "instinct-challenged" people. I hold on, even when someone is standing on my fingertips as I am hanging onto the edge of a cliff. I never know when to quit. Do I think I am superwoman? No, I have just been taught not to back down from a challenge, I am stubborn by nature, and am sometimes afraid to move on.

My challenges are sizable, but not as big as others endure. However, this summer I have been brought to my knees begging for my challenges to end. I have finally reached my breaking point and am calling uncle. What makes the difference in knowing when to go on and when not to? It is different for everyone, but for me, ardent prayers and asking for guidance usually helps. For some people, their body tells them when to quit if they have physical limits; others have their inner voice developed to a point where it tells them. But for most, it will be a combination of all these that will lead them to decide.

Is your body telling you that you have had enough? Do you get headaches, stomachaches, or backaches from muscle tension? Are you always running on low, without adequate time to eat and sleep? Then enough is enough. Persistence is important to get something done well, but if something is interfering with any part of your health, then it's time to rethink your situation and possibly make a change. One of the biggest lessons I have learned in the past four years is that deciding to step down from something or changing your course in life is not always a bad thing. It's using your head and instincts to protect yourself from something that may be hurting you.

Again, hindsight is twenty/twenty, and although everything has worked out for the best, I should have begun thinking of doing something different with my life long ago. I had looked for other jobs within the teaching profession, but never considered changing my career. I had enough long before I retired, but like most single women, I was afraid at fifty to step out of my comfort zone. I didn't realize that when you can't say "when," life may give you a push.

So be honest with yourself. Are you happy or stressed? Is your body trying to tell you something with all of its aches and pains? Can you see yourself trying something else? Don't wait for life to knock you over the head with an illness or an unexpected cut from your current job; listen to what your body and instincts are trying to tell you.

Remember, knowing when to say "when" isn't giving up, but making an informed choice based on the facts at hand. So if your body is telling you to do something different or you dread the Monday alarm clock, then it may be time to listen!

*When an opportunity presents itself, don't wait until you feel you are ready, because you may never be.*

Remember your first professional job when you felt like you were playing at your work or at being an adult? I remember having this conversation with my illustration partner at ShopKo back in the 1980s. We both felt we were playing at being illustrators. Neither of us felt ready for what we were doing, but we were doing it anyway. We had to jump right into our jobs, as the work wouldn't wait.

I finally outgrew the feeling of playing at my job in illustration and didn't even have time to consider it in teaching. Now I am relearning how to do this with writing. I do not feel ready but am doing it anyway. When are we ready then if *feeling* ready isn't an indication? Feeling ready is not a matter of being grown up, but when we have adequate confidence in ourselves. *Being ready* is when we have had the proper training in order to do a job. Ask yourself if you have had the training necessary to move ahead in your life. Some things you are never fully trained for, such as marriage, child rearing, and death. Most other challenges in life pale in comparison.

To begin a new path, it takes a great deal of determination, self-discipline, and a huge leap of faith. And that is it in a nutshell, *a leap of faith.* If you have taken everything else I have already mentioned into consideration, you will then need to step out of your comfort zone into the unknown and test your skills and your faith in yourself. A great many people, myself included, will move ahead without considering the greatest part of the equation, and that is one of soul-searching. Whether it's spending a day apart from your usual endeavors to get in touch with your inner being, saying a silent prayer, or looking to someone else to help you decide, this will help you to know whether you are on the right path if you don't know immediately. However, eventually it will come down to taking a leap of faith and moving ahead with those plans.

A student once asked me if I had any regrets in life. After some consideration, I told her that my regrets were few because I always grabbed for any opportunity that came my way. And even though I may have been afraid to embark upon some of these opportunities or adventures, I screwed up my courage and eventually took the leap of faith.

# Part Nine

## Just Great Advice

*You cannot change someone else's behavior, just your own. Don't take responsibility for other people's actions.*

Because I was the oldest girl in our family, I was always expected to watch out for my younger brothers and sister. However, this became a bad habit, which lasted far too long into my adult life. Then, after my mom passed away, it took on a renewed life when I felt I had to play mother and watch over my siblings until things got better. But it wasn't my job or my responsibility to look out for my brothers and sister. It was theirs.

Many of us take on such responsibility for husbands, wives, nephews, nieces, aunts, uncles, fathers, mothers, and so on. The truth is we cannot be mothers to these people any more than they can be our children. The same thing goes for non-family members: those who want to rob, steal, kill, lie, or any number of other things. They may cause you unending emotional pain, but you can't change what they do. Only they can. You can send students to the office if you work in the school system or leave the company of a rude person, but you can't control how they behave. That's something they must decide to do for themselves.

Although I haven't had children of my own, I have listened to enough of my friends and family to know what to do. When raising children, you can only raise them to the best of your ability: teach them how to be respectful and kind to others and treat others the way they want to be treated. When you do that, you are passing on the Golden Rule and teaching them how to get along as part of the new generation. Hopefully your lessons will become part of who they are and be carried on. But if they aren't, you should remember you have done the best you were able to, and they also have a free will to choose the person they will be. Please don't blame yourself in any way if something goes wrong. This is very hard to do and will take time to work on, but once it becomes a life habit, it will become second nature to you.

Set yourself free from this unnecessary and painful burden. Tell the people in your life you love them, but you won't mother or enable them. If you have done your job, they will eventually find their own way and you will be free to live your life.

*Find your passion in life.
It will keep you young and happy.*

> "Choose a job you love and you will never
> have to work a day in your life."
> – Anonymous.

When you enjoy what you are doing, it not only brings you joy doing it, but you do a better job and your day will fly by.

Passions change throughout life. During my twenties, I was passionate about ice skating and knew everyone who was in the spotlight in the sport. In my thirties and forties, it was photography and drawing. In my fifties, snorkeling, travel, beachcombing, writing, and photography. Now that I am in my sixties, my passions still include everything from the previous decade, but I have added linguistics, and I still write every day. Our passions in life change, especially if we are open to growth.

How do we find our passions? It is both easy and difficult. You must first get in touch with your inner self. Once you have done that, it is easy. What is the one thing you have loved your entire life and what makes you tick? But discovering this is easier said than done. Recently I decided to really look into what I have been passionate about my entire life. When I was truly honest with myself and looked around me, I realized that traveling and seeing the many cultures of the world is what I have wanted to do the most. My passions have always involved everything outside of the normal family life in the U.S.. Even now, I am currently planning a trip to Hawaii to see a friend from Australia. We will be meeting half way on Oahu and traveling to the Big Island. I imagine we will be recalling shared experiences late into the night or nights, swimming with the manta rays, snorkeling, hula dancing, and enjoying the Hawaiian Island rays.

This is my third career. I was an illustrator in my twenties, a teacher in my thirties, forties, and fifties, went back to school to be a travel agent, and now am a writer in my sixties. With this latest career change, I can incorporate my knowledge of writing, travel, art, language, and teaching skills and write about them as well. And even though I am five years into retirement, I certainly feel much younger and more exuberant in my heart than I used to. Without looking within and being truly honest with myself, who I am, and what I want, I wouldn't be where I am. I absolutely love what I'm doing and love my life!

Put what you love into action. Find a way to use this as a way to make a living. If you love helping others as I do, find a way to use what you love to help those around you, such as nursing, teaching, social work, etc. If you love being center stage, find a way to do this in your job. If you enjoy the outdoors, look for a career that will allow you to be outside. Look at your gifts as well as what you love, and then look at what is really needed in this world. The answer will speak to you.

Now my days are filled with pleasure, the passion of youth, and an excitement for life. My passion for what I do is infectious and sells itself. Find your own passion, and you will find that you are blessed as well!

*Without discipline and respect,
there can be no real freedoms.*

Our country brags about the freedoms we have. We *should* be grateful for these, as many of our nation's fathers and mothers have paid the ultimate price for them. Other countries are not so fortunate. But too often we take many of our rights in the United States for granted, such as our freedom of speech, our right to bear arms, freedom of religion, equal rights, and the right to vote. We have freedom of speech, but if we speak our minds in a public forum, such as Facebook, we get slammed. We have the right to bear arms, but so many are killed each year in our country by those who misuse that right. We have the right to practice the religion we wish in our homeland, but often we fail to give those of other faiths the respect we ourselves desire. Even though we are a progressive country, there is still rampant prejudice against African and Native Americans, women, the elderly, those with different sexual orientations and those with special needs.

Without *RESPECT* for others, their life choices, the color of their skin, and the *DISCIPLINE* to control how we use these rights, there can be no real freedom. We are stuck in a stalemate of entrenched hate and violence.

This is something I feel *very* strongly about. I was raised in the sixties, when women spoke of bra burning and their rights. If I hadn't been so young, I would have been out protesting with the others for those rights as well. Things have progressed, but they have stayed the same too. We have had an African American president in office, but there are still so many who hate others for the color of their skin. Yes, we should have the right to bear arms to protect ourselves, but people are still gunning down others in schools and public spaces. We have laws in place to protect the rights of the elderly and those with special needs, but they are still being discriminated against regardless of what anyone says.

We must treat others with respect. We don't need to agree with them, but we should concede they have just as much right to believe what they want and look the way they do as us. We also need to have the discipline to put this into practice so we control our behavior as well.

This must begin with each individual, however. We must put both of these behaviors into practice in our lives and teach these to our children. We also need to put love and acceptance first and use the Golden Rule. In the movie *South Pacific*, a film about prejudice, acceptance, and respect, the song "You've Got to be Carefully Taught" gives us this warning:

> You've got to be taught
> To hate and fear,
> You've got to be taught
> From year to year,
> It's got to be drummed
> In your dear little ear
> You've got to be carefully taught.
>
> You've got to be taught to be afraid
> Of people whose eyes are oddly made,
> And people whose skin is a diff'rent shade,
> You've got to be carefully taught.
>
> You've got to be taught before it's too late,
> Before you are six or seven or eight,
> To hate all the people your relatives hate,
> You've got to be carefully taught!

Let us stop the anger, prejudice, and hate with our generation and apply love, acceptance, *respect, and discipline.*

*Every day* is a special day. Use your fancy dishes, nice sheets, fancy lingerie, and your antique crystal. Don't wait for a special day that may never arrive.

While packing to make my recent move, I had the chance to go through all of the wonderful things I have. These special items had been passed down to me or collected along my life's path, packed away and saved for special days to come; when I married, when I would have a family, or when I retired. I also ran across some items my mom had given to me before she passed. There were many items that had been saved for her special day: scarves and other special items my father had bought her in Korea, etched crystal glasses, and lace doilies she had made and then stored away.

When I saw all of these, I realized her special day had never come. I wasn't going to let the same thing happen to me.

That was an "aha" moment for me. It was then that I realized most people have their lives on hold for that magical day when they would use their special items or go on a special trip to Europe or the tropics. Even though I have done a lot in my life, I had still been saving many things for special occasions. My special dishes I had put on display and only used them once a year, all of the antiques from my ancestors were in storage or packed safely away, and I had money put away that was available for my relatives when I pass from this life. What was I thinking?! It was then I began to dig everything out of its boxes and decided whether I should use it or pass it on to the next generation. My "aha" moment reminded me we are only here for today: that today is our special day because it is a gift and tomorrow is never promised.

Take out those special dishes and use them for supper, put on your special nightgown you were saving, and take a vacation with some of the money you have been saving for your retirement. Today is here and tomorrow may never come. Today is your special day.

*Celebrate the special events
and achievements of your life.*

One lesson I learned when I was younger was to celebrate each special event in life. So through the years I have celebrated birthdays, anniversaries, Thanksgivings, Christmases, Easters, Independence Days, and New Year's, even when no one else was around. What mattered is that I marked the occasion as something special.

Celebrations and ceremonies help us to mark new stages in our lives and remember dates with a special event. These are very important as stepping-stones in our lives. That is why we have graduations, weddings, baptisms, anniversaries, class reunions, birthdays, national holidays, and even religious holidays such as Hanukah, Christmas, Easter, Eid Al-Fitr, and Eid Al-Adha.

I really didn't think very much about why celebrations were important until I went back to college to obtain my teaching license. I was talked into just getting my teaching certificate, as I already had a degree in studio art. I was already taking a full load for the last semester and was out of the country practicing my student teaching, so I opted to just complete my teaching certificate. But because of this, I wasn't able to join in the graduation ceremony. When I went to my friend's graduation at my college that spring to support her, I suddenly felt something was missing; that this was something I needed as well. After all, I had just completed a lot of studying and hard work, and I needed to celebrate my success too.

Even if you are alone in your celebration, you can and should celebrate. Make yourself a fancy dinner on your special dishes, pour yourself some wine or champagne in your crystal glasses, take a picture of your elegant repast and post it to your Facebook page to share your celebration with your friends, and then dig in. If you aren't a cook, take yourself out to a fancy restaurant and afterwards put on your favorite movie and with feet elevated, enjoy.

So whether you plan on having your wedding ceremony in a

hot air balloon or traditionally in a church, or celebrate Christmas in July, give yourself a gift and *CELEBRATE.* Not only will it help you to mark the event, depending on what it is, it will help you to remember the wonderful time and bring family and friends together in the process.

*Cherish each moment because
we are never promised another.*

I was reminded once again we really don't know when we will be called home when one of my good friends lost her husband suddenly this past weekend. I am certain my friends Janice and Judy didn't have a clue they wouldn't be going to school the next day when their brother came home that February evening in 1963 and took their lives along with the rest of his family. Nor did I know on February 1 five years ago my father would be called home to heaven when I went to work that cold winter morning. None of us is ever promised a tomorrow, or another moment, for that matter.

I was down at my sister's house for the weekend years ago when she received a phone call from my father. I was leaving anyway, so I said goodbye to my sister and drove the hour home to see my father. When I got there, my dad was visibly shaken and told me to sit down. Knowing what was about to follow wasn't something I wanted to hear, I quickly did as I was told. Upon doing so, my father broke into tears and proceeded to tell me my uncle had passed away earlier that day. He was the younger brother of my mother and had been best friends with my dad since before I could remember. He had been out surveying with another mutual friend and bent over to pick up something, had a massive heart attack, and died on the spot. He had been fine that morning. No one had any hint he would be gone on that day.

This past week one of my nephew's friends was out, and while running tripped on a curb, fell and fractured a rib. The rib penetrated his liver, and by the end of the next day he was gone at twenty years old.

I could go on and on with stories like this, but we truly don't know how much time we are given on this earth. No one does. No one has a magic book of dates that tells us when to live life and when to expect an end. We must all cherish each of the moments we have been given like a precious child, gently holding them in our arms and caring for them, playing and enjoying our days and watching them change. Then when the time comes, we will have no regrets and will have lived our lives well.

*Everyone needs to let his or her inner child out to play from time to time.*

When I was a child, I had no problem playing. I would jump rope and play hopscotch, four square, kickball, pom-pom pull away, Simon says, marbles, sled, duck, duck, goose, crack the whip, king of the hill, and tag. I was always running, digging in the dirt, building sand forts, playing with blocks, and making what we called "marble machines" with blocks and marbles. I knew how to play and how to play hard. Many times my mother had to hose my brother and I off at the end of the day before we came into the house because we were so dirty! (We thought that was great fun!)

As adults, we often forget it's just our body that has grown older and our spirit is still as young as it always was. It needs to play, sometimes desperately! I recently surveyed a group of students I was teaching. I asked them what they most liked to do as children. These were their responses: Play with pets, play games, explore, play sports, play on the swings, sleep, and play. Do you see the reoccurring theme here? It is to play! How many of us truly play each day? I know of no one who does, with the exception of those who have pets. Even those who have children sometimes find reasons not to toss the football or baseball back and forth. We find all sorts of excuses not to let our inner child out to play: maybe tomorrow, if I have time, or when I am done.

Quite recently one of my old friends and a husband to another friend passed away. I worked with him as an illustrator at ShopKo. The one thing I remember most about him was that he never forgot how to let his inner child out to play. Nearly thirty-five years later, people were still talking about how his humor and ability to play brought joy into their lives. Have you ever considered that playing may be what was keeping you young at heart and bringing joy to others and yourself? When you begin to neglect the child within, that child begins to shrivel, and you forget the part of life that is made for us to enjoy.

So play games, throw balls, play on the beach, or make a fort with your child, and the child within will thank you.

*Although it would be nice to have a companion, you don't need a partner to be complete. You are enough.*

*I cannot repeat this enough.* In a world in which you are encouraged from the time that you start dating to find your soul mate and settle down, you are enough!

Face it, wouldn't it be wonderful if everyone could find a perfect mate, that somehow out of the sea of beings your perfect someone would miraculously appear at just the right time and you would have those 2.5 children we were all promised in fairy tales? However, this is real life, and the people who are out there don't always fit with our desires, lifestyles, or philosophies of life.

As for me, I have only been blessed with relationships, but no marriages. I have had to come to terms with living alone, traveling alone, and being alone. For a people person, this was quite a hard pill to swallow at first. Many others think people like myself aren't whole without a man by their side and feel sorry for me. I was one of those people until quite recently, waiting impatiently for my Prince Charming to come along to complete me. However, lately I have come to like who I am, what I do, and believe I don't need a man to be complete.

Would it be nice to have someone to share my life with? You bet! But if one doesn't show up, I'm not going to fall apart. I can handle my life as a single adult. I can make sure I have a roof over my head and food in my refrigerator, new adventures, excitement that comes from creating pictures through art or the written word, and the love I need each day. If I feel I need more love in my life, I can reach out to my friends, my family, or a little puppy named Lola to give me the love I need. If I need more adventure, I can plan a trip and visit friends and family, or, if I can save enough money, a trip out of the country.

Please do not fall prey to those who push others on you, pity you, or tell you that you are incomplete without a significant other.

You are fearfully and wonderfully made, and the universal plan for us is so much better than what we plan for ourselves. When the right time comes, a companion will appear, and if he or she doesn't, aren't we better off being single than in a bad relationship? So smile, count your blessings and be grateful! Put your feet up at the end of each day, take command of your remote, and turn on your favorite chick flick or football game . . . and chill out.

*You can never predict what tomorrow may bring or what is waiting just around the corner.*

If you had told me even four years ago I would be living in a new town, have finished a course for a third career, editing my first published work, writing poetry, working on a travel blog, and be joyful at this point in life, I would have told you that you were crazy. Isn't it amazing how life can turn on a dime?

We can and should plan for a great future, but life does sometimes take us on a rollercoaster of twists and turns, and we can never know what may happen tomorrow. An example is when I went back to school to get my teaching degree. I was taking two classes my first semester as I was working mornings. In one of the classes, we were given a project in which we were to deliver a speech. When the day came for us to present, one of the girls gave a presentation on Australia. Being curious, I asked her afterward why she had chosen the subject she had. When she told me she was going to practice teach Down Under, I made up my mind right then and there I was going to do the same thing. The rest is history. And even in going there I had no idea it would play such a major role in my life.

Please don't ever believe your life will never get better or change or that the sun will never shine for you again. By doing so, you are depriving yourself of the very thing that you are searching for: happiness. I have learned a bit of wisdom in the past few years, which is whatever you may dream for your life is nothing compared to what is waiting for you if you are just open to it. I was so certain I would be an illustrator when I was young, and now I am an illustrator of my own books. Two years ago I was convinced by going back to travel school I would get a job in travel; I have now begun a blog to help others on their trips. Life is filled with such wonderful surprises!

So if today is a disappointment for you, wait for tomorrow, as it just might bring a new adventure that may change your life. It is a bit like Wisconsin weather: wait fifteen minutes and it may change!

*Don't rent your life.*
*It's not a dress rehearsal.*
*Make the most of it now.*

The English singer Dido has a song called "Life For Rent" on the album by the same title. One of its verses goes as follows, "But if my life is for rent and I don't learn to buy. Well I deserve nothing more than I get. Cos nothing I have is truly mine."

When I was in high school, I was in three plays, and although I never had any big parts because of my shyness and stage fright, I still had fun participating. I remember all of the late-night practices as we ran through our lines, learning to dance and synchronizing our performances. I especially remember the nights of dress rehearsals. This was our last chance to banish stage fright and correct any mistakes that were still being made in preparation for opening night; it was the last time we could perfect the investment we would be making in our public performance.

Although our lives are never meant for us to keep, that doesn't mean that we shouldn't make an investment in them. Lives are so much more than rehearsals or practices. We do enough of that in secondary school and in college. We do that with internships, clinical experiences, and wedding rehearsals, after which we plunge into life. Sink or swim, most of us make it. We begin to really live our lives by investing in relationships, by getting married or partnering with someone, perhaps having children and raising them, buying homes, condos, or renting apartments, building businesses or investing in jobs. It's when we try to make the most of everyday we truly begin to live. If you aren't willing to invest in something in life, you are not going to get the most out of it.

We all talk about what we have worked so hard to attain: our careers, jobs, homes, cars, boats, and summer homes. Then we have friends, husbands, wives, children, pets, and others that are part of our families. Do we rent items and just let them sit or throw them in the corner of our house? Of course not! Renting is expensive, and none of us has money we can afford to throw away. We try to take care of things that aren't ours because we know we will have to pay for any damages incurred while they are in our possession. So too, it is with our lives. Life and everything in it is a gift borrowed, but not rented. We need to invest in it to make it work for us and enjoy it. It is given to us for a while, but never meant for us to keep. Every day is a gift for us to use, and all we have is on loan for us to use: our bodies, our minds, our gifts, the money we make, everything we collect in our lives. They are all precious blessings we borrow.

Let us all use our gifts in an honorable way, investing in them and nurturing them during our lifetime and graciously giving them up or passing them on to those left behind.

*Live life like the Australians:
work hard, play hard, and love life.*

I admit I have had a love affair with Australia since I was old enough to learn about the platypus and the Royal Spoonbill in grade school. But it wasn't until I crossed its shores in 1988 and experienced the Land of Oz and its people that it changed me forever. The Aussies are like no other people I have ever met. They really know how to live life, work hard, and PLAY.

You can see this in the way they are all out on the weekends living life as we all should: picnicking, swimming, surfing, hiking in the bush, boating, and more. Life for them is so much more than work or a job. When I got to Australia, I immediately got down to the business of being the best student teacher I could be. And like most Americans, I wanted to be a good representative of my country to the people and place I had dreamed about all of my life.

About the third week into my stay, my supervisor sat down with me and told me that my visit to Australia involved more than just learning to teach; it was an experience I should enjoy and I needed to learn about Australia as well. So he set me up with most of his staff for a weekend in each of their places. By doing this, I not only got to see how the Aussies live, but I also made several lifelong friends while doing so.

I was treated to a day long wine tasting adventure in Hunter Valley and a visit to Old Sydney Town and the Taronga Zoo. I visited the New South Wales Art Gallery, went to the Royal Easter Show, threw a line out along Forresters Beach, and had many other experiences that are too long to mention here. I had the time of my life!

The Australians I came to call friends know how to separate work from their personal life. They work hard, sometimes in jobs that are very physical and some in offices. But on Friday night you will see many out at the local pub having a fish dinner and a brew. On the weekends, many are out at the local beaches or visiting nearby cities doing something interesting and being physically active.

Many I know in Melbourne and along the central coast are warm and inviting. They would not think twice about letting someone stay with them and would give someone the shirts off their backs. They are community minded and play an active role in world affairs. Many I know are humanitarians, going out of their way to help others in need. They are wonderful people who are constantly growing, loving, and living life.

Australians live life with zest. They are warm and inviting, loving and giving, and are truly an example for all of us to follow. We, in America, could learn a lot from our brothers and sisters Down Under in how they live their lives!

*Sometimes it is only in the middle of the darkness that you see the light to guide your way.*

> "Only in the darkness can you see the stars."
> – Martin Luther King, Junior

I was in a dark place for a very long time. My heart was burdened by everything I carried, and I was so sad I was barely living, just existing. It was at this time that my sister-in-law suggested I see someone. Only then did I begin to see the tiny beacons of light begin to twinkle. It was in the midst of the darkest of darks I was finally able to "see the stars" as Martin Luther King, Junior put it.

Depression, as I have already stated, is a black hole. But it also is a place in which a great deal of learning and growing can take place if it is handled in the proper way. By being in this dark place, I began to learn why I was so broken, and although it might have been nice to have had those answers when I was younger, I was finally allowed to heal. Many people aren't so lucky. I have also discovered what a wonderful family I have and how unique they truly are. And though we aren't perfect, we are family, and all of my siblings, in-laws, nieces and nephews, and relation are amazingly kind, loving, and we are all exceedingly blessed.

I have also gained an arsenal of skills I can use in dealing with situations in the world I didn't have while growing up. And I am finally learning who this Vicki is that I have been living with for so many years and how to love her. This realization alone fills my night with a whole sky of stars!

I have learned all of the items discussed in this book from my depression, and I thank God every day I was able to go through it and come out the other side whole. That being said, however, there are a few key points I need to repeat. Medication is not always the answer or the only answer. Sometimes we must go to a counselor, and sometimes any number of other therapies may help. For me, to get to the bottom of my hurt, I needed counseling. I still take medication, because depression and anxiety have been a lifelong struggle. I have also learned a great deal about relaxation and meditation as a way to help with anxiety. And as a result of having to look at myself closely, I have learned who I am and what I really want out of life. Lastly, I have learned to appreciate every day, even with all of its drudgery and pain.

Although being in the blackness of depression isn't a fun place to be, it has helped mold the person I am today. I can finally sit under the night sky and count the billions of stars for the first time in my adult life.

*In life, we are usually given what we need, but it doesn't always show up in a package that we recognize.*

I am certain you have heard of the joke about a fellow stranded on his rooftop in a flood who was praying to be saved. As he was praying, a helicopter came along and the people inside asked if he needed help. He sent them away, telling them God would save him. Another time a canoe came along, and the same thing took place. Then lastly a rowboat came along and he sent those people away too. So he continued praying as he stood on the roof. Suddenly God's booming voice called down: "Yes, I have heard your prayers. Didn't you see the helicopter, canoe, and the rowboat that I sent?"

As you have probably already guessed, I love to watch movies and television. One movie I watch because of the Italian in it and the story line is *Under the Tuscan Sun*. It always reminds me to be specific in what I pray for and to look for the answers to my prayers in unique packages. Here we find the main character of the movie, Frances, talking with her Italian friend after a wedding ceremony held at her house:

*Frances:* What are you thinking?
*Martini:* What do I think?
*Frances:* Tell me.
*Martini:* I think you got your wish.
*Frances:* My wish?
*Martini:* On that day we looked for your snake, you said to me that you wanted there to be a wedding here. And then you said you wanted there to be a family here.
*Frances:* You're right . . . I got my wish. I got everything I asked for.

Frances hosted a wedding for an immigrant worker who had worked to repair her house. She was also able to witness her best friend have her baby there. Lastly, the people who helped fix up the Italian villa she bought had become her family.

I grew up wanting a little girl. But in reality, I don't care very much for the little tiny ones, the crying and all the late nights and rocking them to sleep. (I had enough of that during my teenage years.) I have never entertained the thought of giving up the things that I like to do, such as traveling, to raise a child.

In retrospect, I see that I was given everything I had wished for; I was truly blessed with the best little sister in the world, and when she began to have children, a godchild. I now have another niece who is incredibly sweet, along with two wonderful nephews, and I'm continuing to be the best and coolest aunt I can be. I was also given the time to travel and to lead the interesting and diverse life I'd longed for. So, like Frances, I really got everything I had prayed and wished for. And although it wasn't in the package I had anticipated, I still was blessed beyond my wildest dreams.

*If you want something bad enough in life,
you will usually find a way to get it.*

As I have already stated, I have wanted to travel since I was very young. Between the talk of Ethiopia in our church and the films of African tribesman on *National Geographic*, I was hooked. So when it came time to plan for a life career, summers off naturally figured into the picture. I also had to adjust my life and spending habits to be able to afford my trips.

During this time, I once went two years with bag lunches so I could afford a vacation to visit my friends in Australia. When I bought a house, it had to be small enough so I could afford my adventures. And when I had to decide between going overseas to teach and a new travel career when I retired, you can guess which one was chosen. I wanted to travel more than anything else. My sister, on the other hand, was dead set on having a family. All the while she was growing up, I remember her saying she wanted a boy and a girl and a dog and a cat. Well, she got all but one, as her son is allergic to cats. She has her family and I have visited fifteen other countries.

If you want something bad enough, you will make it happen, even if you have to wait or turn your life upside down to get it. I have a former student who found a wonderful woman to marry, but they were not blessed with children. So they decided to adopt. My brother found a woman to love in his fifties and has finally found a lifestyle that suits him in a bigger city. My cousin wanted to drive a sports car and race ever since he saw my aunt's Spitfire. He went into medicine and now is on the racing circuit with his son. I will eventually get back to Australia and visit my friends again because it is part of my fabric and I won't stop until I do.

For those of us who are ill, those missing limbs, or born with other physical challenges, wishes and dreams aren't so easily obtained. Sometimes there are many obstacles to overcome before we can get what we want. We may have to adjust our desires or ways of fulfilling them. Those who are handicapped and want to go to the Olympics now have the Special Olympics to strive for. Those who are ill and cannot work out of the house will find a way to work from home, many online. Those who struggle with mental illness and issues of prejudice may also have to work harder and smarter to achieve their goals. But yes, they are still achievable. You may just have to be more creative to reach them.

Again, if you want something bad enough and you're convinced it is meant to be part of your life, you will eventually achieve your goal. But never give up, no matter what anyone says!

*Never put yourself through something today you aren't willing to pay for tomorrow.*

I am just waking up and it's already 11:30 a.m. My first cup of coffee is in front of me and I am just beginning to focus. Yesterday was my nephew's high school graduation party. He is a super kid, graduated with honors, has almost a semester of college classes completed already, and, with almost a full ride to college, plans on going on to get an environmental science degree and eventually a degree that will allow him to make a difference in an administrative role. We are all so proud of him.

My sister and I spent Friday afternoon and Saturday morning preparing for the party. I only had two light drinks in the afternoon, kept myself well hydrated as it was nearly 90 degrees, and sat down most of the time. But still my body started complaining at 3:00 this morning. I woke with a headache that didn't respond to aspirin, my asthma flared up, and even my fingers hurt. My sister just texted me telling me her feet hurt and she couldn't even go near her aging Havanese dog because she was growly as well. But it was well worth it. We will all recover within a day or so, but will never forget the fun, conversations, and new people we met. However, this was a *GOOD* thing. How many of us do things to ourselves we regret, are permanent, or wind up hurting ourselves in a *negative* way.

Always consider what you are doing and count the costs *AHEAD* of time. Senior dogs have an excuse, as they can't count, but we have no one to blame but ourselves when we don't. I can remember so many times in my life when I didn't and paid the cost later. I'm not talking about what we have no control over, but the things that we do and the decisions we make. Think ahead to the consequences. Will this put me in jeopardy? How will this affect my life? Am I going to regret this decision? Will my choices hurt others? I recently had supper with a bunch of my high school girlfriends and, like most of us, we all agreed we were all lucky to still be alive because of some of the silly things we did as youngsters.

Use common sense and always ask yourself *BEFORE* you act: Will this be worth it or not? Our family created memories yesterday and captured them in pictures that will be priceless for years to come. What will *you* create?

*Set goals and dreams.*

I was dead already and didn't even know it. My dreams had either died or had been crushed into nothingness. I hadn't made any new goals to look forward to. Without my job and my significant other, I didn't believe I had any future. I was just waiting to die. How foolish and wasteful! I had stopped dreaming because I believed the lie that I was too old to change and I had been too hurt to believe in my dreams again. But dreams are much like the fabled phoenix; they rise from the ashes of life and reestablish themselves regardless of who we are and what we have been through.

I had never been coached by anyone to plan future dreams for my life. Goals, such as going to school and marriage, were drummed into my head by both my parents and society. But dreams were left up to us as if we would develop them by osmosis. Since then, I have learned that when you get too busy with life and don't set aside time to dream, your heart and soul suffer. Also without alternative goals and dreams, you may find yourself without a bridge to the next path in life.

After teaching for twenty-some years and retiring without plans for the future, I had to first stop, collect myself, figure out who I was and what I wanted, and how to get there. That took a long time. I now have daily goals, monthly goals, and yearly goals. And despite my age, I have many dreams I am determined to accomplish. Some are practical and some are shooting for the moon. But they are *MY* dreams and *MY* goals, and by hard work I will get to them and if not, something better.

When I was teaching and the advisor of our school's yearbook, each student would pick a favorite quote and put it by their senior picture. One of my favorite quotes to this day was by Norman Vincent Peale, "Shoot for the moon. Even if you miss, you'll land among the stars." So shoot for the moon! Set your dreams high and reassess them often. Love yourself enough to set some time aside and dream, then make those dreams a reality by planning a way to reach your goals. In so doing you will make your dreams come true!

*Learn to be flexible and adaptable.
That is the only way you will
not break in life.*

People who are easy going and accept life as it is offered do much better in life than those of us who are rigid. Most people who know me will agree that I don't like to argue and usually go along with others because I don't like to cause waves. They may think I am pretty flexible, but when it comes to the important things in life, I don't deal well with change and never have. I have "broken" many times because of this. Changes hit me like a Mack truck, and it takes me days, weeks, or even years to recover and adjust.

The best example of this in my life was when my last significant other broke up with me. I was devastated and cried for two years. Although a book of poems came out of it, which I have yet to publish, it need not have been so hard on me. I cried for the death of the relationship, the way it ended, and the years of my life lost. If I had looked at it more positively, I could have seen I was being protected from a life that wasn't what I wanted. Also, I have since seen all of the positives that came out of the relationship: a wonderful new set of friends, several wonderful vacations I wouldn't have had otherwise, and a venue to learn what is important in a long-term relationship. My time spent was not a waste at all.

My sister is quite different, on the other hand. She adapts easily and doesn't battle the external forces in her life. She is definitely a glass-half-full sort of person. Lately, her business has begun to weigh heavily on her because of its physical requirements, so she has begun a new business that is less taxing on her. She doesn't break because she has practiced bending and has learned not to fight the winds of change. I was amazed at how she dealt with the breakup of her first engagement thirty-some years ago. Although she was quite upset at first, she was able to recover faster than anyone I have ever known, get back into the dating scene, eventually find the love of her life, and start the wonderful family she has today.

When change comes into your life, do you fight it or adapt? Do you dig your heals in or do you adjust your path? Fighting for what is right is important and necessary, just like not giving up and persevering is important in order to get things done. However, to swim against the tide of change is useless and a waste of time and effort. So when change comes into your life, ask yourself if it's worth fighting for or is it in your best interest to change and simply go with the flow. Will you be happier going along with that change, or do you need to go in a new direction? Your future will depend on your decision and the choice you make: either flip onto your back, relax, and float along with the current, take a side stream when the waters that you are swimming in divide, or take up additional swimming lessons! It's your choice!

*Always try to balance your work, your life, and personal needs.*

Let's be honest: All of us have times when our lives get out of balance. Recently my life involved moving to a new city, taking a major test for a new career, and going on vacation all within a one-month period. Although I had tried to plan my vacation after my training had finished, studying took longer than expected. And these were all *GOOD* events and all were planned.

What happens when events happen in our lives that aren't expected, life-altering, or aren't pleasant? Illnesses, pregnancies, job loss, death in the family, miscarriages, just to name a few, get in the way of living and throw our lives out of balance. My very wise student teaching supervisor gave me an analogy for teaching that can be applied to this area as well. He told me teaching was like balancing spinning plates on poles; you must pay attention to them all. If you spend too much time on one, another will begin to fall. So you have to run over to the one faltering and get it to spin again; then when another starts to fall, you have to run to make that one right.

Unfortunately, during stressful periods in our lives, we spend most of our time on the things that are demanding our immediate attention, and that usually doesn't include ourselves. So we go without meals, sleep, and enjoyment and before long, part of our own lives come crashing down. Sometimes this is an illness, (our body's way of saying, "Pay attention to me!") or broken relationships, a sign they may not have been attended to.

One of my students once asked me what the hardest thing about teaching was. Without hesitation, I told her it was balancing teaching and a personal life. We all need to have money coming in, and sometimes we don't have the luxury of choosing what we are doing or where. We do what we have to do to get by. But after a while this begins to take a toll. After such a time has passed, you will need to reevaluate your life. Can you afford to leave your job? Perhaps you would be happier in a different career?

Much of the happiness in life is based on whether or not we balance our lives correctly. It affects every aspect of our lives, along with our health. I can certainly attest to this. I have seldom taken the breaks that were needed after stressful times in my life. Now I am paying a hefty price. So work hard but make certain you play hard too. Balance your life in every way you can.

*Don't take things other people
say or do personally.*

Have you ever gone into work only to have someone bite your head off? Most likely it had nothing to do with you. So many times we take things like this personally and think it is our problem or we have somehow caused it. However, this is probably the farthest from the truth. There are a myriad of things that might have happened to cause someone's foul mood, least of all your smiling face.

Today is a great example, I am certain that anyone who saw me would have thought, I was going to snap at them! The truth is everything seems to have gone wrong in my life. I am stressed out and all of my own advice is not helping me. I am spinning. But it is a problem related to my situation and not to those around me. Many times while teaching I encountered this with my students. I began to make it a practice to ask them what was wrong. Sometimes they told me, sometimes not. But it was always a problem either at home, with one of their friends, or another classes. It had nothing to do with me 99.9% of the time.

So too other people, despite all of their careful efforts, begin to spin out of control. We have no idea what other people are going through on a daily basis. They may have been abused, overworked, have an illness or hurt. They might have just had a fight with a husband, wife, child, or boss, have cancer, lost a loved one, or are just having one of those days when everything seems to have gone wrong, like mine. You don't know what is going on in another person's life, and most people don't go around announcing their problems to the world. We can ask them, as I did with my students, but many times adults have their shields of protection up, and unless you are extremely close, they may not want to share.

Sensitivity is great to have, as it allows you to be aware and respond to those around you. However, don't let it rule your life.

When you meet another who has a horrid demeanor, ask if you can help them. If your co-worker bites your head off, tell them you are there to listen if they need to talk and walk away knowing you have done your best to help them. If your child is in a foul mood, you can never show too much love. Don't assume the problem lies with you. It is counterproductive and only serves to make you feel bad about yourself.

Cut yourself a little slack, and when people seem to be short with you, don't make it all about yourself, because it usually isn't.

*Don't worry about tomorrow.*
*You have no control over it anyway.*

I am the consummate worrier. I have generalized anxiety disorder and have had it most of my life. Although it has gotten much better with age, it still rears its ugly head at times. However, this disorder does have its good points: it helps me to double check things so mistakes aren't usually made, I make tons of lists to see that things get done, I very rarely leave things behind at hotels, I get great grades, and my planned trips are usually impeccable.

However, those are the good things. The disorder also gives me panic attacks and problems with concentrating when there is noise around. I used to stay up late at night because I was worried the day before school started. My back gets tied up in knots when I am terribly anxious, and when I was young I struggled with OCD to control my anxiety.

So as you can see, anxiety can be a big problem as well. But it shouldn't and doesn't have to be. We shouldn't worry about tomorrow, as it is never promised to us. (Which is easier said than done.) When problems come up, we can only do our best to work through them. We can't control events, so why worry? But this is a hard thing to put into practice and the first thing we do when we are stressed out and worried about what is happening around us. Anxiety is terribly hard to control—it takes a lot of practice.

How do we control worry then? A practical way to handle this problem is to follow the advice of Web MD. (http://www.webmd.com/balance/features/9-steps-to-end-chronic-worrying)

1. Make a list of your worries.
2. Analyze the list. Look at which worry is productive and which isn't.
3. Embrace uncertainty. Life is uncertain and that cannot be changed.

4. Bore yourself calm. Repeat what you fear over and over in your mind.
5. Make yourself uncomfortable. Practice discomfort.
6. Stop the clock. Relax and focus on what can be done in the moment to make life more pleasant; such as reading a book or listening to calming music.
7. Remember that it's never as bad as you think it will be.
8. Cry out loud. By crying or getting angry you aren't focused.
9. Talk about it.

For me, the following actions are also helpful: Take yourself out of the situation until you can calm down, go to a quiet place and meditate or count your blessings, try envisioning the worst thing that could happen in your situation and how it would affect you, sing, run, or walk if you can, or try laughing at the situation.

Everyone is different, so try different strategies to get your mind off of your troubles until you find one that works for you. Anxiety and worry are merciless parasites that eat away at our precious happiness. Don't let them steal yours.

*The secret to traveling in life
and through it is to travel lightly.
You don't need to carry your burdens . . .*

This was never truer than when I moved recently. The move wasn't far, only about fifty miles, but I had collected so much *stuff* over the time I had lived in my house that it was a major chore. I spent more than a year going through my boxes, my parents' boxes, and my cedar chests, throwing out items or giving them away. When moving day came, I was sure I would be ready. However, I was shocked by the amount of junk I was still moving with me. It took the moving company four-and-one-half hours just to load all of it onto the truck, costing me much more than I had anticipated.

My friend in Australia has spent a great deal of time house sitting. Because she has had to move many times from house to house, she gave me some of the best advice I have ever gotten regarding baggage. She told me to be merciless in throwing things away. This may be applied to our emotional lives as well. We collect all sorts of junk along our paths in life and carry it with us: pain, broken relationships, unresolved problems, and much more. Some are very heavy, such as self-blame, and others are light. But whatever the weight, if we keep carrying any burden long enough, it will eventually become too heavy for us to haul around and will wear us down.

When we travel by plane, do we carry a ton of stuff? Of course not! Airlines now slap a huge fee on extra baggage. Also, if you have ever had to go from one end of Chicago O'Hare Airport dragging your luggage behind you as you are running to catch a connecting flight, you will understand too much luggage can be a major problem. After one trip like this, you will most certainly pare down your luggage to help your trip go more smoothly. Why don't we think to do this with our emotional junk? It's just as heavy and weighs us down even more as we carry it continuously. Emotional baggage can make us ill and chips away at the priceless gift of life.

So whatever your load, go through it and pitch what doesn't work for you anymore. Do everything you can to put your problems behind you: write them down, then burn them, throw them away, or call someone you have wronged to make your relationship right. Then experience how much freedom you truly have.

*Don't be so focused on the bad in life
that you miss opportunities to move on.*

As I grew up, I was fascinated by horseracing. I believe I watched the Kentucky Derby every year. I certainly remember the year Secretariat won the Triple Crown. Some trainers use something called blinkers or blinders when training and racing. They seem to help the horse focus on what is in front of him.

Like the horse, we as adults many times tend to focus on one thing as if we have these blinders on. But instead of looking ahead, we often look back over our shoulder as if in a rearview mirror at what has happened in the past. This is most likely because we have either been hurt by something and can't get it out of our minds or we just can't move on. This does two things to us; it blinds us to our future and keeps our past reigned in close.

Several times in life I have found myself in this situation. At times I was so focused on all of the bad in my life, I wasn't aware of the opportunities that were just within reach. But fortunately for me, many of these opportunities were still waiting when I took my blinders off. Not all are so fortunate.

We all need time to heal from hurts, and like I said before, there is no timetable for loss, pain, and grief. However, sooner or later we all have to get on with our lives. We have to say goodbye to loved ones, accept bodies which no longer work the way they used to, and deal with pain that is part of everyday life. We all need to get the help we need and take chances in life again. We need to take our blinders off and *believe* life will get better. My dad lost my mom nearly twenty years ago and he was crushed. I remember him telling a friend of her passing the next morning as he broke down in tears. But within nine months, he had found a female companion and within another four years, he had found another special lady to share his life with. Bless my mom for giving him permission to move on after she was gone and my dad's bravery for putting himself out there!

When we hold onto the past it serves only to keep our hands too full and our eyes too blind to accept the gifts just in front of our faces. Let go of the past, allow yourself to heal, take your blinders off, and accept the gifts life has given you and you will be surprised by how blessed you will be!

*Work to transform your weaknesses into your greatest strengths.*

Every person has something they don't like about themselves, and everyone has weaknesses. I grew up a quiet and shy girl, with a debilitating social phobia, I have slightly bowed legs, and a last name both kids and adults can twist around in cruel ways. I also have a lot of things I like about myself, but these are the things I remember hating when young.

I promised myself when I got old enough, I would change my last name. Kralapp: who has a name like that? I have been called everything from Trollop to Kraplapp throughout my life, both of which are embarrassing and demeaning. But that same last name is now recognized in the art circles throughout our area because of what our family has done over the past forty years in the arts. We turned our name into *a strength*.

I also used those same bowed legs to win three high school track records and one city record, which was no easy task, as our city is the third largest in our state. I took speech classes and participated in musical productions in high school and eventually became a teacher, growing out of my shyness and fear of public speaking.

We can either use our "weaknesses" and turn them into strengths as I did or we can let them control us throughout life. No one would ever know that Julie Andrews grew up painfully shy. She has overcome this three hundredfold. Sidney Poitier came from extreme poverty, had an education only until age twelve, and finally settled in the Southern United States where African Americans were still considered to be subpar. Look at what he has overcome. He is one of the most gifted and eloquent actors of his or any age. They are both inspirations and have left many gifts for us to enjoy.

I believe what you go through in life forms the person you become. For example, if I had never gone through the embarrassment of intolerant and ignorant teachers as a child, I would not have been so careful of the feelings of students with special needs, those who are socially challenged, and those of other races or gender choices. If I hadn't become ill with fibromyalgia, I would never have understood the problems of the physically challenged who attend school or travel. If I hadn't had so many challenges in the past few years, I would never have begun the journey to writing this book to help others!

So please don't let the challenges in life control the person you become. It is up to you to put a bridle on them, rein them in, and use their energy and strength to help you through your life and help change the world.

*Really? Will it even matter in five years?*

"Don't sweat the small stuff" has been a popular phrase during the past few decades. It simply means we shouldn't be troubled by the little problems in life. Still, some of us get so upset when we run into small problems, we blow them all out of proportion.

Life has plenty of big problems to worry about without focusing on small ones. I'm not saying that you should worry. However it *is* human nature to do so. We all worry about the little things, such as whether the new neighbor will like us, whether Junior is going to have a good first day of school, if we are going to have enough food for a party we are throwing, and so on.

News flash! Not everyone will like you, Junior will most probably have things he liked and didn't like on his first day, and yes, if you're like me, you will probably be able to feed an army of guests at your party. Little things just are not worth worrying about. They zap your energy, your strength, and leave you with nothing in return except stress, exhaustion, and, eventually, illness.

Like many other parents, my mom always told me to ask myself if something would matter in five years. Most things that happen to us won't. The items that will matter are what we should be concentrating our efforts on. What are the important things to be concerned with? Memories will be important in five years, so will time with family and friends, not whether you had a clean house or the best furniture. Attending your son or daughter's track meet or graduation is important, as well as being with family when they need you, not whether you have the latest trend in fashion.

So stop sweating the small stuff and remember the five-year rule: if it doesn't make the cut in that time, then forget about it, and don't waste your precious energy. I have always loved the quote from the Bible, "So do not worry about tomorrow, for tomorrow will care for itself. Each day has enough trouble of its own" (Matthew 6:24).

Leave the worries of yesterday behind, because they are in the past, and tomorrow's problems have yet to arrive. Take care of today, and when you begin to worry, ask yourself: will it even matter?

*There are no guidebooks or sizes that come with our lives. Put your life together and don it in the way it fits you best.*

Wouldn't it be nice if life came with a set of rules and guidelines for us to follow? It would certainly make decisions so much easier to make and raising children less stressful on *both* parents and young.

But in truth, life comes with little to no instructions, except what one can find in parenting books or what our parents pass down to us from generation to generation. One size does not fit all in this case. So many complications and variations come into play in life: different personalities, intelligences, and gifts, and when you add environment to the mix, you get farther and farther from a generic size.

In my own family, we had all nine types of intelligences: logical-mathematical, existential, linguistic, interpersonal, spatial, bodily-kinesthetic, musical, intra-personal, and naturalist—just within the seven of us. Two of us grew up in the "Wild West" of our area and the others did not. Some of us didn't fit well in school and should have been placed in a gifted environment, and some had a great experience. Some of us excelled in physical activities and others didn't. We are all so very different due to a combination of genes, environment, gifts, and how we learn.

The best that we can do for our children is to feed them nutritious food to grow and remain healthy, teach them what they need to know to have a productive life, and encourage them to pursue their dreams. You may have a child who loves to watch the Olympics, while another may strive to be in them one day. One of your children may be extremely quiet, while the next may be just the opposite. We will all have to adjust our guidance as a parent to meet their needs.

But remember, if you do this for your children, you should also do the same for yourself. You may find that your battery is recharged beside a body of water in the sunshine, while your husband, wife, or significant other can recharge in a classroom. Some need to be in a quiet environment at home and others in the quiet countryside. You are not your neighbor, your daughter, or your sister. You are unique and need to treat yourself as such. We do not live in a world of paper dolls with cut-out lives. Give yourself some room to grow and find what fits you best.

So if you are trying to fit yourself or those you love into a generic box, look closer. Perhaps you may need to start being more creative with your life and those around you.

*Strive for excellence, not perfection. Perfection is unachievable and trying to be so will only serve to drive you crazy.*

The Native American Navajos still weave mistakes purposefully into the rugs they produce because they believe that it is within that mistake that the Spirit can move in and out. I have heard this story many times since I was young, yet I didn't internalize it until recently.

I have, since I can remember, expected perfection from myself, which is truly unfortunate. But that is the way I was raised, and for better or worse, it is part of who I am. Together with my anxiety, it has caused a multitude of problems in my life. We aren't perfect, and that is the bottom line, so we should stop trying to be. I remind myself of this every day.

Quite recently I have adopted a compromise with regard to this and work daily to implement it. If I am working on a project, such as preparing for a party or studying for a test, I set myself a goal, then do the very best I can to achieve it. I try to set reasonable goals, delegate, and try not to do everything in sight. However, if I miss my mark, which I often do, I don't beat myself up because I didn't get there. I remind myself to be satisfied, because I have done my best. Most of the time I do achieve excellence, because I work very hard, and if the results don't meet someone else's expectations, well, then, that is their problem. I have done my best and still have enough strength left to enjoy myself.

I am a member of a pretty big perfectionist club in America. We all want to look like either Ken or Barbie, to live in a perfect neighborhood like Park Place, and find a perfect school in which to enroll our kids. We expect to be perfect at our jobs, to be the perfect wife or husband, to keep a perfect house, and on and on. Do you see how this can create a neurotic society? Although doing a good job has its place at work, throwing a reception for a wedding, or making a good first impression, living that way is very unhealthy. The truth is, when we stop trying to be perfect, we can relax and enjoy the life we have been given. We will have less stress and anxiety, less guilt, less anger, and more confidence.

If the situation requires exceptional attention, then go for the details, but if it doesn't, take a lesson from the Navajos. Relax, do your best, and stop trying to be perfect—leave that up to your Creator.

*One trait that all successful people share is that they are persistent. By never giving up, you may also discover more than you anticipate.*

"If I wasn't so absolutely certain of my road at this point in life, I would have given up months ago!" These are the words I have heard myself repeat over and over during the past year, especially this past summer. They haven't made my road any easier to travel, just a little more secure.

I will always remember the morning I made the decision to study travel. I was lying in bed pleading for someone to give me guidance as to what to do for the rest of my life. I had just booked a trip to Italy to celebrate my retirement and was learning Italian for my adventure. But even with this wonderful vacation in my future, I was unhappy with life. I couldn't adjust to retirement or being without steady work. So I was asking for help from above in my decision-making process.

I had been struggling with this for nearly two years when it began to dawn on me I could combine my love of travel, art, language, and foreign culture into a totally new career: one in travel. However, that is not the whole story. Later that day, one of my friends sent me a note, one that confirmed my decision by encouraging me to seek out the travel industry. I hadn't yet told anyone of my decision, with the exception of my sister, so there is no way she could have known what I was considering. That was when I knew I was on the right path.

I must be persistent in living my life in order to finish what I want. Today was a particularly hard day. I am very tired. I have worked one-half day, taken care of my household chores, studied at least six hours, organized appointments for next week, and have been in contact with some members of my family. It is 11 p.m., and tomorrow I will do it all over again. But I am determined to see this period of my life and course of study through.

Many people have families to care for, and each day is filled with numerous problems, housework to do, and full-time jobs, and yet these people still find time to go back to school. Now that takes determination! People who want to learn to ski but have only one leg and those who are ill with cancer struggle much more than I. When my dad met his second love after my mother passed away, his new lady friend was still walking two miles a day and she was in her mid-seventies. Again, determination! Anything worth having will take effort, some things more than others. Whether you will make it through the tough times depends on how determined you are!

When I was in my mid-twenties I began taking ice skating lessons at the local ice rink. What I remembered the most was falling, and I fell a LOT! My first lesson was not in how to skate but in how to fall. This probably saved me from a lot of concussions and many broken bones as I went through life. However, my very first experience in skating was on a pond at a Brownie outing when I was very young. I had to borrow skates, as we didn't own any. Sometime later, I recall my mother's friend who had been with us telling the story of my determination and how I kept falling but didn't give up until I could stay on my skates. That is the difference between getting something done and not. It is not in the amount of times you fall but in how many times you get up and the amount of determination you use to accomplish your goals.

*Fake it 'til you make it.*

This is an old army trick, faking the confidence to lead others until you have it. I have lacked confidence all of my life, and recently asked my counselor how to build it. He began with, "Fake it 'til you make it"!

There are several ways to build confidence. But because it takes a while to develop, what are you supposed to do until you have it? I remember one specific day when I was younger. I had to go out and meet a friend at a restaurant, so I dressed myself up in my best clothes, put on my makeup and heels, and danced out of my apartment. By the time I got out of my car to meet my friend, my whole demeanor had changed. Someone I passed on the way from my car to the restaurant, noticed my attitude and said, "We're feeling pretty good today, aren't we?!" The truth is, I actually was! By dressing up, putting on extra makeup, and putting my hair up in a fancy twist, I had made myself feel better about who I was *to myself*. And that, in turn, made a great deal of difference to those around me.

I faked my confidence by how I presented myself. If you go out in grubby clothes, without taking time to fix your hair or face, does it not follow you won't feel as good about yourself and who you are? Many times the way people react to us will have a profound effect on how we feel about ourselves as well. So why not give yourself and your confidence a head start by looking the best you can?

Another trick is called acting. If we can put on a good face and act like we are confident, people tend to think we are. Practice how to behave and act. In time, you will either convince yourself or become so comfortable with your character it will become second nature. Ask anyone who has done well at acting. They usually become their character while they are performing. I was always performing in the classroom, especially at first in teaching my students; they expected a teacher who was confident about herself, and by acting, I gave them one.

If you can, do as my counselor told me to do, fake it 'til you make it, and you will eventually grow into the confident person you were meant to be!

*We are not always given what we want in life, but rather what we need.*

I can remember many times when I have wanted something so badly I could taste it: the relationships I longed for, the children I pictured in my head, and the places I wanted to travel to. However, I haven't always gotten everything I have asked for, but I have usually been given what I needed.

I am reminded of the '60s music many times with its wise and poetic lyrics. And as I am writing this, a song by the Rolling Stones comes to mind.

> . . . You can't always get what you want
> You can't always get what you want
> You can't always get what you want
> But if you try sometimes well you just might find
> You get what you need . . .

So many times we are heartbroken over relationships, jobs, moves, or careers that don't work out. I was disappointed when I didn't have a family or a husband, and when I had my job cut in half and had to change my career. But looking back, I was given exactly what I *needed*. I didn't need a family, as I've helped raise all sorts of children throughout my life. I needed to make a difference with my life in a different way. I didn't need to stay in art or teaching, as it was time for me to use the other gifts I had been blessed with to help others. I don't need a husband, as I have finally learned to love myself and be comfortable with who I am. And in return, now I can do the things I love: write, learn languages, find all sorts of new adventures, and travel as I wish.

What is it that *you* really need in life? Is it a family? Do you need to help others? Do you need the love of another in a marriage or relationship? Or are you a person who needs adventure? Do you have the strength of a leader and long to be in a leadership role? Honesty with yourself is the key as you look deep inside. What you find will help you as you move forward in life and will help you become the person you were meant to be.

So when you wish upon a star for what you want, make sure it is what you need as well. In that way, you are always assured you will be happy with your life and who you become.

*Don't worry about what other people think, as they are not you.*

Many people spend useless hours worrying about what other people think of them, myself included. Although I am much better than I used to be, I have had to work very hard and have struggled to get where I am. Sometimes I still find myself caught in the trap of worrying about what others think.

Along with other problems, I grew up with a moderate form of public anxiety, as I have already mentioned. I was so shy, and so afraid I would say or do something wrong, that I talked very little in school. I still remember the pain of having to sit in a circle with the other children and asked to read the Dick and Jane books in first grade. I would dread having to read aloud, not because I couldn't read, but I was afraid of what others would think if I stumbled. In high school I would walk on the other side of the hall from the boys I had crushes on and struggled to perform as an individual in band and in front of class for fear of looking stupid. My heart would pound and my mind would go blank. Looking back, I am very surprised by how well I did as a teacher in front of a classroom of students.

What other people think should really be of no concern to you, as they aren't you and they have little knowledge of what makes you tick. It is only their opinion, and unless it matters a great deal, you should not let that affect you at all. Once you have learned that basic premise and internalized it, you will be free to live the life you want, including making mistakes, creating your own style, and being your own person.

If you are like many others struggling with this problem, here are some tricks you can use to help yourself. First, practice, practice, practice. Next, try to place yourself in situations that will desensitize you to the problem. Once you are in an anxiety-producing situation, you can try to calm yourself by taking some deep breaths and talking yourself out of your worry. Remind yourself that many people have this problem and you are strong enough to overcome it. Whichever works for you, use it to set yourself free. The truth is, people who really matter will not judge you for what you do and will be there for you when you fall.

Be yourself and live your own life. It's such a freeing and exhilarating experience. Leave your worries and fears of what others may think by the roadside and be who you were created to be.

*Don't give your power away to anyone by letting others dictate how you feel.*

Do you realize you are giving *power* to someone else every time that you feel angry or bad because of something someone has done to you? That's why we use expressions like "You made me mad" or "You are giving me a headache." Do you really mean to do that? Do you really want to give this power to others so they can hold it over you?

Most of us do not wish to give that type of control to someone else. The expressions "pushing my buttons" or "making me embarrassed" are phrases that similarly express the power we give to others. At my previous job, one of the administration liked to push many of the teachers' buttons. He seemed to enjoy seeing his employees squirm. However, I never realized I was giving him power over how I was feeling by how I reacted.

In the light of recent events with all of the shootings around our country, I am reminded of these reactive feelings and of the people who find themselves in these unfortunate circumstances. Many of these shooters have been bullied and victimized themselves. Many feel helpless and are compelled to let others know. Because they are so frustrated and don't know how to express those feelings, they take action and shoot others. They don't take into consideration that they too have choices all along the way to use their feelings and pain positively. They have given away their power and their futures and, in many instances, lose their lives in the process. They are allowing others who have been pushing their buttons to have control over their lives and are continuing the chain of hate and negativity.

We do have a choice in these situations. If someone wants to make you angry or frustrated, just walk away. If you can't, find help or go to a superior. Even if you must leave a job, isn't it much better than hurting someone else, or spending your life in jail? *Do not give your power away by letting someone get under your skin.* You have been given that power for a reason. Turn it around and use it for your benefit and for your future in a *positive way.* What would have happened if some of the people who were the perpetrators of the mass shootings in our country had taken their anger and focused it on *working against* those who caused their frustrations in a positive way to help others?

We have missed the mark in today's wave of violence by not first teaching students coping skills and how to creatively solve problems like these. Also, if we look at other countries that teach students how to behave and have proper respect for others before teaching them the ABCs, it's amazing what can be done. That being said, there will always be bullies and those who like to push our buttons in this world, so learning to deal with them in a positive way is always the best solution.

NEVER, I REPEAT, NEVER GIVE YOUR POWER AWAY, as I have done in the past by getting angry with someone. Use laughter, joke about the situation, or just walk away, but do not give someone else power over your anger by what they say or do to you and how you react to them. Your life, health, and time are too precious for you to waste it on something like this.

*Follow your own path and dance
to your own drummer.*

I will never forget my mom saying, "If someone jumped off of a bridge, would you follow?" Although I did find myself following the crowd at times, I have never been much of a joiner, I'm happy to say. I have always marched to my own drummer, the reason being I have never found very many people I wanted to emulate in this world. Luckily, I have never been attracted to destructive people, and the few people I have truly admired are or were all humanitarians, giving back to the world. I also have always believed I have a special purpose in life, and I have always tried to pursue it no matter where I was on my journey.

What is your life path? Are you following someone else's road set before you, or are you on a path *you* have chosen? I became an art teacher as a natural progression of my gift for drawing. But after my career in teaching ended abruptly and my back hurt too much to bend over a table to draw, I found myself at a fork in the road and couldn't see which avenue to choose. As I've already related earlier in this book, I sat down one morning, and after much thought about what I loved and what I had always felt I should do, the answer came to me. It was within me all of the time, I just couldn't see it.

For those of you who are not spiritual, listen to your inner voice telling you what to do. It will lead the way. Then follow my example: research how to get to the place you want and create a schedule and path to accomplish it. I went back to school for a year at age fifty-eight and got a travel agent certificate and in the process found out how much I enjoyed writing. Recently I figured out a way to combine the two.

What is it that is special about you that you can share with the world? Remember, we are not just here to eat, sleep, and populate the world. We are each here for a special purpose. Where do you see your drummer leading you? Again, you will have to get to know who you are and what it is you want out of life. No one can tell you this, but they can certainly help you sort it out. Spend time by yourself and get to know you and what you want. When you do, you will know. Then make a plan, start marching, sing with all of your might, and let everyone hear your song.

Again, dance to your own drummer and listen to what is right for you. You are a unique individual, not part of a cookie-cutter crowd. There will never be another you. It may take years to find out what you truly want in life, but it is *YOUR* path and *YOUR* song. Write your own score, your own lyrics, and sing and dance it with enthusiasm, from a mountaintop if you can!

# Part Ten

## Healthy Relationships: Friends & Family

*People sometimes outgrow one another.
It is a fact of life, and that is okay.*

I have a friend I have known since high school, and we have kept in touch all of these years. However, lately our philosophies of life have become very different, and we have lost touch with one another. We only write at Christmas even though we live in the same city. And so it goes with many friends. Some come into our lives for a season in order to teach us something, and others remain as lifelong friends. But all are valid and are to be treasured while they are with us.

Sometimes with significant others or spouses, the relationship may be terminally broken through no fault of our own. It's sad, but it happens. I was with my last significant other for four years, and although I first regretted it, I've come to believe it was a very good learning experience. We had many great times together. He is now married to a much younger woman and has a toddler, and I am free to pursue the life I was meant to lead. We outgrew one another. And that is okay.

The main purpose of my life for the past few years has been to heal and grow. When you grow and others aren't on the same path, it is natural to outgrow them. I am learning all about health, why I have fibromyalgia, and how to overcome it. I have learned how to heal emotionally and am passing it on through this and other writing and art I have in the works.

While writing this book and a blog on travel, my true friends know that I am working hard and allow me time to grow. They love me the same as before I began morphing into the person I am now. The friends who came into my life just for a season have also come to me for a reason, perhaps to learn something or perhaps for support, but whatever the reason, we have both moved on.

We are all blessed with two types of friends: those for a season and those for life. Both are valid and both are to be treasured.

*Good friends are those who see you through both the good and bad times. They don't look at your weight, your wrinkles, or how old you are. When choosing friends, do so with care and forethought, as much of your life experiences and happiness will be a direct result of these people.*

I am so blessed with the beautiful friends I have. Several I met in grade school and high school, some are from my many jobs throughout life, and a few are from the last community I lived in. Many of my students have grown up and have made me their friends on Facebook. I have been invited to their weddings, showers, and graduation parties, and I consider it to be truly a blessing to be part of their lives and love them all dearly.

The three female friends I can always count on are in Minnesota, Australia, and an hour south of me. The first one I met in high school. We spent most of our time together from that day forward when we weren't working, and when she moved to another state, we stayed in touch. My other friend I have known since I was thirty-two. We met during the first day of in-service while I as in Australia to complete my student teaching. Who would have guessed that twenty-nine years later, we would still be best mates halfway across the planet! Many people talk about their sisters as being their best friends. I am indeed fortunate to count myself among them. And as my friend Down Under said recently, you truly have the best of friends and sister in her!

These three are all sisters to me, and I can't thank them enough for their love and support through the years. All of these girls have seen me through the deaths of both my parents, illnesses, breakups with boyfriends, the buying and selling of my house, lots of moves, trips abroad, retirement, and the changing of careers. They don't care what I look like or what I am wearing, as long as I'm happy and taking care of myself. They love me for who I am.

All of our friends come to us along life's path. All are gifts given to us, but we must all choose those we wish to keep and develop those relationships. We should all make a conscious choice to make friends who will love and support us in life. It would have been so easy to let the friendships with my friends in Australia, Italy, Germany, and all the others around the world slip through the cracks because of their distance and life's busy days. However, I was fortunate to learn the lesson of how to keep and nourish friendships early in life.

Back in 1978, when I was in college for the first time, way before the time of Facebook and other social media, I had a housemate who would write to friends daily. She also was the person who received the most mail in our house of nine students. In so doing, she taught me one must tend to friends to keep them close and let them know they are special. I can't begin to imagine what my life would be like without my bestie in Australia or some of the others I've met along the road of life. I consider it a privilege to count each one among my friends.

But choosing your friends is also very important, as much of life's joy and happiness will come out of your relationshop with them. Because we spend a lot of time developing values in life, it's very important to choose friends who share yours. It is also very important to choose healthy friends, people who lift you up and encourage you and don't have toxic behaviors. Many of your friends will come to you naturally because you share the same interests and have common goals.

If you are isolated in a small community, you may have to seek those out. Look for individuals who share in your joys and successes and can motivate you. People who seek knowledge and growth are usually interesting people and are often up on the latest events. I find these people the most nourished and stimulating people to be with. Lastly, look for kindness and remember to return the favor. Relationships are always two-sided and, as I said before, must be worked at and tended.

I am truly blessed with the friends I have made along life's path. Whether I have chosen them or they have chosen me, they are my family and I love each dearly!

*No relationship, however brief, is a waste of time. There is always something that can be learned from everyone.*

People who we meet come to us in a variety of ways: through casual contact in stores, in restaurants, at banks, parties, on Facebook, and in schools. Some friends we develop very strong attachments to, get married and have children, some become casual acquaintances, and others, lifelong friends. Some we might meet seemingly by accident or on a trip somewhere. Sometimes a person has been woven in and out of our life until we begin to notice them. However you meet is completely unique to you. They either become a part of your life or they drop out. Therein lies the problem.

If there is a split in a marriage, a significant other, in a family, or a friendship, there is usually a period of resentment, hurt, and ill will, then finally forgiveness and healing. The love or friendship that once was is strained or nowhere to be found, and for whatever reason, there are two or more angry people remaining.

Once the anger and the mourning have run their course, the healing can begin. It is only at that point we can look back and really begin to learn from the relationship. For whatever reason, that person was put into our lives. It might not have been for a long time or for the reason we had wished, but in some way, they have helped us learn something about ourselves.

It finally dawned on me recently, while writing this book, what I was supposed to learn from my last significant relationship. It was to trust my gut instinct. I was also given several wonderful new friends to love and learned a lot about relationships. My best friend from around the world taught me I can have a sister who is not a blood relative and has loved and supported me even though I haven't seen her in years. I even met someone one night at a coffee shop in my last city of residence, and through the beauty of Facebook, we have become good friends despite the fact she lives, once again, in Australia.

You may never know or figure out why someone has come into your life, but when you begin to count the memories, friends, and blessings you have been given as a result of that bond, you will begin to have some perspective on the situation and count them among your treasures.

*You are never too old to need or want your mom or your dad.*

We normally draw security from our parents when we are children, and as we grow older, we rely on their presence and advice to help us make many of life's decisions. But as they age, many slowly leave us because of their advanced years or through illness or accidents. So if you are lucky enough to still have your parents with you at my age, consider yourself very fortunate.

When I went to Italy as part of my retirement present to myself, I had the pleasure of traveling with a mother and her son from Melbourne, Australia. Both were lovely people, but the young man was so kind and loving to his mom that everyone began commenting on what a good son he was. He would hold his mom's hand, help her up on the bus, put his arm around her, and make certain she was always okay. It was truly inspirational.

This is how it should be. Most parents give up so much to make sure we grow up healthy, with a good education, and strong enough to survive on our own. We owe them a great deal. This mother had raised three children all by herself, and her son was returning the love he had been given growing up.

Just before my mother passed away, she and I were talking about her own mother and how she still missed her. She had died of a stroke when my Mom was only thirty-four. Now, over nineteen years has gone by since my own mom passed away, and I know exactly what she was talking about. I have had a full life, with a career and house, have traveled the world, and completed several dreams both of us had, but on a bad day, I still long to call her and tell her how I am doing. Sometimes I still even reach for the phone. Two years ago when I was so sick with bronchitis, anemia, and asthma, I longed to hear her voice say to me," You'll be okay honey, don't worry!

There is no shame in needing your parents' love and support.

If you still have them with you, make certain that you never take them for granted. But for those of us that are not so lucky, no amount of time will stop the longing to be with them or hear their comforting words. Unfortunately, that will never go away.

So never apologize for your love and connection to your parents, whether you are ten or sixty, whether you live with them or they with you, if you call them every night or travel home every weekend to see them. Wherever you may be, your love and need for your parents will continue until the day you are no longer here.

*Family and health should come
before a job or career.*

There are some things I truly regret and wish I could do over in my life. One such time was the weekend before my mom's passing. On Friday, my mom's hospice nurse called to tell me if I wanted to spend time with my mother, I should do so right away. So, like a dutiful schoolteacher, I took time to plan my lessons for the next week and brought them in on Monday. However, I had no idea that would be the last morning I could tell my mom I loved her. She slipped into a coma that night and died at home the next morning. If I could do it over, I would tell the school to get someone who could do their own lesson plans. Such trivial things are nothing compared to a family member we love.

I can remember times when I would go into work with migraines so severe I would have to excuse myself from class and run to the bathroom to be sick. I even put up an art show less than two weeks after having major surgery. This was silly and self-destructive behavior as I look back on it now. When I *would* call into work sick, the person in charge would always say that she would *try* to find someone to fill in for me, as if to make me feel guilty so I would change my mind. Didn't I deserve the same opportunity to heal and recuperate others had received? Of course I did! I have since learned the hard way, family and health come first.

Always remember jobs can be replaced, but parents and family members cannot. Do not shortchange your life; you can never replace precious time spent with family or, oftentimes, health.

*No matter how old you get, family is still important and becomes more important as you age.*

How many of you come home at the end of a particularly hard day and find yourself either talking to family or picking up the phone to talk to a family member? Most everyone does. Family is generally at the center of most people's lives, and they become more and more important as we get older.

My family is everything to me. No, I don't mean my immediate family, as I have no children or husband. I am talking about my siblings and the memory of my parents and grandparents. I love my brothers and sister, sisters-in-law and brother-in-law, all of the significant others, and nieces and nephews. I can't imagine life without them. Changes through the years and the additional family members have only added to our group and brought us closer together. I still miss both of my parents, especially my mom.

I wish she could have met her youngest grandchild and have seen the wonderful men and woman the oldest three have become. I want to tell her I had a house for thirteen years, am writing my ninth book, and that I had an art gallery in her memory. Although I know she knows these things already, I miss the human interaction and seeing the surprise in her eyes. My sister has been there for me more times than not, and my brother and sister-in-law are amazingly giving people. My nieces and nephews are growing up and are in high school, away at college, working, or both. I long for the simpler times when everyone was here to enjoy everyone else.

It's very important for those who have family to try to be there for your children's events growing up: all of the plays, performances, dance recitals, birthday parties, graduations, confirmations, moves, and anniversaries. We want our nieces, nephews, brothers, and sisters to know they were loved. Our parents become more precious as we age, and it's important we show them how much they mean to us.

How can we show our love for our family? Call your parents to let them know you are thinking of them, especially if you live far away. Send family "just because" notes to let them know they are loved. Remember special events in big or small ways. If you become a godparent to a niece or nephew, take an active role in his or her life. They'll always remember the times you showed your love and the time spent together. Shovel out your parents' driveway if you live close. Help out one another during hard times—that's what families are for. Unfortunately, some people have toxic families and need to distance themselves . . . so they develop healthy friendships that serve as surrogate families. These loved ones are very important to remember and cherish as well.

I could recount hundreds of things we have done for each other in our family, but there is neither time nor space for this show of love. It's not unusual for family to miss each other and show love long after someone has passed into the next life. Don't apologize for that affection. People will understand. So if you find yourself missing family who are far away or have passed into the next dimension, don't feel alone.

Family is and should be important, and you will never lose your need for them. Enjoy them while they are here, and remember them after they are gone with love.

*Gather those you love around you, whether they are friends or family. They were given to you to help you in good and bad times, to support you when you are feeling low, and to share your joy when you are blessed.*

Without my family and friends, I don't think I would still be here. They have been my support and guiding light in both good and bad times. I have loved them through all of the events in my life but have appreciated them much more when the light went out. My biological sister has been my rock and support. I don't think that a sister could love another any more than I love her. And my sister at heart in Australia has been an inspiration to my soul, showing me how to find happiness, how to love my fellow man, and how to be strong. Despite the distance between us, I feel closer to her than to some people I know here in my own city.

My younger brother and sister-in-law have guided me through teaching and out the other end again, throwing me a lifeline when I needed it the most. My friend, a state over in Minnesota, knows me better than I know myself and brings me back to still waters when I am drowning. My mentor in Australia has shown me what my parents neglected to and accepted me as part of his family when I was lost. Another couple from my last professional job have always had my back during my years of teaching and have called regularly to check on me since my retirement. I could go on and on. And although my parents are gone, I still hear their voices inside my head and feel their comfort and words despite the worlds that separate us.

There are many others who have been part of my life, some who are relatively new. Many I have met through past relationships, and some I have met seemingly by chance. Some have been keepers of my secrets or have given me skills with which to navigate this world. All of these people have played a part in my life, and I wouldn't be the same without them. I truly believe a part of me would be missing if we had never met.

All of us have a great many people who have been placed in our lives for various reasons. These people are like beautiful flowers in the garden of life. Some of the flowers are fragrant and attract bees and other insects, and some are full of color, bringing beauty and excitement to our world. Others produce sweet nectar and attract hummingbirds. Some produce sweet fruits or vegetables when pollinated and provide nourishment.

Finally, some are the weeds in our gardens that steal from the beauty of the rest. These weeds also take nutrients from the flowers, and if not pulled out will kill all of the other plants. But they are also needed in our gardens, for without them, we couldn't appreciate the beauty of the flowers and sustenance of the produce. All must be tended as they grow or weeded from our friendship garden, or the strength of our relationships will fade and die.

The good people in our lives have been given to us to lift us up when we have fallen, share in our joy when we have succeeded, give us strength when we have none left, and help us appreciate the good in the world. These individuals are our earthly angels on loan. Appreciate them and return their friendship in turn. Tend them as you would a precious garden. Water them with love, feed them with support, and you will reap a great harvest of love, which will nourish you and produce flowers that will give your life beauty well into the winter of your life.

*You can love your parents and still disagree with the way you were raised and not be a bad son or daughter. Most of our parents did the very best they could, and you, in turn, must do your best to try to understand them.*

I was so sure I was a bad daughter when I first began talking about my childhood and my formative years with my counselor. How could I even discuss the secrets we all have so carefully kept locked behind closed doors, especially with someone else outside my immediate family? Not that my parents were bad, but like so many other parents of their generation, they lived in a different world, and that world had a profound effect on the way most of their children live today.

I am reminded of the song by Crosby, Stills, and Nash, and Young "Teach Your Children" as I write this about my mom and dad. The lyrics read, "Teach your children well, their father's hell did slowly go by . . . And you of tender years, can't know the fears that your elders grew by . . ."

My dad was a hero of two wars, earning a two bronze stars the Korean Conflict. He never discussed those times with us when we were young except in brief snippets. However, all of us knew my older brother's middle name was given to him in memory of a friend who lost his life in the war, which one, I am not sure. We heard briefly about a time he had been caught behind enemy lines for three days, living on Hershey chocolate bars. We also knew the man who left for the Korean War never returned, just an angry man with severe Post Traumatic Stress Disorder. People didn't even have a name for it back then. Mom just called it "nerves." We didn't have a lot of money to get my dad the help he needed, so we learned to deal with his situation like so many other families of that era did. None of us understood him or his illness.

During my childhood, my dad would be out on construction all week, and we only saw him on weekends. But when we did, he would be very tired, and we would have to be quiet because of his "nerves." So most of the time, if we could, we would be out of the house so as not to make trouble. My mom was alone with five children much of the time, and although we were very good kids, five was still a handful. Mom naturally didn't have a lot of time for any one child, and we occupied ourselves by playing outside with each other, teaching each other games and things we had learned in school. But I do remember times when Mom would help us build things out of Tinker Toys or Lincoln Logs or show us how to paint or draw.

Because of the tension in the house, we had to walk on eggshells. Some of my friends thought my parents were too strict, and some just remember how quiet they had to be at our house when they visited. But it all had to do with the PTSD that was so prevalent in most of the men returning home from the battlefields. That left us very quiet children, unable to cope with loud or boisterous kids in school. Also, because we were out in the country at that time, there were very few children our own age to play with, and most of us grew up shy, lacking in social skills as well.

My parents were also intellectuals, gifted in many areas and knowledgeable in almost everything you could imagine. I thought there was nothing my mom didn't know. My older brother is a gifted writer and was reading Edgar Allen Poe and writing his own music in grade school while I was running around, trying to fit in. I was the one who took care of everything, watching baby brother, then sister, and then another baby brother as they came along. I was the "responsible one": the one everyone relied on and watched over my siblings.

I learned a great deal, but it never gave me the chance to gain that knowledge in the proper way, by being a child and making mistakes. I had a lot of the responsibility in dealing with food preparation, changing diapers, putting babies to sleep, etc. I was needed for this role, and my parents, like many others, had no other options, end of story. I knew they loved me, and although we had our problems, I loved them too.

So, like many other daughters, although I may have disagreed in part with how I was raised, I felt the love my parents had for me and knew they did the very best they knew how. And when judging your own parents for gaps in parenting skills, please try to understand them and remember they lived lives we can barely comprehend as they were from a different time and space. They did the best they could with the skills and knowledge they had.

*Each generation has been raised in a specific set of circumstances. What happened during your parents' generation, or even your siblings' generation, may have affected them in totally different ways.*

My parents were raised during an exceptionally scary time in history. My mom was born the day before the stock market fell in 1929 and lived a life of poverty, like so many others, until adulthood. During my parents' life, there were two wars, WWII and the Korean War, before they reached their thirtieth birthdays. There was very little credit during this time with the exception of loans for houses. Everything was saved for the future unless it spoiled. Polio was rampant, and there was no counseling for PTSD, trauma, or depression.

My life has been unique too. The Vietnam and Gulf Wars were raging before I was thirty and polio was still around when I was very young (the girls up the street contracted it). As I mentioned before, I struggled with abuse in school and trauma from a neighborhood murder as well as the murder of a classmate in high school. There was Kent State, the Kennedy assassinations, and Martin Luther King's murder. I remember watching the coverage of the assassinations at the Munich Olympics in my teens.

When I was out of high school, I was able to go to college twice and, unlike my mom, earn a degree and a teaching certificate. However, we still didn't have counselors until I was older, and most weren't very intuitive. My parents had five kids by the time they were finished and I have none, unless you count my kids at school.

My brother, who is just four years younger than I, never had to experience the trauma of the neighborhood murders when he was young. The Vietnam War was just ending and the Gulf War was now in the news, and polio had been eradicated as a killer/crippler. He was able to go to an updated school for part of his primary school year instead of our one-hundred-year-old institution. He still experienced all of the assassinations that I did, and his fourth birthday even marks the date of JFK's death. He went to college like me and even got his degree in teaching art, just like I did. However, his experience with teaching was far different from mine. I did my student teaching in Australia and he did his here in the United States. He was an aide during his first couple of years, and I got a job as an art teacher right away. Teaching was his first career and my second. He has a wife and a son who will soon be married.

So as you can see, every person's life experience is very different even within families and generations, and each shapes us into the people we become. Please don't compare yourself with anyone around you, even family members, because you could never be like they are. And don't judge others according to your life, as you couldn't imagine the path of their lives or "the fears they grew by" ("Teach Your Children Well," Crosby, Stills, Nash, and Young).

*If you have children, cherish them.
Not everyone is so blessed.*

Not everyone is blessed with children, for various reasons. Some don't find the right man, like me, some can't conceive because of the ways their bodies were formed, and some cannot because of illness or accident. But for whatever reason, it amounts to the same thing: there are many couples and singles all over the world without children in their lives.

Although I had dreams when I was younger of having my own, I am comfortable with where I am now. As a sixty-one-year-old, I certainly wouldn't have the energy, body strength, or flexibility to run after little ones, much less go through school with them. But as I look back on my life, it occurs to me I had *many* children: all of the babies I babysat for as a young teenager, including my own brothers and sister, and all of the students I had in my classes. They might not have been my biological children, but it didn't stop me from loving them and calling them "my kids" all the same.

If you have your own children, count your blessings. Love them unconditionally and show them how to love others as well as themselves. Spend quality time with them as they grow: go to their track meets, their concerts, and graduations. Take them on trips to explore their world and expose them to different cultures, foods, and music. Share their accomplishments with them, as well as your own. Bring them to work with you and share in theirs. Pass on your traditions and your family history. Teach them how to play and enjoy life, but also to work hard. Bring them up to be good and strong adults so they can thrive.

Being an educator, I have often thought parents should have to pass a test before they are allowed to have children, as I have seen too many who don't treat theirs as the special little beings they are. Children are our legacy, our gifts to the world, and should never be a burden. But so often in life, we see families in which the children appear to be only additional mouths to feed for their parents. Consider all of the events that must occur perfectly in order to even conceive these little miracles. They are truly gifts of creation.

If children are not what you like, then for heaven's sake, don't have them, or put them up for adoption. Let them be someone else's joy. You can be the eccentric aunt or uncle who comes to play with nieces and nephews and then has the freedom to go home. If you can't have your own children, there is always foster care and adoption, or you may consider being a nanny for a family, participating in Big Brothers and Sisters, or spend time babysitting the neighborhood children.

So show your own children that you love them by how you treat them and raise them. Count them as a blessing and invest in their lives with love, and you will continue to be blessed.

*Keep your life free from people who are negative and critical. Toxic people, just like toxic situations, will eventually kill you. Get rid of them before they destroy you!*

How many of you have been in situations or attached to people who made your skin crawl? They are the people who represent everything you abhor. I worked at several places with people like this throughout the years. They made life miserable, eventually making me sick. In retrospect, it would have been much wiser for me to leave each situation earlier than to let their infection spread through me as it eventually did.

Toxic, according to the Merriam Webster Dictionary, is defined as, "Containing or being poisonous material especially when capable of causing death or serious debilitation . . ." Relationships and situations can become toxic because of the unhealthy situations in our everyday lives. So many times it is more efficient to cut your losses and leave rather than stick it out. There have been times when friends have asked me questions such as, "Should I stay in my present situation or should I leave? I am so unhappy! Is it too late to start over? A lot of times we are just looking for someone to give us permission to leave and be happy.

Only you can answer this question for yourself. Ask yourself, is your situation verbally, mentally, or physically abusive? If it is, then it's time to leave. Get some help and leave everything but your children if you have to. Are you being bullied at work and can't stand up for yourself for fear of losing your job? Then it's time to look for other work. Is a friend treating you badly or engaging in dangerous or risky activities and taking you along for the ride? Then it is time to get off of that train. But if you are talking about a subtler problem, you have got to ask yourself again whether it is making you ill or destroying your happiness. Perhaps you should discuss it with the other person if possible. However, many times, the situation can be so toxic you must leave and begin again.

Surround yourself with people and situations that lift you up and not bring you down. Make your lists of positives and negatives, talk to friends and relatives, get advice from a counselor, and make the decision that is right for *you*. But remember, you will have to live with it. So choose the one that will let you live the life you were meant to, happy and healthy.

# Part Eleven

Kindness, Compassion, and the Golden Rule

*Make your life more about love
than anything else.*

Very few lines in movies have moved me as much as one of the last in the movie *Ghost* when Sam was saying goodbye to Molly. As he stood in front of the host of angels, he said, "It's amazing, Molly! The love inside, you take it with you!"

After all of the scenes where the demons carry the souls down to the underworld (which still gives me the creeps, by the way), this scene is so uplifting and finishes the movie with a most remarkable happy ending. I truly believe that *is* what we take with us when we go to the hereafter. We take the love and the caring (the positive energy) we spend in this world.

Whether you believe in the hereafter is not the point. The point is that we, as well as the world around us, need more love. We hear about hate and violence all over the news, whether it's in our own backyards or across the world. What we really need to see more of is the sharing and caring that goes on each day and make it part of our lives.

For me, it's so much more fun to give gifts than to receive them. I love to see the joy giving brings to others. I love to share my time, help others with their lives, or drop a note in the mail or on Facebook to let someone know how special they are. I truly believe I get more out of the deal, however, for I feel this love too. Being on the receiving end is wonderful as well. I still remember the day I moved into my house in Avoca Beach, Australia, and the neighbors brought me a cake to welcome me. The feeling of love and welcome bubbled up in my heart and overflowed, just like it is now.

I have two friends who spend some time each year either working to raise money for third world countries or traveling to them in person in order to help the people who are struggling there. It has been heartwarming to watch the joy on the faces of these people in photos, as well as in the eyes of my friends.

Love isn't so much a feeling or an emotion: it's the *action* of love by which we *show* others. We can see the love in the eyes of the recipients because of *the gifts* of life, education, and love that have been shared with them. Love always begins with an action and will return to us some day in some way. I must admit I have become hooked watching my friends and their humanitarian gestures and hope one day to be able to join them. But for the time being, I will continue to love those around me here in the Midwest.

How can we show love to those around us? These gestures don't have to be on a grand scale, but more often can be shown in the small things we do. You might mow a neighbor's lawn, help shovel their driveway, or put down salt when it's slippery. You may go sit with a friend who is sick or care for their children or dog. There was recently a 24-hour power outage in my city, and although I wasn't part of it, some of my friends were. I read passages on Facebook of how neighbors helped one another through the outage and the sweltering heat they endured following a rainstorm. It was truly uplifting.

Love your family, your friends, your relatives, your in-laws, and your neighbors. Let them know you care about them in any way you can. You will always come out a winner no matter what!

*Always try to put yourself in someone else's shoes and walk around before you judge. You may be surprised by how they feel.*

I remember a family of girls in grade school who lived in a neighborhood near us. Everyone in the school shunned them, mainly because they never bathed properly. Unfortunately, I followed the crowd. What I didn't know at the time was that they were extremely poor. Like everyone else, because I was a child and didn't know any better, I didn't take time to become their friends. This was my loss, as they were the sweetest girls! I don't remember them in high school, so they must have moved away. But I have always wondered what happened to them.

I have certainly been on the other end of this type of behavior in life as well, especially as an overweight and partially disabled senior in the job market today. Many people don't understand what it is like to be in my position or even try to walk in my shoes. It's a different situation as the girls from my grade school, but it has the same results. Many times it's very hard to handle. We tend to judge far too often in our society on what we see without understanding, but the saddest part is we never take the time to even try.

We can never truly step into someone else's shoes and walk around in them, but we can imagine how we might feel in their situation because of what we have gone through in our own lives. I have never been without work since I was eighteen with the exception of when I was in college, so these last five years have been hard on my self-concept and pocketbook. It has taken me all of this time to come to terms with who I am and my situation. However, I have been very fortunate, as I have many others who have reached out to help me make the transition. What happens to people who don't have a support system?!

After what I have been through, I will never look at another poor person, those who lack social skills, those with disabilities, or someone struggling in society in the same way again. I will always remember those girls from my childhood and always try to walk in the shoes of others for a while to learn the pain of their journey first hand. Maybe we can all try to do the same.

*Treat other people as you want to be treated;
Golden Rule, old expression, great advice.*

I am sitting in a doctor's waiting room as I write this, waiting for the first in my series of rabies shots. A dog bit me this morning. I was leaving a drug store when I spotted what looked like a nice young man with his dog. The owner had him on a leash, and wanting to be friendly and polite, I asked if I could pet him. The owner assured me it was all right, but to follow dog protocol and let him smell me first. I slowly reached out a fist so the pooch could sniff me and chomp! Right down on the knuckle of my middle finger. I should have realized this wasn't a good situation when the guy didn't even ask me if I was okay, but instead said the dog was very protective of him. (Well then, why say it was okay to pet him, right?) With blood dripping all over, I told him I would be right back and wanted to clean up before I got it all over my clothing. Second mistake. When I returned, both dog and owner were gone. Long story short, I'm now waiting for my first shots. I'm scared, tired, and hungry, having not eaten since breakfast. I am annoyed at the dog, his owner, myself, and the people who have been making me sit here waiting for four hours.

Why can't people live by the Golden Rule and treat others as they would want to be treated?! If the owner had been more responsible, I wouldn't have to go through the pain of the shots, the cost, and all of the anxiety that comes with them. All he would have had to do would have been to have his dog quarantined for a couple of days, and I could have spent my day and money in better pursuits. Now I have to come back four more times for these awful shots. My hand is swollen, my finger hurts, and the police said without a picture, license plate, or car model, the dog's owner will probably never be caught!

No matter how old I get, I am still amazed by some people's lack of responsibility and respect for one another and what lengths they will go through to cover their own backsides.

PLEASE follow the Golden Rule. I have always stressed this in my classes, and this is what I try to live by. We were taught to do this as children in our home and grade school. So why do we suddenly get amnesia when it might get us into trouble? If you want to make the world a better place and make certain others treat you well, this is the first step. Loving one another means looking out for what is best for others as well as ourselves.

*Pay it forward.*

The first time I heard the phrase, "pay it forward" was when the movie with the same name starring Kevin Spacey, Helen Hunt, and Haley Joel Osment was in the theaters. The concept for this has been around a long time, but the phrase was actually coined by Lily Hardy Hammond, in a 1916 book that she wrote called, *In the Garden of Delight*. The phrase means doing a good deed for someone and asking them to pass it on to others.

The first time I experienced this in practice was in the town I taught in for most of my teaching career. One of the business townspeople paid for my coffee one morning and asked me to pass the favor on to someone else. This was done on more than one occasion. So I have used my move to give away some of my items to neighbors and asked them to do the same for others as well. It felt so good to see the expressions of delight on their faces.

Many people in our society are struggling with money, health issues, and unemployment today because of our economy. If you are one of these, I can certainly empathize. So how can we pay it forward on a fixed or challenged income? To save money, I often put up apples and make my own yogurt. Most people don't have the time or know how to do these things today. Share some of these items with others as a pay-it-forward kindness.

If you don't have time to make something, buy coffee for someone in the line at Starbucks, like my friend did. If you know someone is especially busy, run a casserole over to their house some evening to help and ask them to pass it on. Another way to do this is to re-gift unopened items that aren't being used and give them to families that are in need. Then ask them to be creative to share something with others. Why not use your talents for arts and crafts to pass something on? People always appreciate a beautiful picture or piece of craftwork that is homemade.

Paying it forward gives as much to the person giving as the one on the receiving end, if not more. Whoever pays something forward experiences the joy and warmth of knowing they have done something for someone else and that they have planted a seed that will continue to grow. So if you are out and about, pay for a stranger's snack or soda and watch the magic begin. It will warm your heart and perhaps change your day.

*Be a good neighbor and the first to step up when your help is needed. Your neighbors will always remember what you did for them, and you will always have a friend.*

When I was young, my mother was very active in our neighborhood helping others. But I will always remember her supporting one of my teachers who lost her house and her dogs in a fire while I was in grade school. My mom, together with the neighbors, had a shower to help her with what she and her family had lost. Now, years later, this former teacher is my friend, and she still remembers what my mother did for her. Such a small act of kindness remembered for a lifetime!

The first year after I retired, I had very little to do around Christmas, as substitute teaching was sparse, so I decided to bake cookies and make candy to fill my time. Before long, I had over twenty-five different kinds of treats with at least two-dozen of each type. This was far too many for myself obviously, so I decided to give plates away. I gave them to relatives, friends, and neighbors. When I delivered a plate to one of my older neighbors, she broke into tears as she accepted the cookies. I never realized such a simple gesture would make such a difference to someone else. I went home with tears of joy, and soon this lady returned the kindness by looking in on me when I was sick.

In today's busy world, we don't always have time to know our neighbors, much less establish a relationship with them. This is much different from when my parents and I were young, as we knew everyone for blocks around. But it's so important for us to establish a good relationship with those who live near us, as they are our community family. They will need our help from time to time.

What can you do to help those around you? Some join a church and make quilts, establishing community relationships. Some work in a soup kitchen and help those who are struggling financially to have warm food. Some volunteer in their local schools with the students to establish relationships there. Where does your heart lie?

With your immediate neighbors or community neighbors? Do you find helping out your friends when they are in need fulfills you? My sister spent countless hours watching the neighbor's baby when he was little to help out a young struggling mother because she could.

Remember, the kindness you show to others will always come back to you in some way, if only in the smile on the recipient's face!

*If you make it one of your goals to make others feel good about who they are, you will never be in need of friends.*

As I have already said, I have many friends who are absolutely amazing people, and I realize how very fortunate I am. But there is one friend in particular who has made it his mission to make people feel good about who they are on a daily basis. He knows how to make everyone feel center stage and is always there to give others a compliment.

Wouldn't it be nice if everyone would be this considerate? However, we all know that's not how the real world works. Today we live in the "me generation" and find that very often people forget about their neighbor. We forget sometimes we need to take the first step in making a difference in this world. Our purpose for being here isn't so much in what we do for ourselves, but in what we do for those around us. So shouldn't it follow that we should all try to make this a priority?

How can you make others feel great about who they are? The first step is to listen to what they have to say. This will let them know they are truly important. You also need to make them feel good about what they are doing, even if it is the smallest thing. There is plenty of time for criticism in the future, and when making a correction, it should always be a constructive one so they can learn. All good friends, associates, and bosses need to be great teachers, educating others on how to do a better job at work and how to be a better person in the school of life. By doing this, we will make everyone feel great!

So the next time you are dealing with people, whether friends, acquaintances, or employees, remember what my Australian friend told me so very long ago. If you make it one of your goals to make others feel good about who they are, you will never be in need of friends. If you do this, you will always have people singing your praises and basking in the memory of their time with you and always have a friend.

*Nothing is free in life that takes time.*

Time is truly our most precious commodity, more precious than gold or all of the jewels in the world. Limitless people would gladly give all they have for just one more hour on earth. However, it's not up to us to say when we slip these earthly bonds.

There are so many gimmicks on the Internet and television that tell you something is free, but by the time you fill in all of the blanks, answer all of the questions, and send in all of the forms, you sometimes have spent hours on a "free" item. This isn't free by any means if it takes part of our lives. We can always replace items, but our time is lost forever. Time is very precious and finite. None of us knows exactly how much we have to spend, so we must treat it as the precious item it is and make the most of every second.

Everyone has someone they have lost and would give anything to spend time with again. My special someone is my mother. She was taken from us when she was sixty-seven, which is far too young by any means. Although I was glad I was smart enough to take care of all of the misunderstandings in our lives before she really got sick, I didn't realize how soon she would go or how to tell her how much I appreciated her while she was here. Sometimes the most precious thing we can do with our time is to spend it with those we love, whether it is tucking them in bed, visiting them in a nursing home, or surprising them with a gift.

The same thing is true with your life mission. Once you have found it, don't take your time for granted: run with your mission as if you were trying to make a touchdown. I didn't know what mine was until quite recently, but everything in me tells me not to waste my time, but to get this mission done as soon as possible.

So whether you are young or in the winter of your life, take some of that "free" time of yours and do something useful, lasting, loving, or creative with it. Sprinkle some of your precious hours on others and make the world a more beautiful place than you found it.

*Always have a backup plan in life. You never know when you are going to get the rug pulled out from under you.*

My life plan was to work as an art educator until I was in my mid-sixties, then retire with my 401K, my teaching pension, and my Social Security. I planned to travel every few years and possibly take the yearly winter snowbird trip my parents had taken, only to Florida. *That was the plan.* I had done everything right and worked very hard in a job I believed would make a difference in the world. Then, when everything fell apart, I had NO backup plan whatsoever.

I had forgotten one of the basic rules of the Boy Scout code, "Be prepared." My mother had been the local Boy Scout leader when I was young, and every week we would gather in our living room sitting in a circle cross-legged, in the middle of the floor. I was an honorary member, of course, being a girl, as I needed to be part of everything going on at home.

Like others, I usually followed all of the rules in life, got mostly As and Bs throughout my schooling, and went on to get a college degree and a teaching certificate. I remained in the teaching profession because it used many of my talents, made a difference in the lives of children, and had a good retirement program. It wasn't easy being a teacher, and most people in education can tell you the first few years can be quite challenging. But I stuck it out. My students did well at the local, state, and national levels in competitions, and I was very proud of what they had accomplished.

However, in 2012, when I was suddenly faced with the decision to retire, due to cuts in the arts and education, I wondered what I had done wrong. For those of you facing similar situations, my answer to this is probably nothing, except that most employers have done away with loyalty in the present economy and have opted for cutting those higher up on the pay scale. Is this fair? Absolutely not! But it's something that is a part of our present world we must deal with. Do they prepare you for a transition such as this in school? Again, my answer is no. However, if I had only remembered the Boy Scout motto "Be prepared," I could have saved myself much pain and financial burden.

Therefore, you should always have an alternate plan in mind to make the bumps in the road of life more manageable. Always be thinking two or three steps down the road so that your next step is stable, like playing a game of chess. What could you do if you were to leave your present position? If your answer is nothing, then perhaps it's time to begin looking into a new field or area that would allow you to make your segue to a new position or job easier.

Many people climb corporate ladders to become principals or department heads, but there are also many more like myself who have never had the desire to be in charge of so much. Perhaps you might start a nighttime or weekend business that could take off if plans should change. Working from home without the problems and cost of housing an office staff is quickly becoming a company standard. There are endless possibilities out there if you look long enough.

The secret is to give yourself enough time while you are still in your present job so that you don't panic if your job isn't there tomorrow. Look at your position in life and always give yourself future alternatives so that you don't fall down that rabbit hole. And never forget the Boy Scout motto to be prepared.

*Everything comes at a cost. Some things are harder than others to obtain. It just depends on how much you are willing to work to get them.*

When I was growing up, the thought of *not* attending college never crossed my mind. I don't think we really had an option in our family. But whatever the circumstances, I worked construction jobs to pay my way through. It was tough work, but it was outside summer employment, so I enjoyed it. I never considered the cost or the effort. It was just something that needed to be done, much like stepping up when my mom got sick.

When it came to buying a house, I could have afforded a much more expensive home than I eventually bought, but I wanted the option of traveling and knew I couldn't afford both. Traveling was my priority. I now live in a small, one-bedroom apartment so I can afford to work on my health and take small trips. Most of us will have to forego items in life, unless we are wealthy, in order to get the things we really want or need. What are you willing to do to make money or save for something you want? Are you willing to relocate within your country or move somewhere overseas? Are you willing to work nights, weekends, or holidays? What is the bottom line for your goal?

Some people talk about having it all, but in reality, there is always something that is left behind in balancing our lives. When I was going to college the first time, I left behind nights and weekends with friends in favor of better grades and saving money. Education was most important to me. How hard are you willing to work, and what are you willing to do to see your dreams come true? Always keep in mind how this will affect you, and how it will affect your relationships, your pocketbook, and your other dreams.

Even though dreams are important, we must also keep a balance in our lives. Consider too your physical and mental health. Are you strong enough to pursue these dreams and do the job required to attain them? I certainly couldn't handle a full-time job within the public school system, a travel office, or a cruise ship at my age, regardless of whether I wanted it or not. You may have to consider an alternate route or a modified goal in order to achieve your dream.

But anything is possible. I once met a woman on one of my trips Down Under who married an Australian in order to stay within the country. Although this is an extreme example and not something I would condone, it demonstrates the lengths some are willing to go to get what they feel they need or want.

There are always decisions we will have to make in life: how hard do we want to work, how much do we want to make, do we want a family, do we want to travel, do we want . . . ? Always keep in mind the price you are willing to pay for those choices.

# Part Twelve

## Your Creative Side

*Be creative with something in your life.*

I have been creative since I can remember. Some of my first memories involve building with blocks, sand, and snow and painting with my mom's magic watercolors. One of my favorite childhood memories was building marble mazes out of blocks and watching the marbles go from top to bottom. As I grew, I learned to draw, paint with oils, and build with clay. Now I channel my creativity through writing and photography. I also use Photoshop to create imaginary pictures to go along with some of my poems and stories.

My sister, on the other hand, uses her creativity in flower gardening, designing and creating stained glass windows, and working on artwork for her church. My older brother writes short stories and plays the violin while working with older people in art, music, and writing to help improve their memories. My younger brother is an art teacher as well as a children's book author. He draws a picture a day, works on a comic strip, and writes ukulele songs in his spare time. My youngest brother used to make hobo art, but now builds birdhouses and works with wood.

The truth is we can be creative with anything in our lives. We can use our creativity at home to build tree houses and decks, and paint murals on our walls, or decorate our houses. We can paint with words and create stories or poems. Our trees and leftover tree trunks can be carved into sculptures. Farmers can create mazes in their cornfields or make a tractor out of bales of hay. We can build toy models or learn how to cook and bake or decorate.

Some people use their bodies to be creative in sports, such as figure skating, ballet, or ballroom dancing. We all know of someone who is gifted at playing a musical instrument or singing. We also can take part in acrobatic skiing, gymnastics, or equestrian sports. There is no limit to the length of this list. And if you are extremely creative, you can invent new activities for yourself and others to enjoy.

We were made to be creative beings, so find something that sparks your imagination and let your inner creative spirit go crazy. You might be surprised at what you come up with. You and the world will be better because of it.

*Listen to good music.*

Just as beauty is in the eye of the beholder, good music is too. I am very selective about the music I listen to. All of the CD players in my cars have gotten a workout. When I drive, which is quite often, I usually play my CDs or plug in my iPhone and turn on my Pandora app. Some of what others thrive on today wouldn't be my first choice, and I no longer try to keep up with the latest trends in music. If I hear something that is pleasant to me, I investigate it and usually add it to my playlist.

My music list include artists such as Jack Johnson, Norah Jones, Diana Krall, John Mayer, Sarah McLaughlin, Don McLean, Led Zepplin, Fleetwood Mac, Pink Floyd, Miles Davis, Bob Marley, Leonard Cohen, Josh Groban, Crosby, Stills and Nash, and Procol Harum; albums such as *Dark Side of The Moon*, *Abbey Road*, *Bridge Over Troubled Waters*, *American Pie*, *Tapestry*, *Every Good Boy Deserves Favor*, *Déjà Vu*, *Kind of Blue*; and classical classics such as Pavarotti, *Danse Macabre* by Camille Saint-Saëns, *Night on Bald Mountain* by Mussorgsky, *Peter and the Wolf* by Sergei Prokofiev, and *Bolero* by Ravel. I love good music.

When I am having a particularly blue day or one that is challenging me emotionally, I put on my go-to list of uplifting songs. These include:

"Here Comes The Sun" – The Beatles
"Somewhere Over The Rainbow / What A Wonderful World" – Israel "IZ" Kamakawiwo'ole
"What a Wonderful World" – Louis Armstrong
"In Your Shoes" – Sarah McLachlan
"Ordinary Miracle" – Sarah McLachlan
"Maui-Waui" – Chuck Mangione
"Walking On Sunshine" – Katrina and the Waves

"Good Vibrations" – The Beach Boys
"Take On Me" – A-ha
"Viva La Vida" – Coldplay
"Dancing in the Moonlight" – King Harvest
"Home" – Michael Bublé
"I Am Woman" – Helen Reddy
"I Will Survive" – Gloria Gaynor
"Put Your Records On" – Corinne Bailey Rae
"I'm Yours" – Jason Mraz
"In My Life" (I Love You More) – The Beatles
"Hallelujah" – Jeff Buckley

However, many like country, others opera, and still others serious classical. Although some of these wouldn't be my choice, they are still good music. Whatever relaxes or motivates you, makes you thoughtful or inspires you to do something of your own, listen to it and enjoy. You might even take up an instrument and learn how to play. I played the flute for years, and although my nephew now has it, I had many years of enjoyment playing it through school and as an adult.

Whether you are a musician, or just a listener, or a little of both, remember the old expression that music calms the savage beast, but it also lifts the heart and inspires the soul. And whatever you choose as your favorites, enjoy them as you would a good bottle of cognac: drink it in and savor every minute of it, then share it with others.

*Use your energy to build
up and not to destroy.*

I will never for the life of me understand why some people use their limited energy to purposefully destroy something or someone instead of building them up. It's the one thing I simply cannot wrap my head around. When I listen to the news, there are always stories about some individual or group bombing something, shooting someone, or destroying property.

So much of the beauty and people in the world has been destroyed because of war and hatred. This can most recently be illustrated by the bombings of the World Trade Towers, the approximate seventeen million people who were killed in the Holocaust, and the latest genocide in Syria. But consider the events that happen within our own cities and small towns. What about people who destroy gravestones in cemeteries, or those who create worms and viruses that attack computers? What about arsonists and drive-by shootings? Don't people have better things to do with their time than this? I ask myself this question each time I listen to the news.

As an artist, I sometimes cry over the thousands of pieces of artwork that are no longer here for us to enjoy or are damaged because of acts of vandalism or ignorance: the Sphinx, used by Napoleon and his army for target practice; the *David* and *The Pieta*, both damaged by deranged vandals; the Taliban government who destroyed the Buddhas of Bamyan; much of the Medieval and Renaissance religious art that was destroyed in Protestant areas in Europe during the Reformation; and the tens of thousands of artworks that were destroyed in World War II by Nazi Germany and in Japan with the bombing of Nagasaki and Hiroshima.

How do you use your energies for positive actions when you are so angry and hurt that all you want to do is destroy and lash out at others? Anger is a natural result of being wronged, and we naturally want to retaliate. But this only makes a situation worse. First, we should respond without anger and give ourselves time to calm down and heal. One of the things I see happening now is people reaching out in love. It is hard, if not impossible, to get past the violence on our own that comes with anger and hurt. Ask for help, get counseling, confront those who have wronged you, look beyond the immediate to what caused your hurt to begin with, and use your energies and feelings to protest with positive actions through dance, art, or music. Turn what is ugly into something that sends a message and is beautiful. One of my friends posted a comment on Facebook this morning about the song, "If I Had a Hammer" by Peter, Paul and Mary. I find this a very appropriate illustration to warn people and share our love in today's world.

> If I had a hammer
> I'd hammer in the morning
> I'd hammer in the evening
> All over this land
> I'd hammer out danger
> I'd hammer out a warning
> I'd hammer out love between
> My brothers and my sisters
> All over this land, uh

Just consider this: if all of our angry energy was used for the good, what a wonderful planet we would live in. So if you find you are angry with someone or just in a bad situation, take the time to think about how you can use the energy you have to build up and not destroy. I use mine to create poetry and make other visual art, others may run or swim, and still others may turn their anger into action to help change the world. You can still release your anger, but in a positive way. In doing so, you will be leaving a legacy of beauty instead of hate and destruction. Peace.

*If you find something you are good at,
give it all you've got! Anything less
is a waste of your gift.*

I have been given many gifts, and I am grateful for each and every one of them. At the present time, I am working on two of them; completing one of my books and organizing my photography. I try to put some time aside each day to work on one or both, and despite having a summer job, I will continue to work on them.

Gifts involve discipline to make them shine the way they were intended, and discipline involves hard work. When I was in my last year of school studying to be an illustrator, I would spend at least forty hours a week just perfecting my drawing skills. When I was learning Italian, I spent one-half hour to four hours a day on it, and I have lost track of how much time and money I have spent on getting well. My mother always told those in our family if we did something, it was worth doing well. So too it is with our gifts. If we want our gifts to shine, we must spend time polishing them.

It is true that some gifts are with us only for a season, as age and injury can strip them from us. But that doesn't mean we should give up on them. It just means we need to see what else is waiting for us when one door closes. Because of the arthritis in my back, I can't draw like I used to over a table, but I can use a laptop that is propped up. Though I cannot climb mountains at my age, I can swim under the sea to enjoy a different type of beauty, and though I choose not to teach in the classroom anymore, it doesn't mean I can't teach from inside a book. So we evolve along with our gifts to enjoy a portion of life we never would have seen if we had continued along the same path.

The gifts we are given come back to us as well. I enjoy what I do tremendously. As we grow, we have to let go of what no longer makes us happy or benefits us or others. Holding on to it is a bit like trying to keep a great dinner in the refrigerator; after its time, it becomes toxic and can kill us. So enjoy your gift and share it in its season but be willing to grow and mature. If I hadn't been willing to do so, I would have missed out on so much beauty in life.

Be vigilant when working on your gifts and make them shine. They are blessings for us to use and share with the world. But if they should be taken from you in some way, look around your world for other blessings and embrace them along your new path in life.

*Memories are some of the most priceless treasures we own. Record yours in some way, whether it is through journaling, in movies, or in pictures. Then share them with others to enjoy.*

All of us collect memories in life, whether in our own mind's eye, in pictures, in items we save, or in the things we leave for others to enjoy and learn from. It's part of the human experience. Since humans began to walk this earth, there have been attempts to pass on what people have learned, seen, and experienced for generations to follow. Some of these items can be found in the caves of Lascaux in France and the Kakadu Rock paintings in Australia, in the paintings and sculptures of artists such as Michelangelo and Leonardo da Vinci, and the philosophical writings of Socrates and Thales.

My dad was very good at keeping pictures labeled and creating albums with detailed descriptions of who was featured in the photos and where they were taken. He had numerous albums of the two branches of service he served in and the wars in which he took part. He also kept a picture book of each of us kids. My mother on the other hand, kept a journal during most of the trips she went on and wrote beautiful poems to describe some of her experiences.

I draw and paint some of the beautiful places I have been and have taken literally thousands of photos while traveling. I like to write poetry as well that expresses my innermost emotions for others to enjoy. My older brother writes short stories to capture some of his memories and has priceless films from when we were young. My younger brother creates movie videos of events and gatherings so that we have these in the future. Before my mom passed away, this brother also recorded several hours of her talking about her life and history for the grandchildren to listen to. Also, my brother-in-law had the forethought to take a video of her reading to one of my nieces, a priceless legacy for our family. What precious treasures these memories are to our family and to those who will come after when we have gone!

How are you saving your memories? Are you writing down your life history, your memoirs, travels, creating art, music, or videos for others to enjoy? Will your descendants or your friends know what you have learned in life and pass on your lessons? Today it is so easy to go to a site like Snapfish and in a very short time, and for a reasonable cost, have a priceless family book to share! There are so many ways for you to leave part of yourself behind—the sky is the limit. So what are you waiting for? Choose a vehicle that fits your personality and leave behind a legacy for your friends and family to remember you by!

# Part Thirteen

## Heart Health

*Guard your heart above all else,
for it determines the course of your life.
— Proverbs 4:23*

When I read this, I felt it was something I absolutely had to include in this book, as it states what I learned far better than I ever could. My heart has so many cracks and cleat marks in it that it is nearly unrecognizable. Yet out of the broken shards of my heart a bigger, stronger one has emerged.

I used to think a broken heart would never mend. But now I believe everyone must feel that way. I truly believe all of those cracks and cleat marks have been placed upon my heart for a purpose. They have made my heart more tender and malleable in order to sense other people's pain and help them. Those of you who have been able to protect this precious muscle we call a heart, I applaud you. However, for better or worse, most of us have or will feel the pain of a dead relationship or a serious disappointment sometime in our lives.

How do you guard your heart from being broken in the first place? That is a good question! Our heart is the pump that sends blood-carrying oxygen to our whole body. But it is also that symbolic part of our body that houses our emotions. When people experience a trauma, their hearts literally ache. I have often said physical trauma is much easier to recover from than emotional pain, as it takes much longer for one's emotional self to heal.

However, we can do a lot to protect ourselves from emotional trauma. This can be achieved by, first, staying away from those we know who are not good for us. My mother always warned us to keep away from people who were bad influences on us while we were growing up. She had a sixth sense in knowing when we didn't follow her advice, as these kids and their behaviors would rub off on us. Don't associate with those who might lead you down the wrong path. Many of our experiences will come about as a result of those we befriend.

Next, let your intuition guide you with those you let into your heart. Your subconscious will pick up red flags much quicker than you do. If it feels wrong, it probably is.

Make certain you place guards around your heart and protect it from unnecessary trauma, run away if something feels wrong, and make sure you are ready with a package of bandages if it does get hurt along life's path. Your heart will take you places that are far beyond the imagination in life, so keep it safe!

*Love does not set conditions. It is colorblind, and does not consider age, weight, illness, time, distance, gender, species, disability, or even death.*

There are several people I love like family besides my siblings and relatives. Some live very far away and some, from my childhood, live in different parts of the United States. We all share a bond that cannot be broken. We can go for years without talking or seeing each other and pick up right where we left off. We are there for each other during tough times or times of loss. Some of those I love are in their eighties, and some are much younger than myself. I love men, women, children, and even dogs! Two of my best friends live in Australia, and I am always amazed to realize we have remained like family for over twenty-nine years. Today, in this age of high tech with Facebook and Skype, it is so much easier to connect than years ago, when snail mail and costly long-distance calls were the norm.

You will find out who your true friends are when you are sick, depressed, or struggling emotionally or financially. Friends who love you don't need an excuse to send you a card or a package, or to just say hi. They don't care how you look, as long as you are happy and healthy.

One of the truly unselfish events I've experienced in my life was what my friends did for me when I was in Australia in 1997. My father called me early one morning to tell me that my mom's health was failing and that I must come home right away. My friends immediately jumped into action, both taking off a full day of work, organizing an emergency flight home, and driving me down to the Sydney Airport. Both waited with me until my flight was ready to leave. I cannot think of a better way to show your love than being there for a friend in a time of need!

When my mother had her cancer surgery, it left her disfigured. I helped her change her bandages and still remember with stark clarity the two lines of sutures. I felt very bad for her, but it never changed how I felt about her. In fact, it made me love and appreciate her more. My dad changed his work schedule from on-the-road construction during the summer to a schedule that let him come home every night. We all chipped in to take over some of the work, no questions asked.

When I met my friend Scott, who had Hodgkin's disease, I was quite surprised when he informed me I was the only one who had treated him like a normal person, not like he had a contagious disease. I could not wrap my mind around this concept. Sure, it was a serious disease, but it shouldn't cause that sort of reaction. He had even lost a girlfriend due to it, which still blows my mind. Many people with disabilities from wars and accidents, birth defects, and life-threatening illnesses go on to live relatively normal and productive lives. This shouldn't make any difference to those who truly love them.

People who are minorities in narrow-minded communities have a hard time as well. One of my students came to me crying one day. When I asked her why she was upset, she told me that other students had teased her because of her color and deafness. She was an adopted, full-blooded South American native of Mayan descent. She was beautiful—black curly hair, perfect complexion, big black eyes, with the whitest, most gorgeous teeth you ever wanted to see. My heart broke for her. I told her they were jealous because she was so beautiful.

Age and weight are also disabilities in our society. Being in my early sixtyies and overweight, I see it every day. Dating proved a huge problem in the past because of both. But if someone doesn't like me because I am struggling with my weight, or if someone is turned off by my age and health, then they don't deserve to love me or be in my life. End of story.

Love yourself, and when you find someone else who is willing to look beyond the obvious, you know you have found someone who loves you too and will always stand beside you.

*When your heart is breaking and your whole world comes to a screeching halt, it is hard to watch everyone else's life go on as normal.*

I remember vividly when one of my best childhood friends lost her dad while we were both still in our early twenties. As she walked down our old childhood street pushing her young daughter in a stroller, she made a comment that I have never forgotten. She asked me why everyone else's world got to go on as normal while hers was shattered. I didn't have an answer for her, nor did I totally understand what she meant until my own mother passed away over twenty years later. It took two years for me to stop crying every day over this loss. I learned unless you have gone through a trauma like this yourself, there is no way for you to understand the depth of another person's sorrow. There are very few days that go by during which I don't think of my mother or the lesson my friend taught me.

The death of a relationship is another pain that will bring you to your knees and can leave you grieving for years. Although I am now thankful things didn't work out with my last long-term relationship, at the time I grieved it like a death. The only thing that got me through it was writing poetry about my pain and talking with my family and friends. I knew every one of them had either gone through a painful divorce or the death of a parent, so they were able to understand.

There is one pain I have not experienced nor will I ever be able to because I don't have children. Losing a child, I am told, is the greatest pain of all. Two of my friends have lost children during the past year, and their posts on Facebook are heart-wrenching. I can't even begin to imagine what people go through when that happens. I would imagine it is a minute-to-minute struggle for years.

The one thing to remember is everyone experiences the pain of loss and heartache sometime in their lives, and no one is immune. Some experience it younger, like my friend, but most experience it in their forties, fifties, and sixties when parents, spouses, and significant others pass and they go through the heartache that follows. We are given each other to lean on for support: our shoulders to lean on and our arms to wrap each other in during times of need.

*The best revenge for any painful breakup is to be happy you weren't stuck with that person any longer and to believe there is a better mate for you.*

Many songs have been composed and will continue to be written about breakups and broken hearts. It is something that has happened for almost as long as history has been recorded. And I know everyone, or almost everyone, has gone through this process. Those of you who haven't, count yourself as *very* fortunate! Almost everyone knows it feels like a death has taken place, and so it has: the death of a relationship.

When it happens, you go through all of the stages of losing a loved one: a desire to understand, denial, bargaining, perhaps trying to make the relationship work again, getting angry, acceptance, and then getting on with your life. Most of us will go through a period of sadness or depression. I, like most others, spent more than my fair share of time in depression. But such sadness didn't do anyone any good except hurt me. I wound up putting on a significant amount of weight after my last serious breakup. True, most of mine was illness related, but the feeling of being rejected didn't help. It took me five years to completely recover, and because the relationship had only lasted four years, it wasn't even a fair trade!

I have learned during my forty-five years of dating that breakups generally happen for a reason. They protect us from a potentially worse situation. If someone drops you, you really don't want him or her anyway, as they do not know how to appreciate or treat you. If you break up with them, then you have already decided they are not for you.

So don't be angry. When a breakup occurs, be sad for the loss, but don't spend your life mourning it. Get out and live your life, and remember, the best revenge for any painful breakup is to beam with happiness and look fantastic when *anyone* sees you, and if you *should* happen to run into your ex, it will be obvious you have moved on. They will probably always wonder what they missed out on, and you won't even care!

*Own a pet. They will love you unconditionally.*

Animals are amazing creatures, and their love is unconditional. My sister has a small Havanese dog named Bella Mia, and we love her to death. I never really knew how much an animal could love someone until I met her. I have taken care of her several times while the family was away on vacation, and now when I visit, she gets so excited she literally barks herself hoarse. She is all over me, and her kisses are seemingly endless. We are buddies. But Bella is thirteen, and even though I hate to think of it, she will only be with us a few more years. So she will be getting a little sister to play with and to show the ropes to in about a week. Her sister's name is Lola.

That was a year ago. Lola has moved in, and, unfortunately, our poor Bella Mia has crossed over the rainbow bridge. Although I still miss Bella, Lola has won my heart and has become my irreplaceable little buddy. I always look forward to that five-pound bundle of energy jumping up on me and giving me kisses.

So what is it about having a pet in our house or apartment that can help us? According to the National Center for Health Research (*The Benefits of Pets for Human Health*, Dana Casciotti, PhD, and Diana Zuckerman, PhD) pets can help lower our blood pressure, help us relax, regulate our heart rate and our stress levels, lower doctor visits, reduce loneliness for single people, and the studies go on. WebMD ("6 Ways Pets Can Improve Your Health," Lisa Fields) states that pet owners are more trusting and happier than those who don't have one. Also, pets give our lives meaning and a sense of belonging.

My sister's family decided to fill their house with pups soon after the passing of Bella. They created a home dog sitting service for small dogs. This way they have plenty of puppies to love and take care of beside their new Lola. It has been a perfect fit for them and is similar to being a loving aunt, as you get all of the perks of being loved but don't have to pay all of the bills or do all of the training.

I would never have believed a little puppy could hold such a precious place in my heart, but my baby girl has. Lola is truly what her name stands for: Lots Of Love Always. And I know there will be others in the future, regardless of where my life takes me!

# Part Fourteen

## Spiritual Health

*Prayers are just outer expressions
of the heart, but how powerful they are!
Meditate or pray daily.*

As I grew up, I always believed a person had to kneel down or have their hands folded in order to pray. As a family, we prayed before meals and were taught to say prayers at bedtime. Adult life soon intruded, and responsibilities, exhaustion, and work soon took the place of prayer. I would fall asleep in the middle of prayers as soon as my head hit the pillow, and I soon gave up trying altogether. I began to pray only when I was in trouble or needed something, somewhat like a young college student away from home for the first time calling my parent's for money.

But through the last few years, I have found a relationship with anyone, including our spiritual source, involves talking to that source on a regular basis. Sometimes it is something we consciously do and sometimes it is just in our thoughts. We may have a friend who is sick and we think about them all day, or we may have a test that is coming up and we are worried about it. I believe all of our thoughts and all of our prayers, both silent and spoken, are heard. And for all of those years I thought my desperate cries were going unheard, my Creator had my back!

In 1988, while I was student teaching, I decided I wanted to live in Australia and did some research before returning home with the help of some of my friends. I discovered the only way I could immigrate to the country was to apply in the Independent Immigration Category. I had no family there and was not married to an Aussie, so I had no sponsors. There were some stipulations to the application however, the first being an applicant needed to have three years' experience in their present occupation. So I began a teaching job right away and put my three years in. The moment I qualified I began my application.

Nearly $1,000 and three months later, my mother found out that she had cancer, Stage 4 this time, and I was torn. My heart was in Australia, as I felt so at home there and loved it so. But I also did not want to leave my mother in her situation either. I could not decide by myself, so I said a fervent prayer that if I were to go, everything would have to work out, but if I was meant to remain home with my mom, then the door to moving to Australia would be shut tight. Around the second week after the New Year began, I received a notice from the Australian Government informing me they had since changed their policy with the first of the year and I no longer qualified for immigration.

My prayer had been answered and the door had been shut tight. For those of you who believe it was just a coincidence, that is quite all right. But for me, it was a direct answer to my prayer. I spent the next six years with my mom before she passed from this earth and have never regretted my decision. I sometimes dream of the life I might have had in that country, but you really cannot miss what you have never had. I truly believe in the power of prayer, and although I don't always pray as much as I feel I should, I still make certain it is a part of my life.

*There is usually a great deal of good born from life's terrible events. So for all of the questions of "Why did this happen to me?" in life, we must be patient and look beyond the immediate.*

Why? I have asked this question so many times in the past I cannot count them all. Why did this happen to me? Whether it was, "Why did I have to get braces at fifty-eight?" "Why did I have to get fibromyalgia?" "Why do I have to hurt all of the time? Why? Why? Why?" My friends and family will tell you that I am not the most patient person, and I get more and more frustrated with each passing year. Many times I have to tell myself this too shall pass, tomorrow is another day, and other people have it worse. I use all of the old phrases to deal with the whys in my life. Sometimes I even have to remind myself to just *GET A GRIP!* But that doesn't help too much when I'm hurting from fingertip to toe or when I am dipping into my retirement fund every few months to meet my expenses.

I am still asking the question why, but I *am* getting better about how much I ask. Now my question has transitioned into a loud declaration instead: I hurt, I am tired, or I need a new body! My whys are getting less because I have come to believe there is a plan. However, I still complain occasionally. Fortunately, silent complaints for me are also prayers. I am letting my God know I'm not happy with how my body is feeling and my financial situation needs attention.

Many of my whys have been answered since I began this book, as will yours as you go through life. Many times I am reminded I would never have written this book if I hadn't left my teaching career or would not be such a fighter if I had not had so many people bully me in life. We are all looking for our hindsight before it becomes clear in our rearview mirror.

For me, my whys have turned into joy. I wouldn't have looked for another type of work, I wouldn't have written any poetry or been able to help so many people with my blogs and writing, and I certainly would not be in the place that I am. So I am thankful for the mixed blessing: the pain, the tears, and all of the why's in my life. And I am still working on my patience.

*Our Creator's plans are sure and often beyond our understanding.*

Though this is true, we often don't see His plan when we are stressed, second guessing ourselves, or struggling with why some things happen the way they do. But we should remember all things are *used* for good. Our Universal Creator doesn't make bad things happen, but He does *use* everything for good.

As I've already mentioned, my mom was diagnosed with cancer when I was fifteen. Many years later, when I was an adult, she told me she was glad that she had gotten cancer, as it taught her how to live. Although she eventually died of the disease, she had twenty years in which she was able to have fun, speak her mind, and treat herself as she should have all along, as a wonderful, *important,* and loving woman.

My road has been similar in my struggle to appreciate myself. Although I have had many misgivings along the way, I am happy for the person I am and the road I have taken, as it has taught me many lessons. Without this, I wouldn't be the joyful and content person I am and would not have found my true calling.

It is what we learn from our journey, what we do for others, and where we end up that is most important. My path in life was to find I was worth being loved, to do what *I* loved to do, to heal, and to pass those lessons on to others in this book. It was not to do what I was best at, or to have kids or a husband, or to have a "normal" life. And for that I am truly grateful.

*Our faith is not based on an emotion or how we feel, what is said, or by our situation, but what is unseen and unsaid. Faith is an intimately personal journey and very different for each and every one of us.*

I had lost my trust in my God and the church in my mid-twenties, and this loss of trust has proven to be a struggle for me until recently. Oh, I still believed in a creator, but I thought He had allowed a bull's-eye to be placed on my back and then forgotten about me.

Like many others, I began searching for spiritual meaning in high school and college. During my junior year at my university, I joined a Christian group and decided to work for them after graduation. Although this group may have begun with a pure heart, it had became corrupted. I left feeling disillusioned with both religion and my God. It has taken me nearly forty years to find my way back to trust in my Universal Creator again.

What I have learned along life's path is every person's walk with their spiritual creator is a unique one and *very personal* to them. My walk is not your walk. It is not my place to tell others mine is the right or only way. I have also learned *our actions*, as human beings, "speak louder than words." I know so many people and nations that preach of knowing and believing in a loving God yet continue to behave in such a manner that make the heavens cry. Yet I know others who do the things they do out of the kindness of their hearts and make no mention of their beliefs.

There is something to be said about my mother's life. She made blankets and quilts for those in third world countries, sewed buttons back onto the coats of my underprivileged friends who came to play as children, and made cookies and other food for neighbors who were either too busy or suffering. She did so quietly but her life spoke volumes to those she touched. Though she was not perfect, she made a difference by her *actions*.

Four of my friends have recently lost loved ones very suddenly, one through tragic circumstances. Yet these people have retained their faith in spite of their situations. How is this done, I asked myself? I know it is a struggle every day for them, but they have put their faith in something they believe in and count on. They have made a choice to stand firm. It is their faith that their Creator is ultimately in control of things, and although they cannot see the whole picture, they believe everything will be okay. I don't know that I could be so strong. But it is also their belief that the kindness of their friends and family will help them carry on and pull through in this physical world.

This is the golden lining that will help everyone get through their times of heartache and struggle: friends help friends, give yourself time to heal, and rely on your Uncreated Creator, whoever you believe Him or Her to be. When times get tough and when loved ones die, our health declines, our life is a daily struggle, or the world seems like it is in shambles, it is our personal belief system that is unseen and our Heavenly Creator's presence in our friends which is what will see us through.

*Miracles do happen, especially when you least expect them. Every time I look in the mirror and see a smile on my face, I am reminded they exist! They happen every day.*

I remember waking up one morning about twenty-five years ago with my mother during a beautiful summer morning and noticing the morning dew on the plants in the garden. It was an incredibly beautiful sight I will never forget, as was my brother-in-law's cry from the delivery room, "It's a girl, it's a Katy!" My godchild and niece had been born. The first magical morning I woke up in Australia was another such memory. I remember hearing a magpie call outside my window as I opened my eyes.

These are all everyday events, but for me they are also miracles: the birth of a child, the crisp colors of the trees in fall, the first snowfall in winter, and the first woodland flowers of spring. Even waking up. They are all miracles. Don't think miracles have to be big events like winning a million dollars or seeing someone walk who was paralyzed. We have all heard tales of the person who was inexplicably cured of cancer or the person who found an article on their property worth a great deal of money. Those are certainly miracles, but they do not happen often. However wonderful these are, there are so many more to see if we would just open our eyes to the everyday miracles we often dismiss as luck or circumstance. Sarah McLachlan sings a song called "Everyday Miracle," which speaks to us of these events that happen each and every day.

The everyday miracle I can celebrate today is that I woke up this morning WITHOUT ANY PAIN! I went to bed early last night and took my full medication, as I couldn't tolerate the pain any longer. Even all of my fibromyalgia pain is gone today! I rarely, if ever, have one of these days, even with medication, so I am grateful for this everyday miracle.

Another one of these miracles I experienced is when I snagged my eight-point buck five years ago. I was driving about fifty miles an hour during rush hour traffic just outside of a country town. The deer ran between my car and the one in front of me. After I hit it, it rolled up on the hood of the car and hit my window, covering it so that I couldn't see. Surprisingly, I wasn't panicked but slowed the car and gently pulled over to the side of the road. I even surprised myself by how calm I was in the face of a potentially fatal accident. Another miracle.

Everyday miracles are miracles just the same. We need to see them as such and remember to thank our God who was looking over us. If your child is sick and teetering on pneumonia and suddenly begins to get better, or if you are standing in line waiting to order in a coffee shop only to find out someone has paid your tab, give thanks for your everyday miracle! You have been blessed!

*You can trust in a universal power. If you feel alone, you can call on that power any time, and in any situation, no matter what.*

Throughout life, we have many challenges. No one is immune to what life sometimes dishes out. So when we get into trouble or have difficult times, it is normal to reach out to someone we trust for help. Most of us have our friends and family, but sometimes they can't help us enough with our needs. In these times, we usually go to our Creator, whoever we believe Him or Her to be.

But what happens if you have lost trust in your spiritual power or have lost your way? What happens if your life has spiraled out of control without any foreseeable hope in sight and no amount of pleading, begging, or bargaining with your God seems to make things right?

You may have lived a good life, helped people when you could, given of yourself more than most, tried to raise a good family, and been a good role model. But yet when it comes to something you need or want, such as a job, a child without cancer, or a day without pain, there never seems to be any hope in sight. No sign of a spiritual power, no quiet voice saying it will be okay, or no bolt of lightning from above striking down the person who is making your life a living hell. You can't figure it out. You have prayed for help, yet all you hear is silence, and you feel so alone that it hurts.

I have been in that spot. As I have already said, I was convinced as an adult that my God had forgotten all about me. Oh, I knew He was still there, but I didn't know if I was still remembered. I seemed to have an X on my back as a target for all of the bad that could happen in life. I was still alone, at the end of my fifties, without a permanent job, and hurting physically every hour of the day.

What had I done wrong? I couldn't understand why things had gone wrong in my life, nor was I ready to accept what was going on around me. I couldn't be joyful in the face of my situation, end of story. But the fact is, I was being protected from many of the problems others were experiencing and didn't even know it. I couldn't see all of the gifts I had been given, things others just dream of. I had been looking in all of the wrong places. My spiritual power was leading me along, patiently waiting as I stopped to wallow in my sorrow, as I was so busy, like a child, concentrating on myself that I forgot to look around.

Our Creator is like our shadow that is always with us. When our lives are sunny and bright and full of joy, that Spirit is easy to see and feel. When we see our shadow, we usually feel the warmth of the sun and know it is not far away. But when storm clouds gather, our shadow and our spiritual leader seem to disappear, because dark places don't reflect our Creator's presence. That doesn't mean they are not around. It just means our human eyes cannot see them. We just have to make a conscious decision to believe they are still there until the sun comes out again and they can once again be seen.

I now see my Creator in my friends who work at the soup kitchen in town to feed the hungry, my friends who donate their time to third world countries, the student who called me an angel, and the friend who just this past week wrote me such a beautiful tribute about my time as his friend that it made me cry. My God is in my dreams showing me there is a heaven after life, allowing me to visit family who have passed, and giving me the gift of sleep when my body hurts too much to move. Whoever your God may be, trust that the Almighty is there for you too, holding your hand and helping you through the black places of your life, back into the sunlight.

*Our Creator is too enormous and powerful to fit into one packaged religion. Its spirit is everywhere and in everything — just look around you!*

One of the many lessons I have learned as I've grown older has been to be more open to different religions and cultures. In my many trips abroad, I have encountered many religions and their beautiful churches, mosques, ancient art, and artifacts. Many cultures talk about their God in the same way that we talk about the God in our Western Culture and Christian faith. After much thought and consideration, I have come to this conclusion: whether we call our God the Universe, Allah, Yahweh, The Great Spirit, The Evolutionary Spirit, Shiva, Jehovah, or the uncreated Creator, we are still referring to an eternal presence.

On the website http://universespirit.org/, there are over one hundred names that describe our Creator. I am sure many more can be added to this list when exploring other cultures. It's similar to when we call our own father by his given name, nickname, his rank in service, work name, or proper name. Our Creator is the same being. The Almighty is a great and powerful entity that controls the universe and everything in it. If this is so, how can we enclose Him in such a limiting and confining set of existence as our earthly religions that *we* have created?

I was brought up in a Christian home living in America. But that does not mean that someone else down the road who comes from a different faith is wrong. Whatever you believe your God to be is highly personal, and your journey with Him is too. I think deep down inside, most of us believe there is some higher power. It isn't our job to judge or to say one religion is better than another or that one is right and one is wrong. In the great hereafter, I believe we all will have to answer for what we do and believe. I don't live someone else's life, and I don't have to answer for their thoughts, beliefs, and decisions.

Look around your world. See the beauty that has been created in even the smallest of things—the symmetry, color, and diversity—then tell me that a universal being doesn't exist. Look at the night sky and then realize there are infinite worlds around us. One of the first men to go into space said it like this:

"*To look out at this kind of creation and not believe in God is to me impossible.*" Thank you, astronaut John Glenn!

*Lastly, whoever God may be and whoever you trust yours to be, that Spirit is always watching over us, patching our knees and wiping our tears!*

Whether you are a Christian, a Jew, a Muslim, or of any other spiritual belief, as I've already stated, I believe most of us have the same basic beliefs. We all believe there is a bigger force out there directing our lives and watching over us. We won't know until we meet that being, whether it is a He or She, both, or neither. It is the last great adventure of our lives.

However, until then, let us all agree this Universal Force is here when we need Him or Her the most. Do we get lost along the way? Of course we do! Do we get angry at that Force? Yes, more than we care to admit! Some of us get so mad we do not talk to our God for years. But that Heavenly Force is still here and will continue to watch over us despite our actions and the actions of those around us. Many people continue to ask, where was God when this happened, or why did God cause this? My sister, who has always been wise beyond her years, answers this way: "We live in an imperfect world." God helps us to deal with this imperfect world we live in by helping us to mend our broken hearts and relationships, leading us to understanding and forgiveness and by picking us up when we have fallen.

*This book is for all of you who have fallen along life's way . . .*

# *Bibliography*

Æsop. (Sixth century B.C.) *Æsops Fables. The Harvard Classics.* 1909–14. Bartleby.com. Available at https://www.bartleby.com/17/1/62.html

Adsit, Dennis (2018). *The Story of the Taoist Farmer.*

American Psychological Association. Available at https://www.apa.org/topics/anger/control.aspx

Armstrong, Dido and Rolo (2013). "Life for Rent." *Life for Rent*, Arista Records. DVD

Casciotti, Dana, PhD, and Zuckerman, Diana. *The Benefits of Pets for Human Health*, National Center for Health Research. Available at http://www.center4research.org/benefits-pets-human-health/

Complementary and Alternative Medicine (CAM), MedicineNet, Sources: National Center for Complementary and Alternative Medicine, National Institutes of Health. Available at https://www.medicinenet.com/alternative_medicine/article.htm#tocd

Constantino, Tor. (2015) "How to Read the 3 Signs Telling You Your Purpose in Life." *The Entrepreneur.* Available at https://www.entrepreneur.com/slideshow/299931 (Accessed 2015)

*Crocodile Dundee* (1986). Directed by Peter Faiman (Film). North America, Hollywood: Paramount Pictures

Dinesen, Isak (1937). Chapter titled "Kamante and Lulu," page 83: *Out of Africa.*

Ehrmann, Max (1927). *Desiderata.*

Fields, Lisa (2013). *6 Ways Pets Can Improve Your Health*, WebMD, Available at https://www.webmd.com/hypertension-high-blood-pressure/features/6-ways-pets-improve-your-health#1 Accessed 2017

Forleo, Marie. "Fear vs. Intuition: How to Tell the Difference." Video, Available at https://www.marieforleo.com/2011/08/fear-intuition-difference/

*Ghost* (1990). Directed by Jerry Zucker (Film). Hollywood: Paramount Pictures

Jagger, Mick, and Richards, Keith. (1969)"You Can't Always Get What You Want." *Let it Bleed*. Rolling Stones, London Records

King, Stephen (1977). *The Shining.* New York City, Doubleday Publishing

Kirste, Imke, et al., (2015) "Is silence golden? Effects of auditory stimuli and their absence on adult hippocampal neurogenesis." *Brain Structure and Function.* Springer Link, Published online 2013 Available at: https://link.springer.com/article/10.1007%2Fs00429-013-0679-3

Mann, Denise (2008). *9 Steps to End Chronic Worrying,* Web MD, Published online January 24, 2008. Available at https://www.webmd.com/balance/features/9-steps-to-end-chronic-worrying#1

Mann, Natasha. *The Health Benefits of Crying*, Natasha Mann, Net Doctor, 16/08/2011 Accessible at https://www.netdoctor.co.uk/healthy-living/wellbeing/a10637/the-health-benefits-of-crying/ Accessed 2017

*Mary Poppins* (1963). Directed by Robert Stevenson (Film). "I Love to Laugh," music by Irwin Kostal. Burbank, California: Buena Vista Distribution

Murphy, Tim (2001). *The Angry Child.* Potter/Ten Speed/Harmony/Rodale, Overdrive, Inc.

"Nanny McDead" (2009). *Castle*, TV episode 2009, Series 1, episode 2, ABC, March 16, 2009

Nash, Graham. Crosby, Stills, Nash, and Young (1970). "Teach Your

Children." *Déjà vu*, Atlantic Records, Vinyl

Phelan, Dr. L.F. "Vincent Egoro." October 23, 2013. Available at https://vincentegoroblog.wordpress.com/tag/dr-l-f-phelan/ Accessed 2017

Reddy, Helen, and Burton, Ray (1972). "I Am Woman." *I Don't Know How to Love Him*, Capital Records, Vinyl.

Seeger, Pete, and Hays, Lee (1962). "If I Had a Hammer." *Peter, Paul and Mary*. Warner Brothers, Vinyl.

*South Pacific*. (1958) Directed by Joshua Logan [Film], Music by Rodgers and Hammerstein, "You've Got to Be Carefully Taught." Los Angeles, Distributed by 20th Century Fox

Stevens, Cat (1967). "The First Cut Is the Deepest." New Masters. Vinyl

Dr. Seuss (1969). Happy Birthday to You! New York City: Penguin/Random House Books

*Under the Tuscan Sun*. (2013) Directed by Audrey Wells (Film). Burbank, Buena Vista.

US Department of Veterans Affairs. "What is PTDS?" National Center for PTSD. Available at https://www.ptsd.va.gov/understand/what/index.asp

## About the Author

Vicki Kralapp is a retired art teacher living in Northeastern Wisconsin. She was born into an artistic and teaching family. Although she has spent much of her adult life in the public school system helping others to discover art, she has always had a love of writing. Vicki now spends her time writing poems as well as inspirational and children's books. Her other pursuits include photography, drawing, painting, cooking, snorkeling, travel, learning foreign languages, and adventure.

www.ingramcontent.com/pod-product-compliance
Lightning Source LLC
Chambersburg PA
CBHW020344170426
43200CB00005B/44